An Amazing Autobiography
...because it's all about me

My Life in Movies

By

Paul R Starling

Author Photograph ©Maurice Gray

An Amazing Autobiography
Paul R Starling

First Edition 2017

All rights reserved. No part of this publication may be reproduced, stored in a retrieval system, or transmitted in any form or by any means, electronic, mechanical, photocopy, recording or otherwise, without prior written permission of the copyright holder. Nor can it be circulated in any form of binding or cover other than that in which it is published and without similar condition including this condition being imposed on a subsequent purchaser.

p.starling@sky.com

Thank you to everyone who helped make this book possible, and special thanks to Susan Starling, Matt Fiddy and others for their invaluable contribution. This is for Jimmy and Clive, sadly no longer with us, who would appreciate the humour within. And for Colin and David whose interest in movies is more than just passing time.

A Brief Briefing of What's in Store

So...what's it all about, eh? This self-congratulatory pretentious autobiography from someone working in retail, what do I possibly have to offer you which might he interesting? The answer is that I really don't know.

I love movies. Always have, always will.
I love stories. Always have, always will.
I love life. Always have, always will.

This is my sixth published novel and contains what I hope is an entertaining and unique collection of short-stories intermingled with autobiographical information of interest, my thoughts and observations on the numerous quirks in life, coupled - or should that be tripled - with my own personal homage to movies.

Someone once said within earshot of me: "Why would someone want to watch a film twice that they know is going to make the cry?"

The worst thing a movie can produce in a person is apathy. Whether a movie is good or bad it should hopefully cause a reaction. If we laugh or cry, cringe or thrill, recoil or rejoice, then a movie has succeeded provoking emotion on some level. What works for some people won't for others. A masterpiece of art to some is a boring waste of time to others. Mind-numbing action might be the epitome of entertainment. The point is, everyone's opinion is valid because it provokes a response. If you do not react, what's the point of watching any film irrespective of whether you r others cry or laugh or rejoice?

There a too many reasons why I like movies as much as do to mention in a single paragraph because all aspects of movies fascinate me, but if I would have to pinpoint one single thing as a reason for watching a movie, any movie, and that is that they are transportation devices into another world, an imaginative yet familiar world, where numerous elements come together to entertain and hopefully expand the mind. And even this isn't enough of a description. Oh well, maybe by reading through this collection of stories and events you will discover more explanation, while also being entertained.

All mistakes, errors and imperfections are my own because I am imperfect, but I do accept criticism so feel free to point out all the mistakes because until I get a proper publisher and agent there will be many.

CONTENTS

1. Contactless
2. First Day Nerves
3. A Star(ling) is Born
4. A Brief History of Mine
5. 1981- My Sporting Life
6. Bonding Experience
7. Kid Soldiers
8. Space Trekkers – An Adventure Amongst the Stars
9. Adventure of the Role-Playing Fantasy Game
10. Poster!
11. Wandering Z'Dar – The Face(or chin) Speaks
12. 1990 – Gone in Twenty Minutes
13. Two Become One…
14. Kassiopi – First Flight Holiday
15. Millennium Countdown
16. Electrical Shop of Biblical Proportions
17. Naked Babes in Beach Town
18. My Wedding day – by Susan Starling
19. First Born
20. An Adventure in the Kingdom
21. Checkout 13: Unlucky for Some
22. Using Your Loaf over Spilt Milk!
23. Locally Filmed Produce!
24. Original Sin

Bibliography

CHAPTER ONE

CONTACTLESS

Lightning flashes intermittently on the horizon of a dark but not stormy sky, jarringly visible three miles off the coastline from the quaint Norfolk village of Stalton-on-the-Broads. The sight of nature at work is beautiful, mesmeric, but adds a sense of trepidation to the lingering suspense which Douglas[1] already feels deep inside his gut when he skulks amongst the orange-hazed shadows at the side of The Kings Head, Shoulders, Knees and Toes public house. Doug doesn't snigger at all because of the ridiculously childish name of this particular speakeasy, his local, knowing the exact history of its delusional incompetent owner who named it after a drunken bet.

If Doug were savvy and actually watched any Film's Noir he might mourn the loss of wispy cigarette smoke and the mixture of tobacco with reefer coming out from the door to the speakeasy - yes, pub! - when he opens it, but he doesn't so he doesn't.

The interior is lit with patchy architrave lights which are set above a dozen individual booths, an unusual choice of design in this modern world but best not question its reality. Shady characters with half-lit shadows and dark contrasts of shadowy blackness twitch nervously in the booths, hints of colour, glints of teeth, jewellery and whites of the eye flash furtively.

Doug smiles nervously at Ray[2] the Barman, still finding it hard to come to terms with this establishments layout which practically promotes dodgy dealings, before setting his eyes upon the girl he is here to meet, elicit rendezvous-style as befits the location and genre. And what a dish or dame or doll she is! Gene[3] is all fiery strawberry blonde, alabaster skin, unsubtle red dress with a cleavage which could cause a weak man to have a heart-attack - or other bodily reflex - at ten paces. She grins with her divine lips parting tantalisingly. Does Doug feel like he is the luckiest guy in the world? Do you feel stupid for wondering this? Of course! This gorgeous bombshell is well above his pay-grade and he is hitting well above his weight - more cliches etcetera, etcetera - because Gene would not spare you or I a second glance, let alone someone like Doug. But he has been caught hook, line and sinker, suckered into a date with this unattainably classy broad and what just the hell is she doing in a backwater village like Stalton-on-the-Broads anyway? Unfortunately Doug doesn't realise he is being played like a pawn in a poker game - no, that's wrong, but you knew it! - and he isn't going to be silly enough to miss such a splendiferous opportunity which is knocking on his wooden door like a handle from...something.

'Hello." Gene's rouged lips part sensuously when she purrs with her husky orgasm-inducing voice, revealing perfectly pearly white teeth.

All Doug can do is mumble and splutter and giggle like an incoherent gibbering monkey - don't want to upset the PC-brigade! - but Gene inexplicably deciphers him, maybe she possesses an inbuilt translator.

"Thank you." Gene says. "I'll have a gin and tonic with ice and a twist of lime." All of which she says in a tantalisingly sexualised stereotype of a voice.

Doug nods in a gormless state and glides across to the bar, orders her a drink, takes it to their table, realises in his lust-blind foolishness he forgot one for himself and repeats the process with a different beverage, not feeling at all silly.

If this were some atmospheric forties Noir classic Gene would be smoking teasingly, with a wisp of smoke sensually hazing the light above their table, but the law today deems smoking to be not only bad for one's health but anti-social - and what isn't in this politically correct world gone crazy? - so instead, Gene leans forward in her seat and exposes more of her splendiferous cleavage so as to distract Doug from thoughts other than herself, and causes every man in eye-range to gawp at her which subsequently gets them into trouble with their respective others, yes, even the homosexuals. In some countries this is a greater offence than smoking!

While Doug sits motionless, looking into her eyes like a drooling fool - this PC stuff is starting to get passé - Gene begins spinning her yarn or telling her story depending upon your perspective.

"Oh Dougie," she says breathily, her luminous green eyes luminous in the luminescence. "I- I love you so very much and it aches that we cannot be together until-" She lets the sentence dangle as tantalisingly as the v-neck of her dress. "I don't like to ask, Dougie, but I need you to do something for me and- its something I hope you don't mind me asking," she bats her eyelids irresistibly, "but if you want to be with me as much as I want to be with you I need you to kill my husband."

Without a moments hesitation Doug nods at her request, his volition no longer under his ownership.

"Before you commit yourself," Gene adds superfluously because Doug has pretty much committed himself already, "I must tell you why." Gene takes hold of Doug's under the table. "I- think- no, I know, my husband is seeing another woman." The missing word was sleeve!

Doug spits out a mouthful of drink incredulously! "You must be joking," he says without a Scottish burr for those who understand where the quote is from. "Your husband is obviously blind and stupid!"

"Thank you, Dougie, you are too kind to me." Gene says innocently, acting up to his gullibility - I should add that we know he is being duped but he doesn't, or does he, maybe that's the surprise twist ending although, now I've mentioned it, it won't come as a surprise, unless I am just trying to misdirect you, or not! "Ty(4) has been doing his Personnel Manager, I know he has. Some Personnel Manger she is! Posh-bird name too: Yvonne(5). The last job she had she was caught on security camera stealing money and denied knowledge of the act entirely, claiming stress and depression, even trying to put the blame onto her co-workers. She quit the job and got away without any charge. Can you believe anyone would be such a low-life scumbag to do such a thing?"

Doug isn't very astute when it comes to rhetoric but before he can reply she continues.

"Ty is also a lying, conniving, thieving, no-good scumbag." Gene states with unbridled frankness. "Can you believe he would prefer that floozy to me!?"

"No." Doug splutters, the booze in his glass going to his head before he has touched a drop, transfixed by her beauty and allure, etcetera.

"It started two weeks ago..." Gene begins.

Two weeks ago: it started.

Gene's watery eyes are wide, clear and bright, emotional pupils surrounded by an ever-changing aura of green, promising myriad possibilities, and Douglas is helplessly sucked into her vortex - which is not a euphemism.

"Will you- help me, Dougie?"

At this juncture a looming shadowy shadow looms menacingly before their table, one which they cannot possibly ignore. Doug turns around in his seat to see who Gene is looking up at standing behind him.

"Hey, doll-face." An ugly big lug chews out the words with one eye half-closed, the other droopy-lidded upon Gene - which is obvious because he wouldn't exactly be addressing Douglas with such affection and you no doubt realise who he is talking to so I don't know why I bothered explaining, really!

"Whassup, Burt(6)?" Gene asks irritably which still sounds amazingly sensuous.

Burt's good eye swivels disconcertingly in Doug's direction but shows little interest in the man seated at the table with Gene once the competition is sized up, deeming him hardly worth the jealousy.

"Who's the bozo?" Burt asks.

"His name is Douglas." Gene informs him. "And he's a gentleman, Burt, unlike you, so leave us alone."

Staring with open moist open-mouthed gormlessness, Burt seems like he cannot be bothered to muster a response, while Doug isn't going to intervene because he values his own life.

"Your old man any work for me?" Burt asks with improper grammatical structuring.

Doug is about to respond with confusion until he realises the question is directed at Gene?

"No." Gene purrs. "Now go away."

Burt stumbles away from their table muttering, disgruntled, like a disgruntled muttering stumbling man.

Gene's attention returns to Doug and her eyes magically soften to their previously alluring state of being. Doug leans forward in his chair with conspiratorial awareness, looking furtively at Gene's cleavage before her eyes but she doesn't appear too bothered by his distraction, evidently pleased he is putty in her hands - who wouldn't be?

"If you do what I am asking," Gene says seductively, not that she needs to turn on the seductiveness, "then you will be rewarded with a better view, my love."

Doug almost loses control of something which I need not linger on!

"When-" Doug throatily clears his throat. "When would you like me to, you know, take care of your husband?"

"Tonight."

This time he almost chokes on his breath. He had perhaps expected a bit longer to prepare yet, now, when he thinks about the logistics of the situation, the sooner he gets this task done the shorter the rumination time on the consequences because, like most people, the author included, Doug ruminates a worse fate than that which actually occurs.

"What am I going to do it with?" He asks reasonably. "The killing, I mean?" Just in case she picks up on some unintentional double-entendre.

"My friend Cathy(7) is waiting for you outside." She tells him and pauses long enough to make him wonder if this Cathy is herself a weapon of some sort. "She has a gun."

"And your husband- Ty- he is at work right now?"

Gene nods affirmative: "He is night-manager of TAMS."

"The- supermarket? Next door?"

She nods once more as confirmation.

"I see-" Doug says without real understanding for what truly motivates her.

"Please, Dougie, do it for me now." Gene pleads, and in his mind he has substituted the 'for' with 'to'. "I promise when you get back we shall have a night to remember."

Doug gulps deeply to calm his nerves for what he is being asked to do now, and later, thinking this night is already one which he will never forget for as long as he remembers to not forget that he should remember it.

"Go now, my lover." Gene says irresistibly, the wanton lust on her face almost finishing him off for the night!

As if possessed by a programmed auto-pilot function Douglas departs the speakeasy with coolness - lest you forget this is supposed to be a sophisticated thriller of the Noir variety - and is greeted outside by dark-haired Cathy who silently passes him the gun without saying a word. On through the quarter-lit side-alley he glides, his mind a numb blank slate with its sole purpose set upon killing, he walks straight into the hulking back of Burt.

"What the what?" Burt blurts while spilling some beer from the pint glass which he had earlier taken with him.

"Careful, mate." Fritz(8) the Kneeler coughs somewhere on the floor.

"Sorry." Doug says, panic rising in his belly.

Burt turns his bulky, black-clad body round and faces the person who has made him waste some if his beer.

"Sorry!" Burt snarls, just able to make out the face in the shadows. "You- You were talking to Gene you were." Again with the poor grammar and spelling!

Instead of risking his life by reacting with sarcasm, Doug bites his tongue - ouch!

"Choked me!" Says Fritz the Kneeler with the requisite cough.

Burt lashes out with a fist as Fritz is rising and catches the sycophantic suck-up squarely across the ear, sending him unconscious to the floor.

"What she want you for?" Burt asks Doug in menacingly poor English.

"She- she wants me to kill her husband."

Burt laughs without humour: "Husband! Gene ain't married, mate!"

Doug is confused, dot com, to say the least.

"Let me guess," Burt continues. "Told you he works at TAMS?"

"Thats right." Doug replies. "She said his name is Ty, and he is the night manager."

"Gene is playing you for a sap." Burt laughs ignominiously. "Ty. Ty is her brother-in-law. He's been knocking Gene's sister Yvonne about. I guess they stand to get a big insurance pay-out once you've done him in!"

"Um- you seem to know an awful lot about this."

Burt nods in a manner which Douglas interprets as thoughtfulness but it is quite difficult to tell, not only because of the limited light but because of Burt's limited emotional range.

"Yeah." Burt says after quite some time and another long pause ensues, making Doug wonder if there will ever be an explanation, which could be very irritating if something like that happened in fiction.

...To be concluded.

CHAPTER TWO

FIRST DAY NERVES

The majority of us have been there: butterflies churning in our stomach causing nervous trepidation because we are embarking to a place beyond our comfort zone, on our own and without the relative safety net of home and protection of family. Maybe this feeling also comes coupled with the excited anticipation of beginning something new. And I was definitely no exception to all these symptoms when I started my first job in 1988 in the world of entertainment: there truly is no business like this business, at least no business that I know of, anyway.

To be more precise and to clear a few details I need to explain that like all beginnings I was participating as an entry-level 'extra,' and to a certain extent, I still am performing within that role.

Extra: normally one in the background of a movie, television or stage production, who rarely has a speaking role although there are exceptions, and in the bigger scheme are nothing more than a prop or scenery.

Ironic how I can identify with these criteria.

Everyone has to begin at the bottom and work their way up through hard-work, determination, and a positive focus on goals without restricting oneself by remaining inside the lines, and by taking risks that's exactly what I have done to get to the place I am today. I suppose I must have constructed a fairly worked-out plan for myself back then which, as I have gotten older and hopefully wiser, has been challenged by the knowledge we must live for the moment because who knows what lies round the corner - this 'live for now' declaration might seem obvious because it is an obvious statement, but how many of us actually practice what we preacher? We all know that we must act now not later because later is a fictional non-existence, similar to those movies which try to forecast our future but invariably fail miserably - time-travel hasn't been invented yet so future knowledge isn't possible. And if we learn by our mistakes then why do we often repeat those mistakes – there's a classic 90's comedy which addresses this particular dilemma.

If I have lost you already because between the lines cannot be deciphered, then I apologise now.

I do not know if some situations or characteristics presently within my life have been influenced by the movies which I have seen, I do like to believe I am grounded enough to separate fiction from reality - or should that be vice versa? But what I do know is I enjoy every aspect of movies: story, acting, imagery, music, sound, posters, production and histrionics. More on these things later, though, because this chapter charts my very first job.

September 1988.

I'm not aware of the exact date with this month but I do remember the time: 530 of the a.m. The place was Norwich Cathedral for my first day on an Anglia Television show about life in Norfolk circa late 1900's. Obviously this was to be a period-piece. After being allowed entry thanks to my official dog-tag - how important did I feel? - I followed other extras similar to myself into the Nave which was being used as our wardrobe and make-up department, where I was promptly handed a numbered sack and told to deposit my own clothing, being of the 80's period, within, and return it to the Wardrobe Master.

While feeling slightly awkward stripping to my underwear in front of strangers both male and female - I was shy back then - I considered something useful a teacher at High School once imparted: when you come upon a situation in life which you know is going to pass by in the blink of an eye take a step back on a conscious level and focus fully upon it, absorb the moment, the sights, sounds, faces, feelings, because you cannot get them back once they have gone. And on many an occasion I have attempted to do this, it saves me from missing important stuff which soon disappears into mere memory, and I find its meditation potential to be calming.

So while I discarded one set of period clothes for another, simpler one, I was looking around wishing I more physically resembled Crash Davis or Eddy Calvin "Nuke" Laloosh[1] from the film I had only recently been to the cinema to watch, instead of the form my gene-pool bestowed upon me. But my bizarrely contradictory self-conscious awareness is perhaps something to be addressed in a later chapter, or by a psychiatrist.

Next came Make-up. With all jobs there is an inherent fear of doing something wrong and looking stupid but if you go with the flow one is soon beyond that point, mostly through the learning curve, and how are we actually supposed to learn if we make no mistakes. I had never worn make-up before and dirtying my face was part of the character so it had to be done, and when I awkwardly found a chair the plus-side to my embarrassing endeavour was the make-up girl. She was only a little older than me, very pretty, silky black hair tied in a pony-tail, radiant tanned skin, vibrant eyes, and our friendly banter relaxed me to this whole new experience. She told me how much she enjoyed her own job in the business with enthusiasm, chatting about the stars she has met in the two short years since beginning work, and how she would love to work on a film like Beetlejuice(2) which she saw with friends during the summer because she thought the make-up was so cool and revolutionary.

    I was her enraptured audience, listening and commenting - it has become a pleasant surprise the ease which I find when talking to new people over the years, finding all unique facets about everyone fascinating, particularly interesting and attractive young females, and the fact is I seem to get along with most people even if our backgrounds and lifestyles are worlds apart. Interesting people are not boring; some who consider themselves boring are interesting; those who are full of self-interest are boring. Involve others and others will involve you.

    I only wish I could recall her name - I aren't forgetful, I just don't remember some stuff!

    This is when Danny arrived, the complete opposite to the make-up girl.

I had just got a bacon butty and strong black coffee from the makeshift cafeteria set up in the cathedrals cloisters, of all places, when Danny sat down opposite me after asking with a cheesy-grin if it was fine to do so. He was full of exuberance and bravado, handsome under the make-up, a physical cat to my mouse yet identical to all the other pretty-boys.

    And did he like to talk about himself?

    That was a rhetorical question!

    It seemed that I knew everything there was to know about him in the space of thirty-seconds: "This is my twelfth job, I've done plays too, and I'm only twenty, only child, parents divorced, I play rugby, I like cars and I know everything about movies. (Okay, maybe this isn't verbatim.) I'm a magnet to the babes and I have an enormous penis!"

Anyway, it transpired Danny-boy had just returned from a month long sabbatical in America with his father and step-mother and was clued up on the plentiful quantity of movies which we hadn't yet received on our fair shores.

"One film you must see is Die Hard(3) with that guy from Moonlighting, its (attach 80's slang here!) I also saw the latest one from Arnie(4) and its not his best, directed by Walter Hill too so it should'a been better. Oh yeah, and another couple of films you haven't had here yet are Big(5) and Who Framed Roger Rabbit?(6) They might be for kids but they're worth catching."

From anyone other than Mister Know-it-all this information might have been worth paying attention to.

"I wouldn't mind seeing Willow(7) when that comes out." I told Danny naively, because what I should've come out with was some superior artist endeavour by the likes of Guiseppe Tornatore(8) which he had never heard of, but what did I know back then, hey?

Danny just sneered dismissively at my childishness: "George Lucas could do better too." (Based upon what success indicator I will never know.)

"Doesn't Ron Howard direct it?" I asked knowledgeably.

"Yeah, but it's a Lucasfilm production and its as babyish as his Ewok films, they're all for kids, not like- Coming to America(9), have you seen that?"

I think I nodded just to placate him because looking back I'm not sure if I actually saw the film in a cinema or on VHS.

"Don't see Cocktail(10)." Said Danny helpfully. "That was the last film I saw before coming home from America. Its Tom Cruise. Not worth bothering with unless you love him. Anyway, catch you later."

Saved by the proverbial bell as it were, Danny-boy saw someone he recognised and went over to chat with them.

Maybe it's because I'm not particularly interested in cars, football or ego, I find that conversation with women of more interest. All talk should produce stimulus to the brain on some level and I guess it depends upon what we find interesting, and the general enthusiasm and knowledge of the talker, plus the fact that he or she involves the listener in their chat - there isn't much worse than a person who loves the sound of his own voice to the exclusion, or disinterest, if others.

Anyway, as I have already said, I try to get along with everyone and it's up to them if they do the opposite.

Eventually the call to the set came after about an hour long waiting around, people watching, observing the principal cast and their camaraderie - I did not recognise any of them but that isn't a reflection of their celebrity, or lack thereof.

I found everything fascinating: the crew, lighting, cameras, scenery, props, costumes, the whole set-up. I was captivated by the teamwork which one tends to take for granted if watching a film or television program or play - but that's the whole point, creating the illusion is a part of the suspension of disbelief. No wonder the End Credits can take several minutes of crawl and consist of hundreds of names. It made me, at 17, gain a greater understanding and appreciation for average films such as Crocodile Dundee 2(11), which I saw in the summer of that year and which has to juggle the logistics of location shooting as well as studio work, and big budget action films like Rambo 3(12) with its pyrotechnics as well as globe-trotting. But not just that, to imagine the pre-production and post-production after filming has been completed on a comedy like Police Academy 5: Assignment Miami Beach(13), to get everything together for a finished product and a pre-sold release date must cause a few sleepless nights for the director, producers, the studio and the cinemas.

And here am I in 1988 experiencing a segment of a miniaturised version in this television production.

Wow!

The start of anything new has the opportunity to be a learning curve as I mentioned before, and along the way it presents numerous challenges and discoveries about life and about oneself. One's first real job can be a major component in forming the nucleus of development for a variety of skills, not just in that working life but also socially, psychologically, spiritually and in relationships, no matter what path we choose for ourselves. If you seek back in your mind to the first working experience you had undoubtedly you will see great truths in what I say, even if your path altered considerably based upon that experience.

(1) Bull Durham, 1988, written and directed by Ron Shelton, starring Kevin Costner, Susan Sarandon and Tim Robbins. Poster tagline:

"Romance is a lot like baseball. It's not whether you win or lose. It's how you play the game."
(2) Beetlejuice, 1988, directed by Tim Burton, starring Michael Keaton, Winona Ryder, Geena Davis and Alec Baldwin. From the Warner Home Video trade book Handbook for the Recently Deceased: "Beetlejuice takes you from the surface of Saturn to miniaturisation within a model town. From a bureaucratic nightmare of Afterlife red-tape, to battles with giant polka-dotted sandworms. There has never been a film like Beetlejuice in the history of the cinema."
(3) Die Hard, 1988, directed by John McTiernan, starring Bruce Willis, Alan Rickman, Bonnie Bedelia, Reginald VelJohnson and William Atherton. Cinematographer Jan De Bont went on to direct the similarly styled Speed.
(4) Red Heat, 1988, directed by Walter Hill, starring Arnold Schwarzenegger, Jim Belushi and Peter Boyle. Poster tagline: "Moscow's toughest detective. Chicago's craziest cop. There's only one thing worse than making them mad. Making them partners."
(5) Big,1988, directed by Penny Marshall, starring Tom Hanks, Elizabeth Perkins, John Heard and Robert Loggia. The first Oscar nomination for Tom Hanks.
(6) Who Framed Roger Rabbit?, 1988, directed by Robert Zemeckis, starring Bob Hoskins, Christopher Lloyd and Joanna Cassidy. From 1988's The Official Poster Magazine: "For four years animators and film artists worked and played and learned as thy produced this film milestone, and most of them will agree with Robert Zemeckis when he said: "Roger Rabbit is one of those experiences you only have once in your life.""
(7) Willow, 1988, directed by Ron Howard, Starring Val Kilmer, Joanne Whalley, Warwick Davis and Jean Marsh. Warwick Davis, from the Official Poster Magazine: "Willow is an amateur magician who is finally taught real magic. I was trying to find something he could do to distinguished himself from any other person, but I couldn't really find anything. However, there us a great deal of me in Willow."
(8) Cinema Paradiso, 1988, directed by Guiseppe Tornatore, starring Philippe Noiret and Salvatore Cascio. With a BAFTA winning score by Ennio Morricone.
(9) Coming to America,1988, directed by John Landis, starring Eddie Murphy, Arsenio Hall and James Earl Jones. Poster artist Drew

Struzan was commissioned to design the poster for Crocodile Dundee 2, but when its star rejected the design, Struzan simply replaced Hogan with Murphy and voila!

(10) Cocktail, 1988, directed by Roger Donaldson, starring Tom Cruise, Bryan Brown and Elizabeth Shue. Poster tagline: "When he pours, he reigns."

(11) Crocodile Dundee 2, 1988, directed by John Cornell, starring Paul Hogan and Linda Kozlowski. A worldwide gross of $239million, off a budget of $14million.

(12) Rambo 3, 1988, directed by Peter MacDonald, starring Sylvester Stallone, Richard Crenna and Kurtwood Smith. Stallone quote, from The Official Poster Magazine: " He finds himself spritually. For the first time, we see Rambo in a whole different arena."

(13) Police Academy 5: Assignment Miami Beach,1988, directed by Alan Myerson, starring Bubba Smith, David Graf, Michael Winslow etc. Poster tagline: "Hold Everything! The Cadets are dropping in on Miami Beach for an all new adventure."

(14) Braddock: Missing in Action 3, 1988, directed by Aaron Norris and starring Chuck Norris, Aki Aleong, Roland Harrah III and Miki Kim. Dialogue quote "I don't step on toes, Littlejohn, I step on necks."

(15) Action Jackson, 1988, directed by Craig R Baxley, starring Carl Weathers, Craig T Nelson, Vanity, Bill Duke, Robert Davi and Sharon Stone. Poster tagline: "It's time for ACTION."

(16) Critters 2: The Main Course, 1988, directed by Mick Garris, starring Scott Grimes, Liane Curtis and Terrance Mann. Poster tagline: "Get ready for seconds...they're back."

(17) Deadly Pursuit, 1988, directed by Roger Spottiswoode, starring Sydney Poitier, Tom Berenger and Kirstie Alley. Original US title: Shoot to Kill.

At the time of writing this piece I have been working in retail for twenty-eight years, a job which involves a certain amount of acting as a person evolves into their role, adapting to conditions and progressing in life.

I started this line of work for a family run electrical shop called EXEL - Ralph Daniels Ltd, T/A, my boss and mentor being one Ian Daniels. We had two floors in a unit along Church Road, Hoveton, Norfolk. We specialised in Brown Goods - TV's, VHS recorders etc - and White Goods - washing machines, refrigerators etc. We also had a

VHS rental library during the heyday of the format, when the home video entertainment industry was something new and fresh, and often the most affordable and convenient way for a whole family to watch movies.

During my time working there I lost count of the quantity of movies I saw, but when I turned eighteen there is little doubt I finally caught up with other films released in 1988 that I could not get in to see myself at the cinema, and as my tastes at that time weren't yet attuned to artistic or classic or foreign films, I probably watched the likes of Braddock: Missing in Action 3(14), Action Jackson(15) and Critters 2: The Main Course(16). Not that there isn't a place for films such as these because entertainment is entertainment, while there were and still are the occasional surprising gems to be found in the bargain basement which get overlooked in the crowded marketplace - Deadly Pursuit(17), was one which stood out amongst the instantly forgettable dross for me.

Retail, as I have said, can often involve acting - J.D. Salinger said it well: "Life is fake." - but perhaps not in the traditional sense that one thinks of acting, the shop-floor isn't really a stage and there are usually only security cameras to catch the performance, but one's real personality has to meld with the projected role, the one the customer sees. If we brought all our multi-faceted characteristics to the fore at work, delivering our emotions full-force to every customer, some of us might not last more than a day in the business. Basically, more often than not, our true state is suppressed behind the facade of politeness.

The saying goes: the customer is always right. Growing into the business at an early age and within independent retail means I respect the saying's principal meaning, able to adhere to it appropriately, which isn't easy to project all the time. But in the last twenty-eight years it has become an almost archaic saying with those who are new in retail. Let me say that not all customers are right, we know this to be true because we are all wrong sometimes, but we need every customer to return to us and keep us in a job so on that basis they are always right, no matter how rude, ignorant and irrational they might be at any given time. We take it on the chin. It's never personal, even if it might seem that way sometimes, and I think if people could see a playback of their behaviour they might think twice next time - or maybe not. There is less tolerance toward abuse these days.

On the plus-side, many customers who I talk to on a daily basis tend to enjoy jovial banter and some have similar interests in film to myself, so you never know what you're gonna get.

Every day in retail presents new challenges like any well-scripted movie scenario should! I have always tried to speak to people how I would like to be spoken to, but any performance can break down when human emotions are involved. I am not perfect, I do not live a perfect life, and sometimes the pressures of life can cause my sarcasm to become facetious and pedantic.

Being front of stage to an audience which passes through a shop sometimes fleetingly, occasionally without even registering the workers presence, and sometimes for longer, involves the performance of adapting to many roles across the working day. We can often be the only person someone meets in a day, the only friendly face, the only person they will talk to. It's not easy, but it shouldn't be. Always a challenge, never a chore, to butcher a phrase!

Thank you for your custom...enjoy the rest of this book, and your day, while I go back to the very beginning.

CHAPTER THREE

A STAR(ling) IS BORN

Ooo-err missus, nudge nudge, wink wink.
No more procrastination let's get on with the fornication, procreation, sex!
The late sixties and early seventies saw a relief of more than just moral codes of the past with the advent of Flower Power and the assertion of Free Love when the sex film outgrew its grimy cheapness and exploded into the professionally made glossy feature film. Sexploitation would indeed enter the main stream with a pelvic thrust. Yet all this change did not mean the S word was discussed openly in polite society, that sort of act was still confined to the bedroom with a hint on the big screen, and perhaps only if you visited one of the infamous backstreet cinema's in London's Soho, or a fleapit venue along New York's 42nd Street, with the dirty-raincoat brigade. But as the seventies began deflowering many myths so collars and cuffs were slowly loosened.
I was born one autumnal afternoon in September 1971, the 28th as it happens, and I share my birthday with many people across the world, I'm sure, plus other famous celebrities born during 1971 such as: Mark Wahlberg on June 5th who became an underwear model turned actor; Sophia Coppola on May 14th, writer, director and famous family; and artist Jason Oxer.
Around the time of my, ahem, conception, I am guessing my parents may have watched Carry On Loving(1) or perhaps the more obscure and artistic drama Cover Me Babe(2) to get into the mood, because they were released...well, you know, about the right time. Although my parents weren't particularly voracious cinema-goers it would be rude of me to ask what, um, inspired my creation, plus I am too embarrassed to do so!
I wasn't their first, you know. In fact I was a late-comer or, if you will, an after-thought - I don't like to say mistake because that would be cruel!
My sister was born in 1961(3), while my brother was 1963(4), so they witnessed this gradual change in attitudes first-hand as the swinging sixties became the anything goes seventies with its more open-minded views toward sexual antics, coupled with progressive

relaxation of media censorship which would imperceptibly transform itself as we departed the 20th Century - more of which, later.

Mum and Dad were war- and pre-war babies so both matured post 1945 into the adults they became, a generation away from where we are now, let alone the seventies, and consequently faced transformative times unimaginable even now when viewed through visual and aural records made at that time. I and my generation take for granted how lucky we are to avoid such upheaval and turmoil of a world war, knowing no different, blindly believing the hardships which we face in the present age are bad enough but we have become blinded by capitalist wants and consumer-driven urges, which are incomparable to the struggle faced by our parents and grandparents - I can't imagine them stressing over lack of a Wi-fi signal while bombs were falling around the country!

Brian and Joy Starling set up home in the village of Stalham, Norfolk, population a quarter of what it is today, with a rail-link - since closed in 1959 - and bus route as their only viable means of transportation to the nearest city: Norwich. More people would inevitably have to walk, bicycle, or use public transport in those days because to average workers a motor-car was an unaffordable luxury, and road networks weren't the extensively woven, congested, environmentally destructive conveniences which they are now. Also at this time and right on into the eighties Norfolk was a comparatively isolated county with a quaint, rural infrastructure which has undoubtedly been the appeal for numerous settlers and holiday-makers over the ensuing years – it's a fact that new ideas can take twelve months to reach us here!

Like many villages with a contained society at this time, they had their own cinema. Oftentimes films were projected in the Village Hall's out in the sticks, maybe once weekly or monthly, and you will discover this practise going on even today, but Stalham in the fifties had its own dedicated cinema which my parents would attend as teenagers/twenty-somethings:

The Broadland Cinema 1955-1963

Situated on the Brumstead Road in the heart of the village of Stalham in a barn belonging to Church Farm, the Fisher family set up this 400-seat cinema with their premiere screening being perennial classic White Christmas(5). Run by Edna Woolsey and her husband for its eight years in existence, the cinema got off to an inauspicious start when projectionist John Fisher started to run White Christmas upside down, although this error was swiftly rectified to the delight of the paying audience.

A vast array of movies were screened there, from the aforementioned White Christmas, a May 9th 1957 screening of Hitchcock's The Man Who Knew Too Much(6), epics Ben-Hur(7) and Lawrence of Arabia(8), along with many hundreds of other well-known and more obscure, long-forgotten movie gems.

Fondly remembering his experiences, one gentleman has told me: "I would go to the cinema there three times a week as a lad, and on Saturday with mates to the matinee. I can particularly recall Dracula(9). That was a highlight for me, getting in underage. We were all a rowdy lot and got thrown out more than once for our mischief-making antics. Teddy boy's you might call us. During the interval we would walk down the aisle letting off stink bombs."

Coincidentally another person unassociated with the first verified these details to me and I cannot image such a thing being tolerated for long in today's age, and he also said the cinema was the venue to turn to during courtship because it was possible to share a double-seat at extra cost on the back row so affording the opportunity for rare privacy - I am sure my parents undoubtedly did similar, gross!

After a lucrative run the cinema was forced to close in 1963 owing to its dwindling numbers and the affordability of television, plus the increasing popularity of the Bingo Hall, and across the country today these smaller venues are few and far-between, which is a great pity because their individual distinction has been mostly erased by the huge corporations whose diversity of choice is restricted.

So nothing too heady at this family-run establishment for the cinema-going public of the time to get too excited about and one wonders what midnight programming might have been chosen in a more promiscuous 1971, to titillate those country folk, had the cinema survived that long. Would they come across the shocking likes of The Altar of Lust(10), Four Times That Night(11), I Was A Male Call Girl(12), or A Weekend With Strangers(13)?

Perhaps the four films above might be unknown out in the sticks, or perhaps even the city of Norwich, maybe reaching no further than London owing to their American Grindhouse circuit obscurity and our failure to catch up. We Brits would definitely have to wait until the advent of the VCR to experience such exploitation fare where the posters - or video covers - would be the major selling points to films with a more salacious entertainment agenda, although I don't doubt there was an underground culture somewhere out there which made it possible to watch anything being made during the decade.

There was of course at this time more mainstream fare pushing the boundaries of decency while challenging the British censorship board, offering up imagery to broaden or shock otherwise closed minds, expanding what was considered acceptable. Examples: girls behind bars mixed-race sadistic brutality The Big Doll House(14), frank sexual exposure of relationships Carnal Knowledge(15), controversial rape and violence Straw Dogs(16).

Other envelopes were being pushed while offering deeper audience enlightenment in 1971, opening the publics eyes to new and alternative story-telling ideas and oblique narratives, addressing sex and drugs and language refreshingly, treating the medium more like the art-form it is, although not everyone then as now might agree these changes were good. Examples: gory European erotic vixen's vampiric horror Vampyros Lesbos(17), artful coming of age with tasteful nudity Walkabout(18), explicit anti-establishment anarchy A Clockwork Orange(19).

Innuendo has always been the mainstay of British sex comedy and we haven't always conducted our lives with stiff upper-lip stoicism, although it took a while for our sexual sensibilities to align with the rest of Europe. Bawdy postcard style humour has always fared well within our shores while burlesque shows were prevalent, but usually we treated them with a sniggering embarrassment. For many years it was up to the Carry On series(1958-92) to keep our funny bone tickled with their innuendo imbued scripts, highlights including Carry On Nurse(1959), Carry On Camping(1969) and Carry On Cleo(1964), all of which were directed by Gerald Thomas and produced by Peter Rogers, utilising a stock company which would often include the talented Sid James, Kenneth Williams, Joan Simms, Hattie Jacques and Charles Hawtry . Subtlety was dispensed with in the later entries in the series as they tried to become more relevant in the shocking seventies where their tried and tested formula eventual floundered with the lame likes of Carry On Behind(1975) and Carry On Emmanuelle(1978).

It wasn't until the mid-seventies when the British sex-comedy hit high gear to quickly reach its apex, departing not much sooner than its load was spent. Examples of these are put upon Timothy Lea in the Confessions series(20); the self-explanatory Can You Keep It Up For a Week?(21); Adventures of a Taxi Driver(22) plus its two follow-up adventures; and the pun-tastic The Ups and Downs of a Handyman(23); plus many dozens of numerous imitators of varying quality. All fairly harmless stuff, of course, because by the late seventies plotless hardcore had overtaken the industry and these softer confections soon became passé.

Now we live in an age where full-frontal nudity has become normal on television, with the irony being that the more aware and uncensored society has generally become, there is less tolerance toward old-school innuendo, flirtatiousness and bottom-punching - strewth, theres a court-case right there! - while back in the beginning of the comparatively soft seventies, the initial tentative steps were being taken into an ocean of full monty skinny-dipping possibilities.

(1) Carry On Loving, November 1970, directed by Gerald Thomas and starring Sid James and Kenneth William etc. 20th film in the series.
(2) Cover Me Babe, December 1970, directed by Noel Black and starring Robert Forster, Sondra Locke and Susanne Benton. Poster tagline: "Camera, in his hands it becomes an obscene instrument. He turns the girls on, then turns on his camera." Alternative title: Run Shadow Run.
(3) Defiant Daughters, directed by Ladislao Vajda and starring Barbara Rutting and Luise Ullrich. From The Act of Seeing: "Selected as the Swiss entry for the Best Foreign Language Film at the 34th Academy Awards, when it wasn't accepted as a nominee, Time Films subtitled Ladislao Vajda's 'Problem Girl' drama and launched it on 42nd Street."
(4) Psychomania, directed by Richard L Hilliard and starring Lee Philips and Sheppard Studwick. From The Act of Seeing: "director Richard Hilliard's axe murder thriller shot as 'Black Autumn' the was changed to 'Violent Midnight' before becoming Psychomania."
(5) White Christmas, 1954, directed by Michael Curtiz, starring Bing Crosby, Danny Kaye, Rosemary Clooney etc. Irving Berlin's title song won the Oscar in 1942 for Holiday Inn, starring Bing Crosby and Fred Astaire.

(6) The Man Who Knew Too Much, 1956, directed by Alfred Hitchcock, starring James Stewart, Doris Day and Bernard Miles. The song "Que, Sera Sera" was Doris Days biggest hit.

(7) Ben-Hur, 1959, directed by William Wyler and starring Charlton Heston, Jack Hawkins and Stephen Boyd. Producer Sam Zimbalist died while on location during the making of the film.

(8) Lawrence of Arabia, 1962, directed by David Lean, starring Peter O'Toole, Alec Guiness and Omar Sharif. Dialogue quote: "There may be honour among thieves, but there is none in politicians."

(9) Dracula, 1958, Terence Fisher directed Hammer horror starring Peter Cushing and Christopher Lee, co-starring Melissa Stribling and Michael Gough. Known as "Horror of Dracula" in America. From the 1958 campaign book: "Christopher Lee, the new master of monsters puts new horror into the new Dracula."

(10) The Altar of Lust, 1971, directed by Roberta Findlay and starring Erica Landers and Charles Lamont. From The Act of Seeing: "After discussing all of (Marie's) incestuous daddy issues and possible bisexuality with her shrink, and having a wild sex session with him on his couch as part of her advanced therapy,(Marie) decides she's a lesbian after all. Complete with belly dancing part filler sequence."

(11) Four Times That Night, 1971, directed by Mario Bava and starring Brett Halsey and Pascale Petit. From The Act of Seeing: "Blocked from Italian release by censorship issues, co-producer Alfredo Leone couldn't sell the foreign distribution rights for three years."

(12) I Was a Male Call Girl, 1971, a retitling of German sexpert Alois Brummer's Confessions of a Male Escort, starring Helmut Alimonta. From The Act of Seeing: "I Was a Male Call Girl is a retitling of German sexpert Alois Brummer's Confessions of a Male Escort or Obszonitaten/Obscenity(1971). A Eurotic variant on the Percy(1971) theme, Helmut Alimonta plays a well-endowed Bavarian gigolo offered 100,000 Deutschmarks to part with his penis for a wealthy noble transplant."

(13) A Weekend With Strangers, 1971, directed by Allen Savage and starring Jennifer Welles and David Gale. From The Act of Seeing: "Also know to some 42nd Streeters as Weekend Swingers."

(14) The Big Doll House, 1971, directed by Jack Hill and starring Roberta Collins, Pam Grier, Judy Brown and Sid Haig. From Blaxploitation Cinema: The Essential Reference Guide, by Josiah

Howard: "Female prisoners in a Philippine jail are being subjected to sadistic torture. Five of the women - along with the help of two men - plot an escape."
(15) Carnal Knowledge, 1971, directed by Mike Nichols, starring Jack Nicholson, Candice Bergen, Ann-Margret and Art Garfunkel. Dialogue quote: "What're you crying for, it wasn't a Lassie story."
(16) Straw Dogs, 1971, directed by Sam Peckinpah and starring Dustin Hoffman, Susan George and Peter Vaughan. Poster tagline: "Every man has his breaking point."
(17) Vampyros Lesbos, 1971, directed by Jesus Franco and starring Soledad Miranda, Dennis Price and Paul Muller. Actress Soledad Miranda died in a road accident in 1970 aged just 27.
(18) Walkabout, 1971, directed by Nicholas Roeg and starring Jenny Agutter, David Gulpilil, Luc Roeg and John Meillon. Poster tagline: "A boy and a girl face the challenge if the world's last frontier."
(19) A Clockwork Orange, 1971, directed by Stanley Kubrick, starring Malcolm McDowell, Patrick Magee, Michael Bates and Warren Clarke. Kubrick directed only 16 films in a 48 year career.
(20) Confessions of a Window Cleaner, 1974, directed by Val Guest, starring Robin Askwith, Sheila White, Anthony Booth and Bill Maynard. Followed by ...Pop Performer(1975), ...Driving Instructor(1976), and ...Holiday Camp(1977), all directed by Norman Cohen with the same stars. The quartet of films all have screenplays by Christopher(The Spy Who Loved Me/Moonraker) Wood.
(21) Can You Keep it Up for a Week?, 1975, directed by Jim Atkinson(his only directing effort), starring Jeremy(Star Wars bounty hunter Boba Fett) Bulloch, Jill Damas, Neil Hallett and Joy Harington. Not that the film was in need of a poster tagline, there is one nonetheless: "If you can...then give us a ring!
(22) Adventures of a Taxi Driver, 1976, all three directed by Stanley Long, starring Barry Evans, Judy Geeson, Diana Dors and Liz Fraser. Private Eye, 1977, starring Christopher Neill, Suzy Kendall, Diana Dors and Harry H. Corbett. Plumbers Mate, 1978, starring Lindy Benson, Prudence Drage and Peter Cleall. Each had its own pun intended tagline, you can guess which belongs to which: "He gets more than his fare share." "The clever Dick...who uncovers everybody." "He's always on call for this sort of job."
(23) The Ups and Downs of a Handyman, 1976, directed by John Sealey, starring Barry Stokes, Gay Soper, Sue Lloyd and Bob Todd.

Poster tagline: "Always handy, the odd job man whose services are constantly in demand."

CHAPTER FOUR

A BRIEF HISTORY OF MINE

- 1895- Louis Lumiere releases what is considered to be the first true motion picture: Sortie de l'usine Lumiere de Lyon.
- 1897- Georges Melies builds one of the first dedicated movie studios.
- 1899- Arthur Melborne-Cooper producers Matches: An Appeal, the first use of animation.
- 1903- Will Barker relocates his Autoscope Company and creates studios where Ealing Studios will later reside.
- 1905- The opening of the first permanent theatre showing only films: "The Nickleodeon" in Pittsburgh.
- 1906- The Story of the Kelly Gang is the first multi-reel feature-length movie.
- 1908- Paris-based film company Pathe-Freres is founded.
- 1912- Carl Laemmle's Independent Motion Picture Company merges with several small companies to form Universal.
- 1914- Elstree Studios, Hertfordshire, begins to take shape.
- 1916- Although Paramount Pictures is a distributor in 1914, it is not until after various mergers that the studio is created from this name.
- 1917- Universum Film AG(Ufa) in Germany see's the partial nationalisation of the film industry in that country.
- 1919- Charlie Chaplin, Douglas Fairbanks, D.W. Griffith and Mary Pickford form United Artists.
- 1923- Despite being in business together since 1918, it's not until this year that the Warner brothers form their company.
- 1923- Walt and Roy O. Disney form their company.
- 1924- Harry and Jack Cohn's company CVC, formed in 1920 with Joe Brandt, is renamed Columbia Pictures.
- 1924- Metro Pictures merges with the Goldwyn Company And Louis B Mayer Productions to form MGM.
- 1927- The Jazz Singer is generally considered to be the first Talking Picture.
- 1931- Shepperton Studios in Middlesex begins production.
- 1932- Ichizo Kobayashi creates Toho Studios.
- 1935- Pinewood Studios Limited is formed by J. Arthur Rank and Charles Boot.

1935- 20th Century Fox is the new name for William Fox's company(Fox Film Corporation) when it merges with 20th Century Productions.
1936- A new studio was opened on 30th September on Iver Heath, Buckinghamshire, called Pinewood Studios.
1936- Alexander Korda creates Denham Studios, Buckinghamshire.
1937- Benito Mussolini creates Cinecitta studios.

As I touched upon in the previous chapter the seventies for movies was a pivotal decade in numerous ways and not just with the loosening of censorship and the moral code, bringing more vivid imagery to the screens and pushing the boundaries of decency at that time. It also brought with it numerous globally fortified social and economic upheavals which altered the way in which films were produced, released, presented and marketed.

Economic downturn in the sixties for the movie industry as a whole saw the near-decimation of the major Hollywood Studies and their backlot facilities as they were taken over by the huge conglomerates and the non-media corporations and financiers, without any real feeling toward the history of film, who were primarily looking to make a quick buck by selling the land off for development.

A prime example if this is the once sprawling MGM backlot, which was the envy of the movie producing world. It included its own zoo, all of which was sold off during the seventies to make way for homes, offices, carparks and strip-malls. There were acres upon acres of open countryside utilised in many classic westerns for movies and television, while the backlot facilities were second to none. The book M-G-M Hollywood's Greatest Backlot, published in 2011 by Santa Monica Press LLC, written and compiled by Steven Bingen, Stephen X. Sylvester and Michael Troyan, is a brilliant yet poignant history in words and pictures of this truly magnificent complex. The Irving G. Thalberg building still exists, while various other studio buildings and sound-stages are being used to this day, but there are nothing but famous street-names to denote what else used to be there.

The story of MGM is a similar one at other facilities synonymous with Hollywood and the British studios, while streamlining continued throughout the decade.

Socially edgy cinema, normally associated with Europe, with powerful, realistic and often nihilistic ideas were brought to the fore in the early years of the decade thanks to a new young breed of film-maker coming through, creating more director-led pictures and offering hope to a floundering industry during a period which was shaky at best. Films such as realistically gritty New York City cop drama The French Connection(1); stark urban alienation in Taxi Driver(2); an unconventional gritty nihilistic cop in Dirty Harry(3); tonal obsessive paranoia in The Conversation(4); powerful media satire in Network(5); hardboiled seventies noir Chinatown(6); and I could go on.

All of these films and more would challenge film conventions, altering people's perceptions of what cinema can be with their thought-provoking stories and imagery, stretching deeper into our real world and the often harsh environment we inhabit while also frequently predicting many future events and morals, transforming the movie landscape and paving the way for others.

"Hang about, I thought this chapter was going to have more details about your family history, not all this film stuff!"

But this pretentious autobiography is supposed to be quirky and full of self-important pretension while showing my love for films, presenting it in an engaging yet unpretentious manner for the reader, taking them on a journey of discovery via facts, short stories and adventures.

"Pretentious is right! Quit the jibber-jabber and give the readers what they actually want, not what you blindly believe they want. So- you were born September 28th 1971?"

Did I not mention that in the last chapter?

"Second chapter."

Stop being pedantic.

"I think you will find I was being facetious, while now I am being pedantic laced with a smidgeon of sarcasm! If you had said previous chapter instead of last chapter I would have let it slip."

A smidgeon? Is that a small pigeon?

"You're not funny."

Jeez, and I thought I was.

"Sarcasm isn't funny." (Apparently sarcasm is the lowest form of wit, but at least it is wit.)

You should know.

"Look- let's just get to the point, shall we? People don't want to read your usual waffle! So- your brother and sister first."

Yes, they were.

"How about saying a bit about them, if you can do that! It might help people to understand where you came from, and maybe explain why you are the person you have become, although I doubt that very much."

Okay, if you think it will help. Philip is eight years my senior and has many of our father's attributes, physically as well as characteristically. He is tall and wiry, and a man of few words with a dark sense of humour - presumably - and is quite an enigma really, keeping his emotions closely guarded and prefers life without conflict - a bit like our dad, whose outbursts were rare but explosive. Coincidentally my brother began his working life in retail but I don't believe it suited him as it has myself. He has now worked for the Postal Service for several years, delivering the mail and working in the sorting office. Like our father he has participated in various sports; football, snooker and cricket as player and coach. Philip is father to one son and husband to one wife.

"Very interesting. How about your sister?"

Karen is ten years older than me and more outgoing, perhaps she was rebellious against the quiet country life in her youth, preferring a more noisy and chaotic City existence which is where she now resides. Essentially she followed a similar path to our mum: juggling a few hours work with being a homemaker, three children, which is hard work enough, who now have kids of their own. Married to a Norwich City man who qualified to be a tailor but seems never to have settled on a career path, and why not, there's nothing wrong with being spontaneously unfocused in this crazy world.

"How close were you to them?"

Crucially the age gap made a big difference but that's not to say we didn't get along - as we still get along now - but we couldn't exactly play sibling games because they were into something different to little me, so our social lives never really interconnected. I was a needy, whiny little shoot so I undoubtedly drove them around the twist - some things don't change! They had their teens in the seventies, I in the eighties, so we have different perspectives on life, culture and such, but I'm sure we get along much better than some families.

"So- you say your brother takes after your father, and your sister takes after your mum. What about you?"

Definitely both, although I used to claim I was found under gooseberry bush. I have a good balance of their positive and negative characteristics - we all have a mixture of the positive and negative, don't we, that's what makes us human. But I can define those characteristics which I inherited from my parents, intermingled with a variety of other sources throughout the years. Neither of my parents were particularly artistic in their endeavours yet mum made sails while dad was a gardner by trade, both of which require some form of creative input. But I suppose as for writing, that would possibly come from the time spent playing by myself, creating stories with my toys which were more like full-blown adventures in three acts, and this continued with reading and English through school.

"Your writing is good?"

Excellent, yes. It's almost inherent Shakespearean. I consider myself to be an undisputed literary genius.

"Indeed- sarcasm isn't funny."

I think you will find it's more accurately described as self-effacing, self-deprecating humour used as a defence mechanism to hide my numerous deficiencies.

"You feel insecure?"

What are you, a psychiatrist?

"Something like that! Tell us more."

I couldn't possibly, I'm far too insecure to talk about myself.

"Very funny."

Thank you.

"Tell us more about your parents."

I knew them both, which is quite good in this day and age!

"Very funny also."

Thank you. Dad held three jobs and was most definitely the provider, not wishing anything for himself, really, and seemed quite content doing this.

"So he was a gardner, local league football referee and a retained fire-fighter?"

That's right. And I suppose my Dad's aloofness helped Mum to cope better when he died, being used to spending time alone and with friends, as well as tending house, being an unpaid agony aunt, putting up with her trio of kids and her variety of ailments, which rarely got her down.

"Can you remember much about your Grandparents?"

Yes. Both sets, but mainly my Mum's parents because Dad's passed away when I was quite young.

"Any particular memories?"

Yes. I can recall going with Dad most every Sunday morning to see his parents, usually followed by a visit to Stalham Fire Station so he could do some paperwork - they had a snooker table in their recreation room in those days so I would play while I waited. My Mum's parents lived near us in Hoveton so I would obviously see them more often. They had a big garden with a bridal-path behind it, which I had great fun mucking around the back of. I can remember when they moved not far along the estate into an attached bungalow I helped them move, I can't recall what age I was, but I can remember that Granddad asked how much he owed me for my help, and of course I said nothing so he swiftly pocketed his wallet: tight git!

"What is your first memory?"

This is a tricky one because I seem to recall riding a three wheel trike along a footpath behind our house when I was three or four, but we have a photograph of this event so I'm not sure if its a real memory or just association memory. I do recall my first school, though, if that's helpful. It was Hoveton St.John's Primary which is no longer there as a school, its someone's home now.

"Anything specific from school?"

Nosy aren't you?

"Just curious as to what you can remember."

I can remember quite a mixture of things from Primary school. I know I didn't like it at first, whining and whinging like a crybaby! I can remember Emma Cadamy, my first girlfriend, because she and I went through Middle School together too. There was a big metal dome-shaped climbing frame which was set above concrete, which health and safety would have a field-day over now. Riding on the back of Mum's bike to school, sometimes getting a lift by car with another parent. An outdoor brick toilet block. I know that one day I failed to ask properly if I could go to the toilet so subsequently I wet myself, and lets just say I now always remember the word please! Strangely enough I don't specifically remember any lessons, nor the teachers.

"So it was a waste of time going?"

No. I'm positive there was social value in going to Primary School as there is now, and obviously one began to learn basic maths and English - please and thank you were also taught back then, and one respected teachers more! Maybe it was less of a business model, less target-driven, less PC than the sponsored teaching institutions of today, or am I just being cynical?

"Maybe."

They didn't teach media and there was no watching films in class, unlike today, which wasn't bad thing I suppose because shouldn't one be at school to learn?

"How about secondary school?"

I attended that too.

"Anything else you would like to add?"

Strewth, I wasn't expecting the Spanish Inquisition.

"No one expects them, they just appear!"

Can I get back to what I was talking about earlier, you know, film stuff?

"Its up to you, we are, after all, one and the same person! First of all, though, what is the first movie you can recall seeing at the cinema?"

E.T.: The Extra Terrestrial(7). I'm not going to include the ones I saw at Butlin's in Skegness while on holiday. I went to see E.T. at the Odeon Cinema, Anglia Square, in Norwich. I cannot recall the exact date but I suppose it was possibly the end of 1982, although its 9th December release date in this country might signify I went in early 1983, which is certainly more probable, but I'm not sure.

And as we are back onto the subject of film.

"Tenuous link alert!"

In 1975 along came Jaws(8), followed perhaps more significantly by Star Wars(9), both altering the cinema landscape entirely while creating films which are essentially upgraded Ray Harryhausen, Roger Corman and Irwin Allen flicks only with inflated studio finances - okay, both were risky ventures which might have turned out disastrously, but they didn't.

These effects driven films and others would herald the dawn of saturated-market releasing, conflated promotion and mind-boggling merchandising opportunities, all of which continues today as each film tries to be the next-big-thing or, as is often the case, one-week wonder because after the pre-release hype machine has done its work and the film is released, its soon forgotten when the next blockbuster comes out.

I should like to note here at this point that the use of the terms blockbuster and classic have come to mean less over the last twenty years when, before the film is released or viewed, a certain section of films are already being labelled with either of these words. A true blockbuster should signify a film which has a queue of excited moviegoers waiting with anticipation going into the auditorium while a few blocks away from the cinema. And a classic cannot be deemed as such until, I feel, after many years for the films overall appreciation to grow, and for a variety of reasons, perhaps rising above its original status.

Don't get me wrong, progress and change are both inevitable and in some cases necessary to drive a business, but it isn't always a good thing for art and artists. The seventies saw lots if cutting-edge cinema with some risk-taking and thought-provoking, anti-establishment stories which are no longer facilitated by the conglomerates of today, where they are now focused mainly on the bottom line. There existed in the seventies an opportunity for independent filmmakers like in no other decade before or since, where the B-picture existed on the fringes with exploitation fare well into the mid-eighties.

(1) The French Connection, 1971, directed by William Friedkin, starring Gene Hackman, Roy Scheider and Aldo Ray. Winner of the BAFTA and Oscar for Best Picture. Poster tagline: "Doyle is bad news, but a good cop."
(2) Taxi Driver, 1976, directed by Martin Scorsese, starring Robert DeNiro, Faye Dunaway, Jodie Foster and Albert Brooks. Dialogue quote: "Thank God for the rain to wash the trash off the sidewalk." Poster tagline: "On every street there's a nobody who dreams of being somebody. He's a lonely forgotten man desperate to prove that he's alive."
(3) Dirty Harry, 1971, directed by Don Siegel, starring Clint Eastwood, Andrew Robinson, John Vernon and Harry Guardino. Poster tagline: "Detective Harry Callaghan. He doesn't break murder cases. He smashes them." Frank Sinatra was first choice for the role of Callaghan.

(4) The Conversation, 1974, directed by Francis Ford Coppola, starring Gene Hackman, John Cazal, Allen Garfield, Cindy Williams and Elizabeth MacRae. Dialogue quote: "I'm not afraid of death, but I am afraid of murder."

(5) Network, 1976, directed by Sidney Lumet, starring Faye Dunaway, William Holden, Peter Finch, Beatrice Straight, Robert Duvall and Ned Beatty. Dialogue quote: "I'm as mad as hell and I'm not going to take it anymore."

(6) Chinatown, 1974, directed by Roman Polanski, starring Jack Nicholson, Faye Dunaway, John Huston, John Hillerman and Diane Ladd. Dialogue quote: "What happened to your nose, Gittes? Someone slam a bedroom window on it? Reply: Nope, your wife got a little excited, she crossed her legs too quick." From the multi-award winning script by Robert Towne.

(7) E.T.: The Extra Terrestrial, 1982, directed by Steven Spielberg, starring Henry Thomas, Drew Barrymore, Dee Wallace and Peter Coyote. Reigned as No.1 at the box-office for over ten years. Won John Williams his third Oscar for Best Original Score.

(8) Jaws, 1975, directed by Steven Spielberg, starring Roy Scheider, Richard Dreyfus, Robert Shaw, Lorraine Gary and Murray Hamilton. Affectively launched the modern-day summer blockbuster with a global haul of $470million. Won John Williams his first Oscar for Best Original Score.

(9) Star Wars, 1977, directed by George Lucas, starring Mark Hamill, Harrison Ford, Carrie Fisher, Alec Guinness and Peter Cushing. Won John Williams his second Oscar for Best Original Score.

CHAPTER FIVE

1981
MY SPORTING LIFE

Truth be told it was probably until '83/'84 when I watched more football matches than I watched movies, and certainly my early childhood memories feature more of these games than cinema visits - but if you have been paying close attention its pretty superfluous of me to make this last statement! The reason for soccer watching and attendance is the simple fact that my Dad was a football referee for the local Saturday afternoon leagues to which I would invariably go no matter what the weather was doing, and I didn't complain because I enjoyed every one - amateur football players and supporters are indeed a very hardy lot, with their muddy pitches, minimal or sometimes no shelter, and stark changing facilities probably in the village hall.

    The reason why I have chosen 1981 as the year to settle on the sporting theme is not just because aged ten I probably went more often than before and honed my talent -or lack of - for sport , but because this is the year that Escape to Victory(1) was released. A sort of uplifting, hokey ensemble picture trying in vain to be The Great Escape(2), wherein the POW's stage a football game as a pretext to their escape plan. Not a particularly original concept although the execution was certainly different, while the acting and characters are poorly fleshed-out and its not terribly exciting or inspiring, yet it still remains one of those films enjoyable despite its inadequacies and has definitely stuck in my brain as such. There have been few other football films of real note, except maybe Bend It Like Beckham(3), unless you group American Football in this bracket where a couple of fine and diverse examples are Any Given Sunday(4) and The Blind Side(5), but their germination owes a great deal to Hollywood and its people rather than the sport, perhaps, and are inspiring stories which transcend the genre.

    I must have visited countless Norfolk village playing fields throughout this county in my younger days and swung on a variety of swings, slid down numerous slides and rode many a round-about. During these two-hours of play I would make new friends and have fun while absorbing the sights, sounds and smells which go with these football matches: the grass, the whistle, the ointment, the voracious encouragement with colourful metaphors that sailed over my innocent head. Yet I never actually played the game myself, at least not in the context of playing and I would say I was poorly lacking in skill as a participant, and this is me being generous! In my late teens I was a part of a five-aside team which I didn't offer any real talent to but we were all of a mixed-age and skill, some were disabled so there was a noble cause. Perhaps this was a case of the taking part and not the winning being significant - although no sports coach worth his salt actually tells the individual or team he encourages this belief.

Rugby can also be discounted as a sporting endeavour for me although I did once break my little toe and someone asked if it happened while I was playing Rugby, but unfortunately it occurred doing a less macho endeavour - I was dancing around my lounge with Chloe, my eldest daughter, and ran into the hardwood play-pen of my youngest daughter: ouch!

Team sports really have never been for me, if thats not obvious by now.

I like Raging Bull(6), The Fighter(7) and the Rocky(8) series but I try to avoid confrontation and my physique is unfortunately lighter than light-weight so boxing or any contact sport is out of the equation - although to contradict myself right here and now I have been a student of karate, holding a high level in the Shotokan style so, yeah, don't mess with me, punk- please!

I was quite good at snooker in my own way, I suppose, although again I am reluctant to praise myself. I started playing when I was fourteen at a local members only Men's Club, Wroxham Social Club as it now known and surprising resides in the village of Wroxham - I know this sounds like an obvious fact but you try finding Wroxham Barns in the village! Thanks should be extended to my brother and grandad, who were members there, which meant I could attend before the official accepted membership age of sixteen. I'm sure there is an untapped movie story vain still to be rendered on the big-screen featuring real characters like Alex Higgins or Ronnie O'Sullivan, both of whom could inspire a suitably dramatic story. It is only the game of Pool which has inspired a truly dramatic movie-story backdrop(9).

Tennis was also something which I enjoyed and I did indeed reach quite a good level of competence until injury to my elbow caused a cessation of this sport: I was also quite lacking in patience at this time in my life so coming up against me could be like witnessing one-man warring against himself. Movies of quality on this particular sport are few and far between: Wimbledon(10) being the obvious one, and Match Point(11), are worth seeking out.

The third and final sport which I enjoyed playing but decided to stop because my passion was beaten by ability is golf, and there have been several films made about this sport too: Tin Cup(12), The Legend of Bagger Vance(13) and Caddyshack(14), to name but three. It is a safer proposition for my clubs that I now play pitch and putt, which is a shame, but a man has definitely got to know his limitations and I enjoy golf too much to be happy playing it badly - does that make sense?

So as you see I am not a sports-person although at least I have tried and I do cycle(15) quite a bit, just not competitively unless you include competing with oneself. I used to enjoy watching F1(16) until it became too corporate, technically restricted and boring(17), and I created my own card statistics game using F1 Top Trump's in those days.

A later school report I would receive stated that "Paul needs to try harder." True, perhaps, but I get frustrated because I cannot achieve in sport what my enjoyment dictates, for some reason, plus I do not enjoy losing - this is not an admission to being a sore loser, I would simply prefer to win!

(1) Escape to Victory, 1981, directed by John Huston, starring Michael Caine, Sylvester Stallone, Pele, Bobby Moore, Osvaldo Ardilles etc. Poster tagline: "The Germans planned a spectacular match - the players planned a spectacular escape."
(2) The Great Escape, 1963, directed by John Sturges, starring Richard Attenborough, Steve McQueen, James Garner, Charles Bronsan, James Coburn etc. My friend Jimmy's favourite film: RIP with love.
(3) Bend it Like Beckham, 2002, directed by Gurinder Chadha, starring Parminder Nagra, Keira Knightley and Jonathan Rhys Meyers. Dialogue quote: "Lesbian? Her birthday's in March, I thought she was a Pisces."
(4) Any Given Sunday, 1999, directed by Oliver Stone, starring Al Pacino, Cameron Diaz, Dennis Quaid, Jamie Foxx, Jim Brown and James Woods. Oliver Stone, from The Oliver Stone Experience by

Matt Zoller Seitz: "Intelligence and game planning make a winning team...there's a madcap quality to football that's fun."

(5) The Blind Side, 2009, directed by John Lee Hancock, starring Sandra Bullock, Quinton Aaron, Tim McGraw and Lily Collins. On a budget of $29million it took $290million at the box office, making it the most financially successful female led sports drama.

(6) Raging Bull, 1980, directed by Martin Scorsese, starring Robert DeNiro, Cathy Moriarty, Joe Pesci and Frank Vincent. Producers Irwin Winkler and Robert Chartoff also produced the Rocky boxing franchise.

(7) The Fighter, 2010, directed by David O Russell, starring Mark Wahlberg, Christian Bale, Amy Adams and Melissa Leo. Like many sporting films it is based on a true story, and this film won Bale and Leo supporting Oscars.

(8) Rocky, 1976, directed by John G Avildson, starring Sylvester Stallone, Talia Shire, Burt Young, Carl Weathers etc. Stallone was nominated for an acting and screenwriting Oscar.

(9) The Hustler, 1961, directed by Robert Rossen, starring Paul Newman, Jackie Gleeson, George C. Scott and Piper Laurie. A sequel in 1986 directed by Martin Scorsese co-starring Tom Cruise won Paul Newman the Best Actor Oscar.

(10) Wimbledon, 2004, directed by Richard Locraine, starring Kirsten Dunst, Paul Bettany and Jon Favreau, Sam Neill and Bernard Hill. Poster tagline: "She's the golden girl. He's the long-shot. Together they're a match made in...Wimbledon."

(11) Match Point, 2005, directed by Woody Allen, starring Scarlett Johannson, Jonathan Rhys Meyers and Emily Mortimer. Poster tagline: "There are no little secrets."

(12) Tin Cup, 1996, directed by Ron Shelton, starring Kevin Costner, Rene Russo and Don Johnson. Director Ron Shelton has made a career from making sporting movies: American Football(The Best of Times, 1986), Baseball(Bull Durham, 1988), Basketball(White Men Can't Jump, 1992), Boxing(Play it to the Bone, 1999), to name but a few,

(13) The Legend of Bagger Vance, 2000, directed by Robert Redford, starring Will Smith, Matt Damon and Charlize Theron. Dialogue quote: "The question on the table is how drunk is drunk enough, and the answer is that it's a matter of brain cells."

(14) Caddyshack, 1980, directed by Harold Ramis, starring Chevy Chase, Bill Murray and Rodney Dangerfield. Poster tagline: "Some people just don't belong."

(15) American Flyers, 1985, directed by John Badham, starring Kevin Costner, David Marshall Grant and Rae Dawn Chong. Star Kevin Costner clearly has a screen sporting aptitude, particularly in baseball(Chasing Dreams, 1982, Bull Durham, 1988, Field of Dreams, 1989, For Love of the Game, 1999).

(16) Senna, 2010, directed by Asif Capadia, compiled from actual footage of F1 stars including Alain Prost, Nigel Mansell, Jackie Stewart and Frank Williams, to create a stunningly original documentary feature on the life and career of Ayrton Senna.

(17) Driven, 2001, directed by Renny Harlin, starring Sylvester Stallone, Burt Reynolds, Kip Pardue and Gina Gershon. Poster tagline: "Welcome to the human race."

CHAPTER SIX

BONDING EXPERIENCE

Since 1964's Goldfinger the James Bond phenomenon has been critic-proof whilst becoming a global box-office behemoth where every entry makes a profit, even those amongst them which are, politely said, below par action films. So it was almost inevitable that in 1982/3 the media circus would make much hype of the rival James Bond films Octopussy and Never Say Never Again; one an official entry in the Eon series, the other unofficial, both with self-explanatory, if unappealing, titles. The Battle of the Bonds continued throughout the duo of films entire production periods and into their release - Roger Moore: "there was no animosity between Sean and me," and "It's the first time I've ever been panned for a film I wasn't in," - ultimately benefitting neither on a critical level while at the box office they both performed adequately if not spectacularly - Octopussy $183.7million on a budget of $27.5million/Never Say Never Again $137.5million on a budget of $36million - particularly by today's standards where competing comic-book films rule the roost and rake in millions despite their criticism, which must have irked the producers of both Bond's at the time because of the potential opportunity which was missed -   although marketing was much different in the 1980's - and it is quite possible to imagine how the hype-machine would salivate in this present age of excessive budgets and multi-platform cross-promotion.

Sean Connery circa 1983: "I wouldn't mind appearing with Roger Moore in a double-Bond adventure, sort of a Dr. Jekyll and Mr. Bond."

Sadly it's too late now.

Familiar elements struggle in this competition between two very different actors in the role of the ageing hero, while the stories and structure create a pair of eighties films which are indicative of those which become unstuck by formula, plus a lack of risk-taking and much imagination.

While re-viewing, analysing and reappraising these two films I have indeed concluded that they are both critic-proof, a bit like the Transformer films of the new millennium which clean up at the box-office despite their lack of depth, because fans of all things James

Bond - myself included - shall always garner some enjoyment from them, while also being able to admit to their quirks, because in the wider movie pantheon even a fan is not blinkered enough to realise the James Bond are nowhere near to approaching artistic masterpiece status.

James Bond's All Time High

The name of this James Bond films main female character might be utterly ridiculous - although maybe not so much in this age of celebrities naming their babies Sage, Peaches or Moon, to name but a few - but at least the film itself is a decent entry into a franchise which has often seemed to lack the bravery to develop beyond the usual formula. Octopussy tries to avoid using a world-dominating megalomaniac in its attempt to more accurately mirror the decades Cold War world affairs, making the characters feel as though they could perhaps exist in the real world, yet the script still runs afoul of cliché and humdrum action sequences because it doesn't move quite far enough beyond this tried-and-tested formula.

Cubby Broccoli: "A problem loomed on the horizon involving Kevin McClory, Sean Connery, and a rival Bond picture they were making."

The dilemma was how to proceed with their own film.

Octopussy is based on an Ian Fleming short story with little plot or elements familiar to readers of the main novels, yet it does possess a good enough hook for the title character of the future film: her father is given the chance by James Bond of a noble death over personal disgrace. In the short story Octopussy is not a woman.

Many of the familiar elements are in place: action-packed pre-credits sequence with John Barry underscore; powerfully rendered song; an insidious villain blindly hell-bent on destabilising world affairs; a villains glorious lair; gorgeously filmed action set-pieces; nick-of-time perils; 'surprise' denouement.

Maybe returning director John Glen sums this era up best: "A Bond film is quite unique; you don't start with a script, you start with an idea."

What makes this film different to the usual Roger Moore over-the-top adventure of, say, Moonraker or The Spy Who Loved Me, is its focus on situational realism. Moore's previous film in the series, For Your Eyes Only, sought to bring Bond back to earth with a story more indicative of the spy genre with its elements of subterfuge, double-cross and token justice, but still providing enough set-pieces to keep the 70's Bond fan happy. In other words the changes were not too jarring, it still utilised Moore's adeptness at eyebrow-raising humour, as does Octopussy, but they were unfortunately significant enough changes to put a dampers on the box-office triumph of Moonraker - one of the franchises most successful entries based on ticket-sales. This film tries the same approach but less successfully than From Russia With Love, sticking with formula, and from 1995 to 2002 Pierce Brosnan would utilise pretty much the same elements in his portrayal of Bond and the producers would rehash these formulas for him, Brosnan's often wooden acting style being more akin to Moore than Connery.

Octopussy's team of craftsmen and women have been working together for several years now so the production went along comparatively smoothly, even the hijacking of an airplane with production designer Peter Lamont onboard couldn't put them off, and this ability to function as a unit does show in glaring comparison to Never Say Never Again's lack of cohesion throughout.

The trouble lies in the franchises unwillingness to leave the comfort zone of its history. Yes, everyone equites themselves like a well-oiled machine but maybe there isn't enough inventiveness involved to push any boundaries. Octopussy feels stale and unexciting, the Bond films at this point scream out for reinvention and with a clear rival in the shape of Never Say Never Again and the Producers' of that film's threat of beginning a cycle Bond films themselves, you would think Broccoli and co. might just try a little bit harder. Or maybe the filmgoing public were not ready for change - look at Timothy Dalton's hard-edged approach in his two Bond films, The Living Daylights and Licence To Kill, whose box-office failure almost signalled the death-knell to the Bond franchise, although I maintain both of Dalton's films are still better on many levels then Brosnan's quartet. Even John Barry's music in Octopussy feels somewhat stale but, still, it's John Barry's brilliance rather than a poor imitator.

Reviews for Octopussy at the time were decidedly mixed:
"...on better form than it has been for some time." TimeOut.

"This is the thirteenth film and the series luck is palpably beginning to run out." The Sunday Telegraph.

So the conclusion is theres nothing really new here but it still entertains more than numerous other action films and it is this familiarity which kept the franchise alive.

Sean Connery IS James Bond

If you have watched this 'unofficial' entry into the Bond movie lexicon and been disappointed by the fact it possesses none of the 'official series' elements - Monty Norman's theme, familiar production values, tried-and-tested structure - then I believe this is good reason for reappraisal and perhaps offers a refreshing alternative to Roger Moore's nonchalant flippancy in the role of James Bond.

First things first, though: this is not the best film in the world by any stretch of the imagination but there are far worse you could consider watching and, curiously, the missing familiar elements are frequently the high-lights of this sometimes flawed action film. And if you haven't seen this Bond film...well, maybe I can offer you reasons to do so.

Search deeply within this broth and there is potential for greatness bubbling under the surface yet unfortunately the production had too many obstacles to overcome, so when it did eventually begin filming it was a case of too many cooks spoiling its cohesion. The estate of Albert R. Broccoli set many restrictions before this film's tenacious figure-head could even get his project of the ground.

That figure-head was one Kevin McClory who, along with screenwriter Jack Whittingham and James Bond author Ian Fleming concocted the original story which Never Say Never Again is based upon: Thunderball. Together this trio formed a production company to develop a project for the first James Bond movie, the story eventually evolving into Thunderball with a script by Whittingham but after much financial wrangling the project collapsed. This setback did not prevent Fleming from turning their story into his next novel, but through his almost amateurish failure to credit its true source a court-case ensued, during which Kevin McClory was given filming rights to the plot and characters which he and Whittingham helped create, with a few restrictions imposed upon him, and the future Bond producers Harry Saltzman and Albert R. Broccoli.(For more detailed information on this case and its intriguing outcome, see the book The Battle For Bond.

Unfortunately due to its much-maligned script by Lorenzo Semple, with "A magnificent job," done by the rewrites from Dick Clement and Ian Ka Frenais, the film is tonally uneven, but this is undoubtedly because dialogue needed checking by studio lawyers to ensure no repercussions from Albert R. Broccoli's camp.

So are we supposed to be amused or sympathetic towards this ageing James Bond who struggles to fit into the 80's mindset, himself and the audience oftentimes uncomfortably watching these sharp shifts in character. Some if the supporting cast give performances more befitting an entry in the Carry On series; jarringly they sit more comfortably with Roger Moore's Bond circa 1979's Moonraker, especially Q substitute Algernon and Rowan Atkinson's inept secret service liaison officer.

All this despite Sean Connery's claim that: "I made it absolutely clear that my major concern was to make a film of quality."

Connery has always been tough on incompetence and has frequently made clear his feelings on studio politics - which would reach their zenith upon his retirement from the business - so maybe his annoyance saw him lose patience with the projects producers, and he became disinterested in the finished product which caused conflicts of ego with the director.

Irvin Kerschner, director of Never Say Never Again: "A really good actor will challenge the director... Sean challenges me and I have got to come up with the answers."

First-time producer Jack Schwartzman, who wife, Talia Shire, is an Executive Consultant on the picture, also seems a bit daunted and unsure by the task at hand: "I wish it didn't cost so much, but I think we're ending up with a very fine picture."

With so much money and talent lavished upon it why are the action set-pieces and photographic elements so uninspiring?

But don't let me put you off because this is certainly not my aim by pointing out its flaws - I shall discuss Michel Legrand's music stylings later.

So where are the plus points?

Klaus Maria Brandeur's villainous portrayal of Largo is pure OTT Bond villain madness, giving his sometimes leaden dialogue a definite gravitas. Barbara Carrerra is possibly one of the best female villains in a Bond film, or any other film, for that matter, and she gives a lurid and maniacal performance - "Fatima is like a bad child who does not see the evil in what she is doing, she just enjoys it." – it's almost a shame when she killed off. Kim Basinger is suitably gorgeous, acting(?) the part of the dumb-blonde to perfection in her debut film. Sean Connery of course makes a much welcome return to what is certainly his signature role, playing the older, although not necessarily wiser, not-so-secret agent with relish and a spirit which belies his age.

There are several scenes which stand head-and-shoulders above the rest: the reintroduction of Bond during the title sequence; the plot device which instigates the theft of the nuclear warheads; the computer game duel between Bond and Largo; Bond's Tango with Domino; Fatima's explosive demise; the Tears of Allah escape sequence.

The production design is fine enough and the cinematography adequate, but there is a definite lack of a unique signature on the screen by either department, while its director Irvin Kerschner seems to be serving too many masters to stamp any mark of his own on the film - similar to his serving George Lucas' vision on The Empire Strikes Back, only with greater success on the sci-fi saga than with Bond(on the Blu-ray commentary he sounds positively unenthusiastic about the project, which unfortunately makes the film seem a bore to have worked on).

So...Michel Legrand's music. It has the inglorious distinction of being voted the worst score ever. Tonally it is frequently out of place, as if the composer is scoring for a different film entirely, and this does certainly hamper many of the action sequences: the title scenes could definitely be served better without the song, a more action-orientated instrumental is called for. But there are strong motifs throughout and the score doesn't fail through its lack of familiar themes - David Arnold's score for 2005's Casino Royale uses the James Bond theme only in its final scene, but in that instance, the music sits well within the film. And this is where Legand's score unfortunately fails, in its distancing from the expectations and emotions within an action film, which is a great pity.

Maybe Never Say Never Again does not differentiate itself enough: familiarity breeds contempt, after all. If the film had perhaps deviated from Broccoli's formula it might very well have been more of a critical and financial success to rival that particular empire, then who knows where the two potential franchises might be in the 21st Century. But this wasn't to be and it took the successes of the Mission: Impossible and Bourne films to force the Bond producers to rethink, and reimagine, their product, which has duly benefitted the action thriller genre and not just reinvigorated 007.

So why single out these two James Bond films for a chapter by themselves? The answer is quite simple: the James Bond films are almost a genre by themselves. They have transcended the decades in they were made by constantly adapting to audience expectations and by appealing to each new generation, while also maintaining some resemblance of familiarity, and bare out repeated viewings. They began as adventure spy movies before mixing in comedy, thriller, hard-edge action, lacings of drama and tragedy, revenge and even sci-fi. They can be nostalgic period pieces when seen today, high-octane petrol-head chase movies, inspiration to technology lovers, and fascinating movie-music documents. Basically, they are many things to many people and some people have never actually seen a single James Bond film - hard to believe, I know! - despite there being so many variants to choose from, because some people can only look upon them as adolescent adventure fantasies aimed at a male audience. But they are more than this, and they are more to me than just time-wasting exercises.

Below are all the appearances of James Bond followed by their IMDb rating, whether you believe in the validity of such ratings or not, to aid your choice of Bond film.

1954 Casino Royale(Non-series Climax! TV episode)	
1962 Dr No	7.3/10
1963 From Russia With Love	7.5
1964 Goldfinger	7.8
1965 Thunderball	7.0
1967 You Only Live Twice	6.9
1967 Casino Royale(Non-series)	5.2
1969 On Her Majesties Secret Service	6.8
1971 Diamonds are Forever	6.7
1973 Live and Let Die	6.8

1974 The Man With the Golden Gun	6.8
1977 The Spy Who Loved Me	7.1
1979 Moonraker	6.3
1981 For Your Eyes Only	6.8
1983 Octopussy	6.6
1983 Never Say Never Again(Non-series)	6.2
1985 A View to a Kill	6.3
1987 The Living Daylights	6.7
1989 Licence to Kill	6.6
1995 Goldeneye	7.2
1997 Tomorrow Never Dies	6.5
1999 The World is Not Enough	6.4
2002 Die Another Day	6.1
2006 Casino Royale	8.0
2008 Quantum of Solace	6.6
2012 Skyfall	7.8
2015 Spectre	6.8

CHAPTER SEVEN

KID SOLDIERS

"A film is like a battleground: its love, hate, action, violence, death. In one word: emotion." Jean Luc Godard's Pierrot le Fou(1965).

Everything was black and white to us kids in the year 1985. Not long far back in time, really, but a world away from where society is in the 21st Century. There were no grey areas for us to consider in those days, it was simply the good-guys versus the bad-guys. Adults, the police and teachers were accorded respect. There was no back-chat without consequence or disrespect without recourse. What we were fighting against back then is lost to memory, at least it is to mine. Our battlefield was a strip of unclaimed woodland approximately the width of a football field and three times the length, although two-thirds of it was overgrown and tangled so required more effort to fortify and reconnoiter, and thus much more fun for a fourteen year-old to be amongst. A farmer's field covered several acres on one side, while there was housing on the next. We never had any complaints from our neighbours from their backyard despite our inevitable battle commotion and when the field was set to corn or turned into bales at the end of summer it offered more opportunities for cover from the enemy.

    There were times when the farmer might disagree with our war or some other youthful shenanigan, and the police may occasionally back him up on this point, but we were not really causing any particular harm to anyone at all. It's not as if our war was creating damage to property or frightening innocent women and children with its aggressiveness, and the combat drew no blood, only on occasion to our carefree selves! We were actually fighting a war where the real good-guys, us, won a decisive victory for no reason other than because we did - we weren't after land, money, oil, religious domination or power. Our war was for nothing more insidious than fun!

    If I recall correctly we nearly always played good-guys - how noble were we back in '85, fighting the good fight for the betterment of...well, who knows what, really? We most probably gathered the majority of our inspiration from whatever television program we had watched Saturday evening - because our war usually dominated

Sunday - which may very well have been The A-Team(1). So on this basis who were we at war with actually: the system? No, I doubt our thought processes and philosophy would have been so deep at this time in our lives to realise this was what The A-Team truly represented.

Our John 'Hannibal' Smith was David. He was chief orchestrator of our plans for den construction, while resources facilitator, or Templeton 'Faceman' Peck, clearly belonged to Brian. Now...not wishing to do an injustice to my friend Ivan, or myself, really, its impossible to say which one of us was BA Baracus or 'Howling Mad' Murdock because we all go a little mad sometimes!

The dens which we built grew more elaborate in their execution the more we made and subsequently destroyed them, learning from our mistakes, bigger being better as far as we were concerned. Fallen trees were our foundation while branches and bracken became the walls. Sadly I cannot recall the types of tree involved so as to enlighten the reader in the style of our endeavours, and there will be not point checking now because the woodland has been razed to the ground, destroying years of hard work - although I would be intrigued to find out what was discovered in the earth itself, some hidden treasures(2) are undoubtedly buried there because...well, that would be revealing one secret too many.

A boys' own war film which we definitely would've used as inspiration, and maybe the den fortification was our own Schloss Adler, was David's favourite film Where Eagles Dare(3). Our story wasn't set at such lofty heights or even remotely snow-tinged, but its all about the shooting and defeating the enemy, and this film would definitely have stirred our creativity. I do not know if its still David's favourite film, and although watching it is a bit of a labour at two-hours thirty-eight minutes, a running time which tends to ruin the film's suspense, it remains essential viewing.

Obviously we couldn't possible have hundreds of friends portraying the invading hordes, or Nazi's(4), as we undoubtedly stereotyped, so our imaginations would inevitably provide the enemy - I wonder what the politically correct, children padded with cotton wool brigade would preach about such choices of villain now. The defenders numbers would sometimes rise from four to most probably a total of seven in our elite unit of combatants, which isn't even enough to qualify us for The Dirty Dozen(5) status, although our unclean and dishevelled appearance owing to crawling on the woodland floor, laying in dirt or climbing sticky tree branches, may very well qualify us for the 'dirty' moniker - incidentally, I am no great fan of this much-lauded male-posturing war film, I find its overstuffed running time renders it a listless epic, but maybe that's just me!

So here we were in our fortification of tree branches - which would offer no real protection against bullets, I might add, so maybe we should've imagined an attack by arrows instead, cowboys and Indians style, which would provoke yet more political correctness! We brandished guns of various sizes furnished out of appropriately shaped tree branches and pine-cone grenades, pretending we were The Wild Geese(6) while protecting ourselves and our imaginary rebel leader from capture. The above mentioned film was one of my favourites, a highlight of the three-act boys' own war movie where soldiers return for one final, desperate mission - if we would've set our adventure on the Norfolk Broads itself perhaps our story would emulate in The Sea Wolves(7) which is a story in a similar vain. At the time of watching The Wild Geese, probably on VHS, I did not know the primary cast members were permanently drunk, and certainly watching the film now with this knowledge adds an edge to their performances, wondering about their alcohol-fuelled on-set escapades because for the most part they look like they are having genuine fun.

Probably about three-quarters of the woodland would have been quite dense with foliage, as I already said, offering ample cover for the enemy, so often we would deem it necessary to set tree-top spotters to alert us when the enemy was in sight. Climbing these trees for a thirteen year-old was comparatively simple, while jumping from tree to tree twenty-feet in the air like an untrained circus acrobat was also no problem, although slipping off mid-jump and relying on comparatively soft branches and leaves to cushion the blow could be risky - these caused some of the injuries sustained in combat, and I received my fair share.

These were fun adventures, thrilling in our youthful exuberance to prove that the good-guys always won - like I said, there were no grey areas, we were naive - and usually only ceased for Sunday lunch.

We were a mixed bag of combatants from different backgrounds and ages working together for the common good(8), a dynamic group, one might say. Ivan was the eldest, Martin the youngest.

Occasionally we might have female combatants with us and this brought along an altogether different set of challenges and dynamic to the story. I'm not sure these young girls were part of a resistance unit(9), freedom-fighters(10) or an alluring Barbara Bach character(11) who is more eye-candy, totting her gun sensually. Yet invariably the fairer sex would be treated like most female characters in male dominated war films: they were nurses. Which often forced a curious occurrence in that when either Christine - a year older than I - or Raylene - my then girlfriend - took part, I would inevitably find myself wounded in action and require their attention. Perhaps they were a jinx or there was some other strange force at work, who can say?

David is now a car mechanic, while Brian is an architect, so they were both developing their skills at a very young age. Ivan is in the food processing business and, when I read this chapter to him, his recollections have more to do with me playing James Bond and us talking, rather than playing war, in our dens: it was more the trio of myself, Ivan and David discussing the creation of THE Game – a board game created by the three of us - which Ivan recalls.

But to me these outdoor adventures will forever be etched in my memory as fun times when we cared not if it was cold or hot, wet or dry, and the main focus was playing together. Perhaps there was some subliminal value in our wars: establishing a higher learning of functioning in a structured society, discovering the hierarchy, building boundaries for ourselves, sharing a camaraderie which undoubtedly helped our development beyond these times. But I could never fight in a real war when I was old enough to enlist because I have an aversion to confrontation, I am too placid, although in my late teens I might have been able to adapt, but certainly not now.

I think the main reason why I might very well have watched several war movies when I was younger is the fact my Dad watched them on a Sunday afternoon. He was not a particularly discerning movie viewer and I couldn't say what motivated his choice because he kept his thoughts very much to himself, although it may he because he was of that age, but the one film which I might knowledgeably claim as a favourite of his in the genre is The Bridge on the River Kwai(12). What were his reasons for enjoying this film particularly? Well, I will never have the answer to that question and I wouldn't wish to note the many virtuous points of this film, that would be putting into words what someone else's motives might be, and my father would certainly not have the cinephile vocabulary to give a dissertation on the movie. Whenever I watch it now I cannot help but remember my Dad.

It wasn't really until years later, probably when I saw the VHS release of Platoon(13), that I appreciated the more meaningful aspects of war movies, because back there I was more interested in seeing stuff getting blown up amidst the thrilling stories, usually typified by ensemble movies based on novels by Alistair MacLean(14), which may involve a more adventurous, less prosaic, premise. One might say they are more Boys' Own films with a wartime backdrop, or MacGuffin, rather than those with a message or purpose other than merely to entertain a predominantly male audience.

(1) The A-Team television series,1983-1987, 97 Episodes, starring George Peppard, Mr T, Dirk Benedict and Dwight Schultz as soldiers of fortune accused of a crime they didn't commit.
(2) Kelly's Heroes, 1970, directed by Brian G Hutton, starring Clint Eastwood, Telly Savalas, Donald Sutherland, Don Rickles etc. According to the poster it was pretty epic: In 70mm and full stereophonic sound.
(3) Where Eagles Dare, 1968, directed by Brian G Hutton, starring Richard Burton, Clint Eastwood, Michael Hordern, Mary Ure and Patrick Wymark. Poster tagline: "One weekend Major Smith, Lieutenant Schaffer, and a beautiful blonde named Mary decided to win World War II."
(4) The Eagle Has Landed, 1976, directed by John Sturges, starring Michael Caine, Donald Sutherland, Robert Duvall, Jenny Agutter, Donald Pleasance and Anthony Quayle. The story is set in the fictional local village of Studley Constable, on the North Norfolk coast apparently near to Blakeney.
(5) The Dirty Dozen, 1967, directed by Robert Aldrich, starring Lee Marvin, Ernest Borgnine, Charles Bronson, John Cassevetes, Jim Brown, Robert Ryan etc. Poster tagline: "Train them! Excite them! Arm them! ...then turn them loose on the Nazi's."
(6) The Wild Geese, 1978, directed by Andrew V McLaglan starring Richard Burton, Richard Harris, Roger Moore, Hardy Kruger, Stewart

Granger etc. Dialogue quote: "Good luck to you, you Godless murderers."

(7) The Sea Wolves, 1980, directed by Andrew V McLaglan, starring Gregory Peck, Roger Moore, David Niven, Trevor Howard etc. Connections to James Bond are strong: not only with star Moore; editing was by Bond director John Glen; production designer Syd Cain; stunts by George Leech, Bob Simmons and Martin Grace; actors Patrick Macnee and Martin Benson.

(8) The Great Escape, 1963, directed by John Sturges, starring Richard Attenborough, Steve McQueen, James Garner etc.

(9) Escape to Athena, 1979, directed by George P Cosmatos, starring David Niven, Telly Savalas, Roger Moore, Stefanie Powers, Claudia Cardinale, Richard Roundtree, Elliott Gould etc. Poster tagline: "The patriot, the professor, the comic and the stripper...were fighting for what they believed in...GETTING RICH!"

(10) The Guns of Navarone, 1961, directed by J Lee Thompson, starring Gregory Peck, David Niven, Anthony Quinn, Anthony Quayle, Stanley Baker, James Darren etc. Seven Oscar nominations including Picture and Director, winning for Visual Effects.

(11) Force 10 From Navarone, 1978, directed by Guy Hamilton, starring Robert Shaw, Edward Fox, Harrison Ford, Franco Nero, Carl Weathers, Barbara Bach, Richard Kiel etc. Another film with strong Bond connections, including its director and four of the stars.

(12) Bridge on the River Kwai, 1957, directed by David Lean, starring Alec Guinness, William Holden and Jack Hawkins. Based on a novel by Pierre Boulle, also responsible for Planet of the Apes. Won seven Oscars from eight nominations.

(13) Platoon, 1986, directed by Oliver Stone, starring Charlie Sheen, Tom Berenger, Willem Dafoe, Keith David and Forest Whitaker. Oliver Stone, from The Oliver Stone Experience by Matt Zoller Seitz: "When you've gone through three, four days of bad sleep, you get very antsy. You get in a killer mood."

(14) Such as... Ice Station Zebra, 1968, directed by John Sturges, starring Rock Hudson, Ernest Borgnine, Jim Brown.

  Bear Island, 1979, directed by Don Sharp, starring Donald Sutherland, Lloyd Bridges, Richard Widmark

  ...plus several others already mentioned above.

CHAPTER EIGHT

SPACE TREKKERS
AN ADVENTURE AMONGST THE STARS

In the year 2324 journeying into space from Earth has become a regular occurrence through necessity while a flight to Moonbase Alpha is as commonplace as driving to the supermarket in the 20th Century - and if you are wondering, yes, a food franchise does exist there too! Over population has drained the resources of our planet almost to buckling point so two centuries ago humans were forced to take drastic measures in order to continue - you know the reasons why because they exist in their infancy in our world today. A fleet of vast spacecraft called Earthships were constructed, capable of holding a thousand explorers to seek out new planets with possibly new civilisations able to sustain future human generations, and in those two-hundred years we have encountered a variety of new species of life, some friendly and others not so much, as we human's boldly go about our quest. The people who crew these Earthships come from all corners of our planet, tasked with performing jobs and skills to the best of their abilities without prejudice in a mostly Utopian society.

Anyway, that's more than enough backstory to give you the picture, you can create the image if the Earthship according to your own imagination without threat of copyright infringement so now, on with the story...

Captain Karina(1) stands in the middle of her bridge on Earthship Five and studies the huge forward viewing window, a blanket of stars brightly shining and a planet, Earth-like in its greens, blues and white clouds, enticingly looming in the foreground. At their stations on the bridge of the Earthship her crew tend to numerous tasks which might be deemed superficial to the uninitiated but are essential for the smooth running of the ship, while their Captain is well aware how alluring the planet's appearance is, so they will be as excited with anticipation as she is: they haven't seen a planet with this many Earth-like features for almost three years.

"The planet's atmosphere," Commander Pizer(2) informs his captain, "consists of seventy-eight percent nitrogen, twenty-percent oxygen, with traces of argon and carbon dioxide."

"Meaning it's breathable!" The ships doctor, Benson(3), sighs loudly with irritability. "Why not simply cut to the chase and get to the point instead of superfluously spouting technical jargon to all and sundry?"

Earthship Five's captain grin inwardly at this familiar camaraderie between her first officer and doctor, recalling with fond memories the similarity with visual entertainment records from the 20th century which she enjoyed watching when her younger brother was researching for his media studies.

"And the planets population?" Captain Karina asks with barely contained anticipation.

"There is life on the planet's surface," her Commander informs, "but not as we might know it. There are no humanoid forms detected, yet we do have readings of structures and possibly a settlement of some description."

All eyes on the bridge turn expectantly to their Captain, hoping they will be the ones chosen to join her on the inevitable landing expedition, and Karina cannot help but break out into a grin. It has been many months since her crew were able to safely enjoy shore leave and she is aware of the dangers of getting ones hopes up but nevertheless, this immediately looks like a very promising location.

"Commander," Karina finally says," Doctor, Lieutenant Penny(4), you're all with me. If we encounter no danger during our initial reconnaissance then fingers-crossed we can remain here a short while."

A whoosh of real air enters the confined space of the Earthship's transport shuttle's cabin when the sealed hatch slides open to reveal the outside world, and what an exhilarating breathe of fresh-air it is to the quartet within, unlike the recycled conditioning which they have grown accustomed to and it takes them all by surprise - this is a stark reminder of the unnaturalness in which they spend most of their time.

Centauri(5) blazes in the blue sky where a few clouds hang like cotton-balls, warming the air to a very pleasant eighty degrees. A lush carpet of blue-green grass lays at their feet when they disembark the transport shuttle, woodland surrounding the glade, a range of mountains behind and who-knows-what else around them. Discernible sounds of unidentified wildlife reach their ears.

Commander Pizer consults the readings on his wrist tablet: "Everything would appear to be Earth-normal at the present time."

"It's simply amazing." Lieutenant Penny breathily adds her pennies-worth. "Just like- being home."

"I agree." Captain Karina agrees, adding. "But remember that looks can be deceiving." She recalls events not long passed when an expedition team leapt before looking with tragically fatal consequences. "We must use extreme caution and remain alert until we can be absolutely certain there is no danger to us here."

Her team acknowledges the warning.

"The settlement is one-hundred yards that way.' Commander Pizer indicates a direction toward the trees. "I am able to detect insect-sized lifeforms in the immediate vicinity but nothing larger- yet we all know how deadly some Earth and non-Earth-"

"Quit yammering, Commander!" Doctor Benson sighs irritably and strides forward. "If anything bites you just let me know, that is why you brought me along."

They fall in behind the Doctor, moving steadily across the glade, all senses attuned to their new surroundings while trying not to let the familiarity of this alien planet overwhelm them, whose atmosphere and flora are uncannily similar to those of Earth.

Tree-tops rustle from the faintest breeze, while high above and on the distant horizon a flock of winged creatures are visible - birds to me and you - soaring gracefully, apparently unaware of the human newcomers wearing inappropriately bright garb.

Doctor Benson feels the urge to utter 'fascinating' but doesn't wish to get himself into trouble through word association.

Thankfully for the team the woodland floor isn't overgrown, presenting a relatively easy trek amongst the trees which are equally familiar in colour as they are alien, hues of greens and blues vibrant owing to the clearness if sky, branches twisting and entwining themselves in the dotted canopy. Insect noises emanate around, above and below, another familiar element on this world which is otherwise utterly new to the quartet. Ahead, through the trees, they can see shapes of abodes which are achingly familiar: log cabins with thatched roofing.

When they exit the woodland, passing between two such huts, they emerge into what is obviously the community square, a well for drawing water from as its centrepiece. There are a total of twelve huts encircling the square which all appear deserted yet there have clearly been recent occupants judging from the utensils and general appearance. A full half-mile distance, breaking the natural beauty of the scenery is a towering black fortress(6), a hundred-feet high and twice as round with menacing turrets and a viciously foreboding entrance.

"Welcome to Carillon(7)." A voice states emotionlessly.

Every one of Earthship Five's reconnaissance team looks about, startled, unsure at first where the voice emanated from, while Commander Pizer is unable to locate any life-signs except for the themselves.

"My name is Kane(8)."

A humanoid dressed in a loose-fitting tan coloured shirt and trousers combo stands unmoving in the doorway to one of the huts, almost blending in seamlessly with the interior so as to be unnoticed. He stands five-feet ten inches, is slight of build with a bald head and pleasantly smiling face which is unnervingly false.

"Hello." Captain Karina says with curious politeness, looking to her Commander, who shakes his head with puzzlement. "My name is Karina, Captain of Earthship Five, representative of the Sol Alliance."

"Welcome." Is Kane's stoic response. "I am an android based on Carillon dwellers not unlike yourselves. I was constructed in Mine World(9)," he lifts an arm to point at the fortress, "sixty-three thousands, one-hundred and eleven sun cycles past."

Captain Karina nods with thoughtful acknowledgement, noticing Commander Pizer's wry smile of irritability at not having recognised this Kane as a robotic life-form.

"My first officer," the Captain points first to Pizer then each in turn, "Commander Pizer, Doctor Benson, and Lieutenant Penny."

It is when the Captain points at the Lieutenant that a bizarre anomaly occurs which, under normal circumstances, she might have put down to a blink of her eye because for a split-second it seems as if Benson flickers from existence. Captain Karina turns to her two other colleagues. The Doctor seems oblivious to what has just transpired, but Commander Pizer's puzzled expression and playback of data on his Tab indicates to her that he saw it too.

Before the Captain can voice her question the smart-comm buzzes to life and she immediately takes the call from her ship.

"What is it, Lieutenant Baxter(10)?"

"Ma'am," the man left in charge of Earthship Five while the Captain is on the reconnaissance mission speaks hurriedly yet without panic: the consummate professional. "We have just received a communication from the planet's surface. Someone claiming to be The Emperor(11) of Carillon demands we leave the planet's surface immediately or face dire consequences."

"Stand by." Captain Karina acknowledges, facing Commander Pizer expectantly because the first officer is rapping away at the ever-reliable Tab. She notices Kane's posture is unaltered.

"Nothing, Captain." Pizer eventually informs her. "I am unable to locate any source of communications in this vicinity."

"And the- spatial distortion we witnessed?"

Commander Pizer shakes his head, annoyed with his inability to be helpful.

"What are you pair wittering on about?" Doctor Benson asks irritably - his usual demeanour. "It's a bit obvious, isn't it? This Kane robot is playing games with us, stalling for time. Whoever built it and the fortress obviously don't want us here! If they have the tech to eject us from this planet they wouldn't have let us land in the first place! Threatening us is a bluff!"

At this instant the ground and air about them rumbles deeply and when their attention is directed toward the fortress its huge entrance is yawning open, dispelling an orange glow from within, casting the shadow of a wheeled object which slowly ejects itself and approaches the settlement.

Commander Pizer glances up thoughtfully from his Tab: "There are two human life sources onboard that transport. I am unable to detect any weapons onboard."

The quartet observes in silence the approaching motorised vehicle which resembles nothing like they have seen before. Kane is unmoving, a lifeless automaton even when the vehicle has drawn to a standstill and its two occupants disembark. They are a human man and a woman, attired similarly to the robot but with distinctly different sashes about their waists, and cause the group to collectively gasp at this surprising revelation.

"Good morning Captain Karina." The man says with a sincere smile and a hand held out in front. "My name is Jake(12)." The

Captain shakes the proffered hand warmly, sensing a relief from the man and woman. "This is my partner, Amanda(13)."

Captain Karina introduces her crew to them, although judging from the knowledge which Jake had regarding her name, she realises they probably know the others too.

"You must have many questions." Amanda states.

"Yeah," says Doctor Benson. "For starters who is this Emperor guy threatening our ship," shooting a glance to Kane, "and what's his beef?"

"Kane is harmless." Jake offers with a reassuring smile. "A relic activated by your presence, and the reason we knew of your arrival. The Emperor is also a- distant relic of a time before now, an automated warning activated too by your presence. You see our ancestors, who were like yourselves, from earth, were part of one of the very first colonies. The Emperor of Carillon, this planet, found their home world one day and decimated most of the population save a few, who he brought here. Legend has it the Emperor was overthrown during a rebellion whose leader, Overdog(14), butchered him and his family, including his wife, Dhyana(15). They promptly abandoned this planet for reasons lost to history where our grand-parents were forced to eke out a new life."

Commander Pizer nods after a moment and confirms these two are human with DNA concurrent to their existence.

"The fortress protects us during storms." Amanda says. "Which is why you couldn't detect our presence."

"And there are just the two of you here?" Doctor Benson asks skeptically.

Jake shakes his head: "There are fifty of us."

"Including our children," Amanda adds, "Nestor and Cayman(16)."

"You say you return to the fortress for shelter?" Captain Karina asks. "But we see no signs if any inclement weather system."

"The storm is- difficult to describe unless you have witnessed it." Jake replies. "It comes every day at the exact same time, as our ancestors discovered and recorded for our own protection. It is more like an- atmospheric or spatial anomaly which cleanses the planets surface."

"Which would explain what we saw." Commander Pizer says to the captain.

Captain Karina's smart-comm activates.

"Lieutenant Baxter." He announces. "Is everything okay down there? We have detected several life signs additional to your own."

From the entrance of the fortress a group of people throng, the human ancestors to those abducted a hundred years ago. They point and the quartet from Earthship Five can sense the excitement, and hope.

"Yes," says Captain Karina, "everything is going to be fine now."

(1) The Ice Pirates, 1984, directed by Stewart Raffill, starring Robert Urich and Mary Crosby. Synopsis: In the future, a princess recruits two pirates to help find her father in a world where water is the greatest commodity.
(2) The Black Hole, 1979, directed by Gary Nelson, starring Maximillian Schell, Robert Forster, Anthony Perkins. An Earth exploration ship discovers a missing vessel, and uncovers its secrets, on the edge of a black hole.
(3) Saturn 3, directed by Stanley Donen and starring Kirk Douglas, Farrah Fawcett and Harvey Keitel. A killer and his robot disrupt the work of scientist lovers on one of Saturn's moons.
(4) The Adventures of Buckeroo Banzai Across the 8th Dimension, 1984, directed by WD Richter, starring Peter Weller, John Lithgow, Ellen Barkin, Jeff Goldblum and Christopher Lloyd. A multi-talented adventurer must stop an alien invasion of Earth.
(5) The Last Starfighter, 1984, directed by Nick Castle and starring Lance Guest, Robert Preston, Kay E. Kuter and Dan O'Herlihy. From 1984's The Last Starfighter Storybook: "Greetings, Starfighter! You have been recruited by the League to defend the frontier against Xur and the Ko-Dan Armada!"
(6) Krull, 1983, directed by Peter Yates, starring Ken Marshall, Lysette Anthony, Francesca Annis, Bernard Bresslaw and Liam Neeson. A prince sets about rescuing his bride from aliens who have invaded his world.
(7) Battlestar Galactica, 1978, directed by Richard A Colla and starring Richard Hatch, Lorne Greene and Dirk(The A-Team) Benedict. Searching for Earth, the last Battlestar encounters resistance from the Cylon's.

(8) Buck Rogers in the 25th Century, 1979, Daniel Haller, starring Gil Gerard, Erin Gray, Pamela Hensley, Henry Silva and Tim O'Connor. An astronaut from the 20th Century is revived from suspended animation into a future Earth which is constantly threatened from aliens.
(9) Starchaser: The Legend of Orin, 1985, animated film directed by Steven Hahn, voiced by Joe Colligan and Noelle North. A band of escaped slaves return to the world which mistreated them.
(10) Forbidden World, 1982, directed by Allan Holzman, starring Jesse Vint, Dawn Dunlap and June(V)Chadwick. On a distant world, a failed genetic experiment threatens its scientist creators.
(11) Starcrash, 1978, directed by Luigi Cozzi, starring Marjoe Gortner, Caroline Munro, Christopher Plummer and David Hasselhoff. The Emperor of the Galaxy recruits two outlaws to rescue his son.
(12) The Cat From Outer Space, 1978, directed by Norman Toker and Starring Ken Berry, Sandy Duncan, Harry Morgan and Roddy McDowall. A UFO, a cat, and its collar which allows human communication.
(13) Space Raiders, 1983, directed by Howard R Cohen, starring Vince Edwards, David Mendenhall, Patsy Pease and Thom Christopher. A boy is accidentally kidnapped by space pirates.
(14) Spacehunter: Adventures in the Forbidden Zone, 1983, directed by Lamont Johnson, starring Peter Strauss, Molly Ringwald, Ernie Hudson, Andrea Marcovicci and Michael Ironside. On a disease plagued planet, an adventurer sets about rescuing the stranded crew of a ship.
(15) Metalstorm: The Destruction of Jared-Syn, 1983, directed by Charles Band, starring Jeffrey Byron, Michael Preston, Tim Thomerson and Kelly Preston. A self-proclaimed messiah tries recruiting mutants on a desert planet, two revolutionaries set out to stop him.
(16) Battle Beyond the Stars, 1980, directed by Jimmy T Murakami, starring Richard(The Waltons) Thomas, George Peppard, John Saxon, Robert Vaughn and Sybil Danning. A farm-boy recruits a disparate band of mercenaries to defend his planet from the Empire.

In approximately 1986 I wrote my first novel. It was my space adventure homage/rip-off to Star Trek and Star Wars and is both naive and poorly written - no change there then! The above story is newly formed yet plays along the themes I was envisioning only on a smaller scale, of course, while the films mentioned within owe a great deal to both Star's Trek and Wars themselves. I still enjoy the big-budget blockbusters, including both Star's, incidentally, but like many people when re-watching old favourites my opinion and perception has altered with time, and my tolerance for visual effects heavy plot-light movies has waned.

CHAPTER NINE

ADVENTURE OF THE ROLE-PLAYING FANTASY GAME

During the 80's I liked to read the Fighting Fantasy series of books and wrote a few similarly structured role-playing narratives myself, usually filled with copious amounts of adolescent sex and violence - there is definitely a pattern going on here.

    If you are aware of these role-playing books then you will be familiar with how to play/read them, and I need not explain, but if you are unfamiliar with them all you need to know is that you are the hero of the story, you choose the path you take and hopefully succeed on some grand quest. The remainder of this chapter is set out like a mini adventure beginning at number 1. I have placed these numbers against the margin so as to avoid confusion with page numbers etc - and as you follow the story as it goes along, making your choice, you turn to that number not the page number. If you still don't understand what it's about, I don't wish to be rude but it's not rocket science, and I would give up now if I were you!

    Good luck, and may you reap untold rewards...

1

Mysteriously you have just awoken on an exotic tropical island in the very middle of Whoknowswhere. You do not know how you have gotten here but you are here now so don't ask questions! The golden sandy beach you stand upon is soft and warm, idyllic one might say. It is in a crescent shaped cove with the calm sea visible in front, waves gently lapping the shore, and there is lush woodland behind you in a glorious array of greens, and clear blue sky above. Birds twitter, insects chirp and animals call to each other in a beautiful chorus of delectable sounds. You are dressed in whatever your imagination permits, there is nobody here but you so who knows, maybe you are naked - shock horror. All you possess is a satchel to place those items inside you may find on your forthcoming adventure. If you have ever dreamed of such a perfectly splendiferous desert island location to be one with yourself, then this is the place for you. If not, then don't worry, the bad will come soon enough! So, do you:

    Sunbathe naked on the sand. Go to 5
    Enter the trees. Go to 10

Enter the water. Go to 20
Remain where you stand. Go to 30
Quit, because this sounds boring. Go to 74

2
Poseidon(1) smiles benignly at your choice and you begin your swim through the clear azure waters, into the swaying mouth of the dark and gloomy rocky entrance into the underwater passage with nary a light to illuminate your way, but you do not care about the danger because this is what fantasy adventure stories should be like. You grope blindly for the rocky walls with careful awareness, afraid to break a fingernail or cut your hands! You shiver. Is the water cooling? It seems thicker and tastes of urine, making you wonder if you have made the wise choice. Abruptly your right-hand touches a loose, fleshy object with seems to come apart to the touch and suddenly a pair of yellowy eyes open widely before you. Do you:
Swim away. Go to 41
Stand your ground. Go to 68
Ask for a kiss. Go to 60

3
Horney(2) Mountain rises majestically ahead of you beyond the tree-lined roughly trodden pathway which is quite easy to negotiate. As you casually stroll along you try identifying the variety of trees, foliage, sounds of the woodland to no avail because this is a place truly unique in colour and wonder, an exotic place etcetera. Suddenly the trees rustle and burst apart on your right, the finely chiseled epitome of manhood Maciste appears, blocking your path with his masculine frame. He says something to you in a language which has hints of Italian but might be gibberish for all you know. His posture is aggressive, body language confrontational, and his bearing indiscernible. Do you:
Cry like a baby. Turn to 11
Fight him. Turn to 23
Try reasoning with him. Turn to 74
Ask him for a kiss. Turn to 60

4
The Grayskull(3)Vulture continues circling until the glint from Maciste's mighty weapon is enough to deter it, so it flies away to find a different victim. You sigh with relief - go on, you know you want to! - and determine which path to take. Do you:

    Enter the mountain. Turn to 52
    Encircle the mountain. Turn to 24

5
Although there is absolutely nothing wrong whatsoever with being free of clothes as nature intended us to be, on this particular occasion it does nothing to aid the story and you die an ignominious death, sorry.

6
Unfortunately your close proximity is enough to offend on this world so your head gets sliced off but never mind, eh, you were getting fed up with this adventure anyway!

7
You stride with confidence but unfortunately for you, unseen on the ground, is a massive hole which you fall uncontrollably into...plummeting to a hideous, grisly death.

8
It is with huge relief that you leave the Bridge Over Sarr Chasm behind you. Now you stride briskly onward through the rocky corridor whose light steadily increases on intensity until, finally, you reach a sturdy wooden door set royally in front of you. Without hesitation you turn the big gold handle and pull open the door to reveal a large circular room with high ceiling, Goblin minions at food-filled tables on the perimeter, both male and female dances gyrating in the middle of the room, while the Goblin King(4) himself us seated on a raised dais with, presumably, his wives seated either side of him. Two doors, not including the one by which you enter, lead off from this royal chamber, either side of the dais. Gold, silver and a vast variety of jewels shine and glint, sported by the Goblin's and the table-wear; this is indeed a treasure trove.

    The performers cease their routine upon your presence and all eyes are upon this new, strange, arrival.

The King clears his throat: "Yes. Can I help you?" Do you:
Possess the Parchment of Lyra. Turn to 56
Possess Parisa's Amulet. Turn to 65
Possess the Ring of Suna. Turn to 73
Ask the King for a favour. Turn to 60
Ask the King help leaving. Turn to 74
Or, none of these. Turn to 29

9

Sucking in a deep breath of oxygen to calm your nerves you step onto the rocky Bridge Over Sarr Chasm, half-expecting the three-feet wide, railless natural construct to sway or, worse still, crumble, but fortunately for you it has been here for thousands of years so it's quite solid! Treading softly so not to awaken anything which might lurk here - earghh, bats! - when you are approximately halfway across the hairs involuntarily stand erect all over your body. Imperceptibly at first, the air begins stirring until it feels like some giant thing is breathing down your neck. Do you:
Continue onwards without looking back. Turn to 7
Stand stock still. Turn to 14
Soil yourself. Turn to 28
Turn back whence you came. Turn to 74

10

You walk along the soft sand, sucking in the fresh tropical air like you haven't ever breathed air before, the clarity buoying your spirits like alcohol to the brain, wondering if anything can possibly be more splendiferous than this. The leaves of the dense woodland, their myriad exotic shapes, sizes and colours, gently rustle in the light breeze at their upper reaches. A roughly hewn pathway lined with flowers leading into the trees presents itself to you welcomingly; this is the way for you.

As you idle along without a single care in the world, admiring the visible flora and fauna, you become aware that it has become almost twilight in dimness beneath the heavy canopy. Sounds of larger mammals worryingly become louder, more intense in the calls, and you wonder if this route was the best choice after all.

But, after a half-mile of twists and blind-turns, the pathway widens and brightens into a splendiferously colourful circular glade filled with flowers, a pool of shimmering water, cool, calm and inviting at its very centre. The flowers appear to be like oversized roses only these are much more exotic in their array of colours. Truly, this takes your breath away with its beauty.

A voice startles you: "I am Kira(5), Goddess of the Sun."

At first you are unable to pinpoint the source of this voice which is new, yet familiar, calming yet equally authoritative.

"Oh stranger from afar." Kira says as she rises mystically from the pool, water cascading off her as she steps onto the bed of roses without damaging a single one of them; she is human, entrancing, corporeal, and a vision of what might be considered beauty in your eyes. "What do you seek?" Do you:

Move nearer to her. Turn to 6
Ask for a kiss. Turn to 60
Want to know where you are. Turn to 42
Ask for help returning home. Turn to 51

11

When you begin whimpering and blaring like a crybaby the tears start rolling, boo-hoo. At first Maciste stares at you disbelievingly, then the chuckling begins, followed by a guttural belly laugh. He is laughing raucously at your patheticness! Aren't you going to do something about it, for goodness sake!?

Riled into a broiling rage of fury and by the will of the very Gods themselves, who take pity on your pathetic plight, a sword and shield magically spring into existence in your hands. The tears abruptly cease, a grin replacing the quivering to your lips. Are you really going to let this dumb brute humiliate you? No, is the answer.

Slicing and slashing like a pro you launch your attack, taking Maciste by surprise but he puts up a strong fight as your swords clash in a blur of speed and ferocity until you, yes, you, deal the death blow by lopping off the man's head. Well done you.

Bloodlust you were formally unaware was in your temperament salved, you pick up the sword of the vanquished man as a token of victory, pumping the air with your fist. YES! Do you:

Dance a naked victory jig. Turn to 5
Turn back. Turn to 22
Continue onwards. Turn to 61
Kick the corpse at your feet. Turn to 74

12
You do not get very far before stumbling to the ground on some loose rocks, losing your balance and falling into some sun-scorched bracken. The vulture circles upon high, beady eyes upon your gleaming flesh. You can sense its hunger.

Something deep in the bracken catches your eye: the glint of gold from the Bow Of Liliput(6), and a quiver of golden arrows.

Remembering your long-forgotten expertise in archery, knowing that someday all those lessons would prove useful, you snatch up the bow, position an arrow, draw the string back tightly and loose off one of the golden arrows just as the vulture drops from the sky to claim you. Instead, the enormous bird thumps to the ground beside you, dead.

It is with great relief that get to your feet. Magically, the Bow Of Liliput and remaining arrows shrink to a convenient pocket(or satchel) size. Do you:

    Continue circling the mountain. Turn to 24
    Approach the dead vulture. Turn to 44
    Enter the mountain. Turn to 52

13
"You are lying!" Bellows the King of the Goblins accusingly. "There is no such person in this realm." He studies you studiously and you stare back sarcastically! "It takes a brave soul to lie to me in my own Kingdom. Are you so brave to lie so bravely?"

You nod bravely.

"In that case," the Goblin King says, "if you should choose the door on my left you shall find victory is yours. Your adventure here has reached its end, my friend, well done, enjoy the taste of success." Do you:

    Dance around in naked victory. Turn to 5
    Hug the King gratefully. Turn to 6
    Take the door on your left. Turn to 67
    Take the door on your right. Turn to75

14
Standing stock-still while holding your breath until it feels as though your lungs are going to burst bears rewards because your

dauntlessness means the danger has passed. Phew! Thats a relief. Do you:

    Turn back. Turn to 7
    Continue onwards. Turn to 8
    Soil yourself. Turn to 28
    Shout a suggestive expletive. Turn to 60

15

"You are in the water!" Poseidon states in a facetial manner.

You politely - or not, it's your choice - ask him to be more specific - maybe using a hint of sarcasm in your voice.

"Kael." Poseidon informs you reasonably. "The Land of Kael. Forged by us: the Gods!" The water seems to roil with subjugation. "But be warned." He says warningly! "There are many dangers here, in the Land of Kael, on land, not here in my waters, and trust only those whom you meet who are trustful, not those who are not." Poseidon says helpfully! "Avoid Murtagh at all cost for he shall lead you onto the wrong path to becoming the Hero you can be. You do want to be a Hero, don't you?"

You wisely nod.

"Good." Poseidon says proudly. "Because otherwise what is point living if you are not willing to be be the Hero on you Journey through life, hey?" Do you:

    Take the tunnel on left. Turn to 2
    Go back to the shore. Turn to 10
    Tell Poseidon to stick his philosophical nonsense. Turn to 68
    Or, give up. Turn to 74

16

You rapidly load the arrow into the bow when they spring magically to fill size, drawing back and firing a clean shot into Murtagh's face, which is a wise move for you because he is an untrustworthy cretin! As proof of your victory and heroic action you claim his axe: well done!

But not what will you do? The desert seems an endless yellow sea of rolling sand as far as the eye can see, while the sun burns ominously high in the sky. This is a dead man's paradise. The flume of sand from where Murtagh arrived is invitingly open, walls of rock visible through the swirling haze. Do you:

Bask naked to top up your tan. Turn to 5
Enter the Flume. Turn to 52
Possess the Carpet Of Aladdin. Turn to 73
Wish you were doing something more constructive. Turn to 74

17
"The axe of Murtagh is cursed." She warns you. "It has the power to transfer a trusting mind into a deceitful one. Throw it away now or be fully consumed by the depths of the Horney Mountains." Do you:
Ignore her. Turn to 7
Do as she warns. Turn to 27
Suggest you and she 'couple'. Turn to 60

18
When the scary rumbling eventually ceases all of the Goblin's present are most impressed by your indomitability in the face of danger.
"Well done." Congratulates the King of the Goblin's. "Take this door on my left because you truly are a warrior if extraordinary heroism, and receive the rewards you justly deserve. Do you:
Open the door on your right. Turn to 38
Open the door on your left. Turn to 67

19
Holding the feather aloft you are magically elevated above the Bridge Over Sarr Chasm, rising upward until the domed roof is almost within touching distance. You discover that by flapping your free arm you can propel yourself slowly forward. Dare you look down? Yes, of course you do, hero that you are! Unfortunately the vertiginous view is too much to stomach, even for you, and you vomit violently. This provokes a rapid response from far below, in the very depths of the Chasm, where the creature stirs. Do you:
Descend back onto the Bridge. Turn to 8
Continue using the magic feather. Turn to 53

20
Strolling across the lovely warm, soft sandy beach you enter the water which is as gloriously temperate as you hoped it would be on this tropical paradise where you have found yourself. Soon you are chest

deep and the healing powers of the ocean are cleansing your very soul: splendiferous, one might say.

Confidence and a sixth-sense overwhelms you, so like some mythical Mer-person you dive the waves. Swimming comes easy to you, as does breathing underwater because this magic ocean has caused gills to temporarily form. This place is simply amazing!

Swimming deeper the ocean floor comes alive with vibrantly coloured fish and coral worth taking time to admire, which is exactly what you do, enjoying the wonder and splendid beneath the waves.

Continuing onward and down the coral is overwhelmed by rock and through the clear water you are taken aback by the mesmerising sight of a statue of Poseidon, which must be at least fifty metres high off the seabed. Two openings in the rocky undersea cliff are situated either side of this monument to sea God.

To your cynical lack of surprise this mythical creature opens its eyes then mouth, before the voice comes to your ears: "Hello, friend. I haven't seen a human like you here before. What do you seek?" Do you:

Ask Poseidon where you are. Turn to 15
Tell Poseidon you want a kiss. Turn to 60
Ask Poseidon which passage to take. Turn to 70

21

The experience which Lyssa(7) provides is absolutely, indescribably mind-blowing, leaving you hearing heavenly choirs and this is enough reward for your bravery doing this adventure so far. Wow, one might say. Or, if feeling extremely grateful, this is better than splendiferous!

Several hours later, fully sated, you know without a doubt that there will never be a dull moment again!

Swimming upward you find yourself back on the beach where you started, basking in the sunshine, drinking in the wonderful view like it's the first time you have ever witnessed such beauty.

While contemplating your magnificence a giant shadow looms overhead and before you can look up, a green and brown dragon swoops onto the sand.

"My name is Djinn(8)." The dragon announces with deep, guttural growl. "I can offer you three Choices, one of which is right." Do you:

Ignore him and go to the woodland. Turn to 10

Ask Djinn for a kiss. Turn to 60
Ask Djinn to transport you home. Turn to 74

22
Through the colour-splashed trees to trot until reaching the very edge of the woodland itself, where a vista of sand and dunes greets you. You have definitely located the desert, and it looks foreboding. Do you:

Turn back. Turn to 3
Continue. Turn to 45
Procrastinate. Turn to 74

23
Maciste(9) frowns deeply when you adopt a fighting stance with no weapons or defence against his mighty sword. Feeling ever so slightly trepidatious you will the Gods themselves to provide salvation but, despite this island being enchanted, there are limits! Maciste simply unsheathes his lengthy weapon. Do you:

Cry like a baby. Turn to 11
Bravely stand your ground. Turn to 43
Ask him for a snog. Turn to 60
Run away screaming. Turn to 74

24
As well as the ever increasing incline to contend with the path becomes pitted and treacherous, you stumble onward despite it all. The view of the island from height is spectacular; the entire island is surrounded by the Ocean and is green and gold. You shiver. It's definitely becoming colder, now, the higher you climb.

Did you imagine you were naked upon arrival on this island? Turn to 5

Do you carry on regardless of the cold? Turn to 31
Do you possess Grayskull's Crimson Feather? Turn to 62
Do you possess Sinbad's Protective Cloak? Turn to 73

25
Whipping out the mighty weapon in one fluid motion you enter a ferocious battle with Murtagh which wears both you and your

opponent down almost to the point of exhaustion until finally, thankfully, gratefully, Murtagh's axe shatters and you lop his head off.

Phew.

You can do with rest but the saying goes: 'no rest for the wicked,' and unfortunately I know how naughty you have been!

Desert sand surrounds you in all directions and your hopes seem hopeless except for the flume of air from which Murtagh arrived. Inside the flume you can see the stony walls of a cavern. Do you:

Bask naked in the sun. Turn to 5
Enter the flume. Turn to 52
Possess the Broom Of Potter. Turn to 73

26

Parisa's Amulet not only offers physical protection to those within its proximity it is self-illuminating and thank goodness it is, the glow shows the path ahead ends with a bottomless pit. As the amulets light fades you realise you only have one option left to you: turn to 39

27

Tossing the axe away behind you it shatters with a loud and slightly over-the-top explosion.

"Now you are worthy." She hands you a parchment. "Give this to my King when you meet him. It will help you avoid any of his tasks."

You thank this mystical creature profusely as she steps aside to let you pass by. Do you:

Attack her. Turn to 6
Ask for a kiss. Turn to 60
Continue onward. Turn to 71

28

Ah, the delightful stench of excrement! On this world it is a delicacy, its perfume acting as a elixir for the Land's residents. When you realise your unfortunate mistake you are already being chewed upon like an A la Carte appetiser, dying the most hideous and painful way possible.

29

After staring at each other for an inordinate amount of time the King finally asks: "Do you know Tyrian(10) The Great?" Do you:

Approach him apologetically. Turn to 6
Say 'yes'. Turn to 13
Say 'no'. Turn to 55
Possess the Axe Of Murtagh. Turn to 59
Tell him to shut his cake-hole. Turn to 68

30

While you stand admiring this wonderful tropical beach which you have unexpectedly round yourself upon you become away that the air about you is starting to waver and shimmer. At first you think it's heat exhaustion - or the booze you are drinking! - or the sun okaying tricks upon you until the shimmering increases to the point of a tall man materialising on the sand before you, his presence and bearing Godly.

"I am Zeus(11)." He smiles balefully without a hint of superiority! "Your quest is now beginning," he informs you superfluously, "but you must not dither because Princess Lucy is in dire danger and needs your help, plus, evil stalks your presence here on this very beach. Not my evil, of course, because I am a nice God." He quickly adds, awkwardly. "Is there anything I can provide you with so you might shift your posterior in a less lackadaisical manner from your normal routine?" Do you:

Ask which route to take. Turn to 40
Ask where you are. Turn to 50
Tell him to fornicate himself. Turn to 60
Pucker up for a kiss. Turn to 68

31

Shivering and shaking to the bone from cold like you have never experienced before causes even your shoes to slip of your feet - if you are wearing any! - and you tumble, falling uncontrollably down the mountain like Jack or Jill, but by some wholly enchanted miracle you are alive when you reach the bottom.

Phew!

When you eventually gather your wits about you enough to stand, you discover something warm is stuck to the sole of your foot - no, it doesn't smell!

Holding up the Amulet belonging to the Goddess Parisa(12) you realise this fantastical object has saved your life. Hows that for luck!

Unfortunately you are now back at the foot of the mountain. Do you:
>   Take the woodland path. Turn to 22
>   Stamp your feet impatiently. Turn to 68
>   Use the Staff Of Odysseus. Turn to 73

32

"Bah!" Grumbles Murtagh before angrily stomping off into the desert like a petulant child - or yourself on a bad day!

Fortunately this cretin has left open the flume of air from where he originally arrived and within it you can see a rocky cavern which is much more inviting than this infernal desert sand. Do you:
>   Bask naked and top up your tan. Turn to 5
>   Call Murtagh names and chase after him. Turn to 6
>   Enter the air flume. Turn to 52
>   Possess the Wand Of Persia. Turn to 73
>   Make a wish to be elsewhere. Turn to 74

33

Reaching the surface of the Pool Of Tranquility you pull yourself onto its sandy shore, happy to be out out the dangerous water.

You are now in a domed cavern with an unreachable opening at its peak that lets in light, illuminating the splendiferous sight of diamonds, emeralds and rubies set into the wall. Wow. What a spectacular trove of treasure, it's just a pity you haven't yet found any tools for removing the stones.

A single passageway indicates the exit.

From the corner of the undersea cavern a chirping, tuneful creature the shape and size of a harmless Chinchilla appears. This creature is an Amar(13), indigenous to this island only. It cautiously approaches you. Do you:
>   Dance around like a naked loon. Turn to 5
>   Reach down to fuss the Amar. Turn to 6
>   Leave via the exit passageway. Turn to 52
>   Dive back into the pool. Turn to 63
>   Possess Poseidon's Trident. Turn to 73

34

Upon drawing out your mighty weapon Lyra the Goblin grins with vicious, pointy, needle-sharp, blood-dripping, white teeth, while also pulling a wicked scythe-like sword from the scabbard at her waist - pity you didn't notice that detail earlier, hey!?

Let battle commence, which is exactly what happens, hacking and slicing until you destroy her in a spectacularly dramatic and pointless display of fizzling lights and explosions which destroys both weapons.

On the floor beside her powdery remains in a parchment, which you pick up and place safely in your satchel for future use. Turn to 71

35

With your sinews as taught as the string on Liliput's Bow, senses on the alert, cautiously you begin traversing the Bridge Over Sarr Chasm - no really, you do!

The blackness of the void is all-encompassing save for intermittent phosphorescent glows, and of course the fiery red glow from below. You feel like you are and ant on a telegraph wire above twin skyscrapers.

The air seems to stir nearby. The hairs on your body warningly spring to life. It feels as though someone, or something, very large is breathing rest next to you. Could this be the creature of the chasm, you wonder? It is an effort to keep you wits about you. Do you:

Panic. Turn to 7
Continue onwards. Turn to 8
Soil yourself. Turn to 28
Fire Liliput's Bow. Turn to 64

36

Drawing the blade from its scabbard too quickly results in you fumbling dangerous, mercifully not cutting yourself, but the sword tumbles through the air. You cannot make out its downward flightpath but you definitely hear the result of it landing: a thunderous roar bellows, echoing deafening about Sarr Chasm. You have found the creature, well done!

The air stirs and buffets you as wings beat, talons claw and breath billows like...bellows! Do you:

Soil yourself. Turn to 28
Possess Murtagh's Axe. Turn to 48
Continue onwards. Turn to 69

37

"The Bow of Liliput is of no use to me." The Goblin King snorts dismissively. "My arms are too short to draw back the string! What do you suggest I do with it?" Do you:

Offer advice for inserting it where the sun doth not shine. Turn to 54

Tell him to fornicate with himself. Turn to 60

Give up because you've had enough. Turn to 74

38

Opening the door you step inside without second thought and discover the room is empty. Mirthful laughter behind you is instantly silenced when the door closes, and is locked from the outside. Oh, its also pitch black. Do you:

Dance about naked with maniacal glee. Turn to 5

Walk forward. Turn to 7

Stand still. Turn to 47

Possess Grayskull's Crimson Feather. Turn to 68

39

Cautiously approaching the wall of phosphorous gems, not wishing to gash your feet or fall down a concealed hole, its will relief when you are in light once more.

Phew!

You are very brave...until your heart leaps into your mouth when an ethereal shadow blots the passageway in front if you like a whirling wraith, followed by a blinding white flash and, standing not much more than six feet in front if you is a ghostly apparition.

"I am Lyra(14)." She informs you, taking on a more corporeal Goblin-like form while you watch, stunned yet again by what this magical island has to reveal to you. She seems harmless enough so you tell her your name. "Such a noble name. Are you here to see my King?" Do you:

Say no. Turn to 6

Possess Murtagh's Axe. Turn to 17

Say yes. Turn to 49
Tell her to fornicate away. Turn to 60
Possess the Shield of Elohesra. Turn to 73

40

"By Khrakannon's(15)beard you are an annoying fellow, are you not!" Zeus exclaims with a jolly, jovial laugh. "Would you like me to hold your hand for the rest if your journey?" Before you idiotically reply 'yes' he continues: "I will advise you on two things. Hmm, on second thought, I shall advise you on three things. If you go into the Ocean you shall learn of powers you never dreamed of. If you go into my woodland then you shall discovers if such wonder like never seen by your eyes. And, thirdly, if you should choose to remain here you will experience satisfaction of individuality." Do you:

Enter the woodland. Turn to 10
Go for a dip in the Ocean. Turn to 20
Stay exactly where you are. Turn to 74

41

Glowing algae illuminates your way through the comfortably warm water, its exotically cheerful colours bringing a smile to your face - if thats a possibility! You are starting to enjoy this adventure - yes, you are! - where your inhibitions are freed to experience-

Floating in the water not far in front of you is a mermaid. She is the most beautiful creature you have ever set eyes upon in your entire life. When you get near to her you are away of a shaft of light from above, and she smiles, pointing upward to indicate what you can already see.

"I am Lyssa." Her voice carries through the water like a heavenly choir. "You must be a brave warrior to venture here, these waters can be treacherous for those unworthy. I can offer further protection from the enchanted dangers which lurk here if you couple with me." Do you:

Accept without hesitation. Turn to 21
Ignore her and swim upward. Turn to 33
Ask her for a kiss. Turn to 60
Decline her offer. Turn to 74

42

"This is the Land if Kael(16)." She informs you helpfully. "A place forged by Zeus himself. Upon it he has created many wondrous things, but also many dangers for the unworthy. Seek out the Goblin King and he may grant your victorious return but not without first proving yourself a hero. He lives in the Horney Mountains. In the desert resides the Dwarf, Mucklebones. He can provide unimaginable services for you. Remember, this is your adventure, do not turn back now." Do you:

    Take the mountain path. Turn to 3
    Take the desert route. Turn to 22
    Ask her for a kiss. Turn to 60
    Turn back now. Turn to 74

43

Running forward headlong you try barrelling into this man but he is an unyielding immoveable object compared to yourself, so these actions achieve nothing more than a headache.

    When you eventually regain consciousness Maciste is nowhere to be seen, having left you for dead.

    Feeling ever so slightly embarrassed by your foolishly ill-conceived idiocy, you continue onwards. Turn to 61

44

The corpse of the giant vulture reeks of something more vile and disgusting than mankind should ever have to smell. You vomit uncontrollably for what seems like hours amidst a maelstrom of pain. Is it worth it? Well, you do find a Crimson Feather which has fallen from the creature - you never know, it might possess mystical powers - so you place it in your satchel. Do you:

    Continue along the mountain path. Turn to 24
    Enter the mountain. Turn to 52
    Shout a lewd curse. Turn to 60
    Give up. Turn to 74

45

Trudging through the fine sand in whatever footwear you imagined you arrived on this island wearing - unless you imagined nothing! - the heat on your soles soon begins to become unbearable, forcing you to stop. When you turn to look back the way you came it somehow appears that you have walked miles already, because all you can see is desert.

This must surely be an illusion?

Despondently you trudge until before you the very surface of the sand swirls and whirls like the funnel of a tornado, bucking and falling like a flume of sand before, in a dramatic crack of light, the Dwarf called Murtagh(17)appears, brandishing a silver axe.

"Hello, friend," the Dwarf says like a cheerful dodgy car salesman. "Do not fear me. I am Murtagh. I travel from from the mountain kingdom and can help you. Thats a nice satchel you are carrying." Do you:

    Agree to his help. Turn to 6
    Possess the Bow Of Liliput. Turn to 16
    Possess the Sword Of Maciste. Turn to 25
    Possess the Balls Of Balthazar. Turn to 73
    Or, none of these. Turn to 32

46

The chamber falls silent. Oh dear!

"Well done." The King says. "Not all tests involve fighting. It is a noble warrior indeed who is capable of shedding off such insults with wit of their own. Now, if you take this door," he indicates the wooden door on his left, "you will receive the reward of a true champion." Do you:

    Dance around naked with joy. Turn to 5
    Approach him to thank him. Turn to 6
    Tell him to fornicate himself. Turn to 60
    Open the door on your left. Turn to 67
    Open the door on your right. Turn to 75

47

Silence. Claustrophobia. Darkness.
    All your worst fears are upon you.
    Are you bored. Turn to 57
    Do you possess Maciste's Sword. Turn to 68
    When you arrived on the island did you
        imagine you were naked. Turn to 75

48
Oh dear! The axe is utterly useless. It ignites brightly and gives away your position to the creature who promptly eats you up...yum yum!

49
"First you must prove yourself worthy."

This curious Goblin creature steps aside. You wonder if her intentions are truly genuine. Do you:
>Attack her. Turn to 6
>Possess the Bow Of Liliput. Turn to 7
>Possess Maciste's Sword. Turn to 34
>Walk past her. Turn to 71

50
"You are in my Land," Zeus tells you in a Godlike voice. "I have named it Kael. There are many wonders to be found on this island of the Gods." He promises in a powerful, authoritative, important, big-boy voice. "This place which I have created is the most splendiferous you will ever see." He says modestly! "There is an underwater Kingdom, an enchanted Woodland paradise, a majestic Mountain treasury, and a desert."

You want to exclaim 'oooh' and 'ah' but don't want to come across as sounding a bit childish!

"But I shall offer you a choice." Zeus says importantly. "Well, more than one choice, really, but I have called the above the first choice so the next thing will be another- ONE CHOICE! If you choose not to explore my land of Kael, then the alternative is the vast wilderness of unexplored imagination which you possess in you mind, which s also worth seeking out." Do you:
>Enter the woodland. Turn to 10
>Enter the ocean. Turn to 20
>Call him a pompous, arrogant bighead. Turn to 68
>Use your imagination. Turn to 74

51
"Cease your blubbering, crybaby!" Kira laughs condescendingly.

Promptly you do as she says, feeling hugely silly for proving you are nothing more than a wimp - sorry, it's not an affirmation of being in touch with your emotions in the world of a hero!

"Zeus himself forged this island for your sole purpose." She tells you, and you smile meekly. "If you go to the mountains seek out the Goblin King. If you go to the desert find Dwarf Mucklebones(18). You are in an adventure, so do not give up now." Do you:

    Take the mountain path. Turn to 3
    Take the desert path. Turn to 22
    Mess you pants excitedly. Turn to 28
    Ask for a kiss. Turn to 60
    Give up now. Turn to 74

52

The mountain cave is sporadically illuminated by phosphorescent rocks dotted sporadically(yes, I know!) along the walls, visible for quite sone distance, which is advantageous because otherwise you would be in pitch darkness.

    Your feet on the ground is the only sound - aren't I clever, I made a rhyme!? The going is flat and smooth, the air inside is stagnant and damp with an acrid warmth, as if you are entering a volcano, not a snowcapped mountain.

    After several hundred metres of straight passage without any alternative direction to take, the illuminate gradually begins to thin out, dimming appreciably, forcing you to slow you pace as a precaution, until you stop because of void!

    To your left there is hope because you can see along another passageway, in the distance, there is yonder light. Do you:

    Continue forward. Turn to 7
    Possess Parisa's Amulet. Turn to 26
    Break wind. Turn to 28
    Take the left-hand passageway. Turn to 39
    Shout a sexually suggestive curse. Turn to 60
    Do absolutely nothing. Turn to 74

53

Drifting steadily onwards you gradually become aware of the shifting in the air currents at this height and wonder what can be causing it. Its the creature. His blazing blood-red eyes glow beneath the Bridge Over Sarr Chasm and you can hear him huffing and puffing with what can only be described as agitation. Do you:

Soil yourself. Turn to 28
Possess Maciste's Sword. Turn to 36
Continue onwards. Turn to 69

54

"That's precisely what I shall do!" Says the Goblin King much to your surprise - he is not joking! "You have completed my test. Now, take this door," he indicates to the one on his left, "and you shall receive your reward.

At first you think this is a wind-up, but its not, the Goblin King really is serious. Do you:

Soil yourself with glee. Turn to 28
Suggest he 'goes away' impolitely. Turn to 60
Go through the door on your left. Turn to 67
Go through the door on your right. Turn to 75

55

The King frowns as deeply as a Goblin can frown and at first you wonder if you made the right choice: "Never mind, I didn't like him anyway!"

Suddenly there is a rumbling beneath your feet which gradually works its way through the entire chamber. Its as if the Horney Mountain is either going to erupt or there is some magical earthquake at work. Do you:

Dance around in naked hysterics. Turn to 5
Heroically stand your ground. Turn to 18
Make a mess in your undergarments. Turn to 28
Possess Grayskull's Crimson Feather. Turn to 68

56

A hush descends upon the chamber and you look around at the Goblin faces with uncertainty.

"Ah, the parchment." The King eventually acknowledges. "You are indeed a worthy brave noble heroic valiant adventurer." He indicates the door to his left. "You reward is well earned, my stouthearted friend, and should you pass through this door your journey shall come to an end befitting your stature." Do you:

Soil yourself with excitement. Turn to 28
Ask for a kiss. Turn to 60

Go through the door to your left. Turn to 67
Go through the door to your right. Turn to 75

57
That is very honest of you. Do you:
    Think this story is rubbish. Turn to 66
    Think this story is good. Turn to 72

58
The Goblin King mocks you with a variety of insults including: pathetic, stupid, weak, loser, imbecile, and every possible put-down ever conceived. After over an hour of this, and with his minions laughing in your face, do you:
    Leak excrement. Turn to 28
    Agree with his insults. Turn to 46
    Possess Maciste's Sword. Turn to 68

59
Unfortunately Murtagh was not at all trustworthy, hence you cannot rely upon his axe to save you, so you die, sorry!

60
Unfortunately your one-track mind does you no service on this occasion because whatever you have said is translated differently amongst the God's and their people, so you have signalled the death-knell and your body is torn asunder before being consumed by the Islands inhabitants, sorry.

61
The pathway is gradually inclining as you approach the Horney Mountains, the prominent Koenig(19) Mountain rising in the middle of three. This the hone of the Goblin King. But you must take care. Be aware. The going may be treacherous, there are traps and obstacles to befuddle the unweary traveller! Let's hope the altitude doesn't play havoc with you also.
    Strewth, so many things to consider!
    Thankfully before you set off on this fantastical adventure you consumed nourishing, protein enriching energy producing foods to

sustain you - no need to worry about fatigue caused by e-numbers or caffeine deficiency lackadaisical spells, so well done you.

The trees thin out - a bit like your hairline - and the ground is stoney with dried, dead shrubs and weeds the only vegetation. The mountains are now imposing, looming obstacles on your journey, which hopefully won't require too much ascension before you reach the Goblins dwelling.

Piercing the air above you is a high-pitched screeching, alerting you to the presence of the grotesque Greyskull Vulture. It is encircling you way up high and its monstrous wingspan casts an ever-increasing shadow. Obviously, you are its prey. Do you:

Possess Maciste's Sword. Turn to 4
Run along the right-hand pathway. Turn to 12
Run for the cave entrance up ahead. Turn to 52

62

The magical fire ignites with a glow which sets a fire of warmth within you also - yes, the Greyskull Feather might smell of putrified rotting flesh but it keeps you alive until you reach the entrance to the cave not far along the pathway. Your only option is to go inside. Turn to 52

63

Mysteriously the Ocean water has cooled off considerably and now becomes less comfortably to swim in, while the current too seems stronger than before. You now believe you have made an unwise choice when, after swimming laboriously for several yards you realise there shimmering light ahead of you. Phew! You have reached the sandy beach where you started once more. For a few moments back there you thought you were a gonna - trust me on this, I know things! Turn to 10

64

Spinning on you heel the same time as you draw back your bow it takes just a split-second to sight-up and loose a magical arrow, which pierces the gleaming eyeball of the creature, itself letting out a bellowing roar of pain and anger before descending back down into the depths of Sarr Chasm.

Phew! Turn to 8

65
"What am I supposed to do with this piece of junk?" The King of the Goblins asks with mirthful disdain, eliciting a cacophony of laughter from his minions. Do you:
    Offer him the Bow Of Liliput. Turn to 37
    Suggest he inserts it where the sun doesn't shine. Turn to 54
    Shrug your shoulders flippantly. Turn to 58

66
You chose...poorly. Do you:
    Die naked. Turn to 5
    Mess yourself. Turn to 28
    Laugh. Turn to 68
    Quit. Turn to 74

67
Obviously the door on your left is the one in the Goblin King's right, not like he suggested, so clearly being stupid you step straight into the Oven For Stupid People and the Goblin's feed on your roasted corpse for supper.

68
As if that's going to help you! You die. Sorry - only I'm not sorry, really.

69
Moving forward undauntedly works to your advantage because the creature cannot locate your lofty position so gives up his search. Phew. Eventually, you descend back to the Bridge Over Sarr Chasm. Turn to: 8

70
Poseidon furrows his brow as much as an animated statue possibly can: "I would say the tunnel to your left is the safest option, but, hmm, there again, you seek adventure so the one in the right provides more of an adrenaline rush. If I were you I wouldn't be me, so then I wouldn't know which tunnel to take!"
    His reply has been most helpful in an unhelpful way, so do you:

Take the tunnel on Poseidon's left. Turn to 2
Empty your bowels. Turn to 28
Take the tunnel on Poseidon's right. Turn to 41
Ask him for a kiss. Turn to 60

71

The tunnel opens into a gaping opening with a stone bridge traversing a huge pit. This is the Bridge Over Sarr Chasm, below which lives a creature of the lowest form called Ustane(20).

It is eerily quiet as if something of importance is about to transpire. You can see through the depths of blackness thanks to an orange glow from below, but images and shadows remain feint, ghostly, wraithlike, etcetera.

You are now on the very threshold of the King Of the Goblin's lair, and this is his first test. Do you:

Walk onward. Turn to 9
Possess Greyskull's Crimson Feather. Turn to 19
Soil yourself. Turn to 28
Possess the Bow Of Liliput. Turn to 35
Possess Murtagh's Axe. Turn to 59
Curse luridly. Turn to 60

72

Good for you. Turn to 75

73

Liar, liar, pants on fire - quite literally because this is the death which awaits liars in this enchanted place - there is no such thing!

74

You have now returned to you own world without so much as an explanation, having learned nothing, gained no tales to tell about your adventure, except the truth about your boring choice!

75

Congratulations! You have succeeded in becoming the heroic adventurer you always knew you were, winning where others lose, gathering all the spoils of your victory which a warrior like yourself deserves, and being revered by men and women across the world like

you are a living God, nobly and selflessly accepting the accolades bestowed upon you. Big-headed bragging rightly ensues.
    The End.
        Well done.
            Please call again.

(1) Clash of the Titans, 1981, directed by Desmond Davis, starring Laurence Olivier, Harry Hamlyn, Judi Bowker, Claire Bloom, Maggie Smith, Ursula Andress etc. Ray Harryhausen, from his epic autobiography co-written by Tony Dalton, An Animated Life: "By the end of Clash of the Titans I had reached grand old age of 61... You have to live, eat and breathe pictures... I hardly saw my family during the endless months of production, and there eventually comes a point when you say: 'is it worth it?' Having said all that, I regret none if it."

(2) Munchhausen, 1943, directed by Joseph von Baky, starring Hans Albers, Wilhelm Bendow, Brigitte Horney and Ferdinand Marian. From the book The Third Reich's Celluloid War, by Ian Garden: "Munchhausen was undoubtedly the most extravagant film produced during the time of the Third Reich... At a cost of 6.5 million Reichsmarks, it is a fascinating epic... Above all, it was only the fourth German film made in colour..."

(3) Masters of the Universe, 1987, directed by Gary Goddard, starring Dolph Lundgren, Frank Langella, Courteney Cox, Robert Duncan McNeill and Meg Foster. Poster tagline: "A battle fought in the stars...now, comes to Earth." Dolph Lundgren, from 1987's Official Poster Magazine: "He is an old-fashioned hero of great strength, sensitivity and humour. He-Man is truly a Renaissance man, and this makes him a tremendous role model for children in these confusing and changing times."

(4) Labyrinth, 1986, directed by Jim Henson, starring David Bowie and Jennifer Connelly. Dialogue quote: "I ask for so little. Just fear me, love me, do as I say and I shall be your slave."

(5) The Dark Crystal, 1982, directed by Jim Henson and Frank Oz, starring Henson, Frank Oz, Dave Goelz. Cinematographer Oswald Morris's final film after a glittering career which included: The Man Who Would Be King(1975), Fiddler on the Roof(1971), Oliver!(1968), Lolita(1962), Moby Dick(1956), and Moulin Rouge(1952) to name but a few.

(6) Gulliver's Travels, 2010, directed by Rob Leiterman, starring Jack Black, Emily Blunt, Jason Segel, Amanda Peet and Billy Connolly. Dialogue quote: "There's no small jobs, just small people."

(7) Krull, 1983, directed by Peter Yates, starring Ken Marshall, Lysette Anthony, Freddie Jones, Francesca Annis, Bernard Bresslaw and Liam Neeson.

(8) The Thief of Bagdad, 1940, directed by Ludwig Berger, starring Conrad Veidt, Sabu, June Duprez, John Ingram and Rex Ingram. Deservedly won Oscars for Cinematography, Art Direction and Special Effects. Dialogue quote: "I am Abu the thief, son of Abu the thief, Grandson of Abu the thief."

(9) Maciste nella valle dei Re, aka. Son of Samson, 1960, directed by Cario Campogalliani, starring Mark Forest, Chezo Alonso and Vira Silenti.poster tagline: "It's beyond belief."

(10) Dragonslayer, 1981, directed by Matthew Robbins, starring Peter MacNicol, Caitlin Clarke, Ralph Richardson, John Hallam and Peter Eyre. Poster tagline: "In the Dark Ages, Magic was a weapon. Love was a mystery. Adventure was everywhere... And dragons were real."

(11) Jason and the Argonauts, 1963, directed by Don Chaffey, starring Todd Armstrong, Nancy Kovack, Gary Raymond, Honor Blackman and Laurence Naismith. Ray Harryhausen, from his epic autobiography co-written by Tony Dalton, An Animated Life: "The earliest written notes I have relating to Jason were made(in 1961)...entitled Sinbad in the Age of Muses."

(12) The 7th Voyage of Sinbad, 1958, directed by Nathan Juran, starring Kerwin Mathews, Kathryn Grant, Richard Eyer, Torin Thatcher and Danny Green. Poster tagline: "The sheer magic of Dynarama now recreates the most spectacular adventures ever filmed." Kerwin Mathews, from An Oral History of Sinbad: "When it came to shooting any footage that involved special effects, Ray(Harryhausen) would take over... He was such a dear man that we always respected his ideas..."

(13) Prince of Persia: The Sands of Time, 2010, directed by Mike Newell, starring Jake Gyllenhaal, Gemma Arterton, Ben Kingsley, Alfred Molina and Steve Toussaint. Based on a successful video game.

(14) The Golden Compass, 2007, directed by Chris Weitz, starring Nicole Kidman, Daniel Craig, Ben Walker, Dakota Blue Richards,

Freddie Highmore etc. Poster tagline: "There are worlds beyond our own - the compass will show the way."
(15) Sorceress, 1982, directed by Jack Hill, starring Leigh Harris, Lynette Harris, Roberto Nelson, David Millburn and Bruno Rey. Poster tagline: "An age undreamed of...An age if fantasy and magic...Of swords and sorcery."
(16) Willow, 1988, directed by Ron Howard, starring Val Kilmer, Joanne Whalley, Warwick Davis etc.
(17) Eragon, 2006, directed by Stefen Fangmeister, starring Ed Speleers, Sienna Guillory, Jeremy Irons, John Malkovich and Robert Carlyle. Movie debut of singer Joss Stone. Dialogue quote: "Thats the spirit, one part brave, three parts fool!"
(18) Legend, 1985, directed by Ridley Scott, starring Tom Cruise, Tim Curry, Mia Sara and David Bennent. Jerry Goldsmith's original score was rejected, replaced by one from Tangerine Dream.
(19) Die Nibelungen, 1924, directed by Fritz Lang, starring Paul Richter, Margarete Shon, Theodor Loos and Gertrud Arnold. Innovative Austrian director Lang also directed: Metropolis(1927), M(1931), Fury(1936), Scarlet Street(1945), The Big Heat(1953), plus many others.
(20) She, 1965, directed by Robert Day, starring Ursula Andress, John Richardson, Peter Cushing, Christopher Lee and Bernard Cribbins. "Hammer Glamour! Hammer Spectacular!" ...the poster tagline when it was double-billed with One Million Years BC(1966).

CHAPTER TEN

POSTER!

I should like to hazard an educated guess based upon the fact I was there that during my time spent working at EXEL Electrical I discovered diverse movie posters and grew to appreciate the art form as something more than a mere marketing tool for the medium. These weren't all flash'n'grab floating-heads of stars but real artists were creating images from their imagination to stir our imagination, making the film appear better than it probably truly was, especially for those rented based solely on the cover and brief synopsis. Of course some VHS covers and posters used photo-montage as their selling point as they still do today in increasing number, promoting either a familiar star visage or a specific scene from the film which they are selling to attract an audience, any audience.

Most films which had success in the cinema reused the poster art for the VHS cover but owing to the size of the box - rental cases were bigger than a Blu-ray case today, while sell-through was about the same - these images had to compete with a wall of titles so had to stand out from the crowded shelves. In this case the cover might be rejigged for maximum impact with a particularly spectacular superlative review quote, or they might be repackaged by one of the local distributors - CIC or Entertainment in Video, for example - capturing something more basic yet bold, perhaps adding a few positive critical review quotes which may or may not be the genuine article.

EXEL Electrical was a family run business under the Ralph Daniels Limited umbrella, which also had a local boatyard and supermarket to its credit, at the time I joined. My boss was the youngest of two brothers: Ian Daniels; Steve, the eldest, had the boatyard. Ian's wife Caryn was in charge of the video library while Ian's sister, Sally, worked there too but her passion for horse-riding would soon see her open Wroxham Saddlery, initially on the first floor of the building - the Saddlery is still in existence today but is now accommodating both floors.

I owe them all a great deal of gratitude for shaping parts of my character into the person I have become, more than they probably realise, in point of fact. Many of my late-teens and early-twenties experiences were influenced by the Daniels clan and their characteristics and quirks, not all of which I emulated because they are not me, but certainly their working ethics and philosophies to retailing I carry with me today. Also it was Ian who took me for my first driving lesson and introduced me to karate, both of which undoubtedly went some way to break down my theretofore lack of confidence.

Eventually I would help a lot more with the operations of the video library, my naive excitement for new releases regularly getting the better of logic - and the Daniels family were exemplars of logic. Caryn might say I interfered above my knowledge and station, and I should have to agree, but I knew no better back then, so sorry for that. We would occasionally fail to see eye-to-eye when it came to the necessity of ordering particular films for rental, and you must bear in mind that in the eighties and early nineties a film could cost in the region of £50-90 to buy, so it was often a gamble on the tastes of our customers to what we should, and shouldn't, stock. As well as the films with a known history and surefire profit status there were many duds, oh yes - or quirky curiosities, if you will, some of which would inconceivably make their money back. Others wouldn't, but thats the risk.

These were the days when Cannon, Corman and New Line churned out direct-to-video cheapie's at a mind-boggling rate yet many of their sleeves were gloriously decorated even if the content was questionable, such as: Allan Quartermain and the Lost City of Gold(1), Sahara(2), Caribe(3), Eye of the Eagle II: Inside the Enemy(4) etc.

People would rent the likes of these films based on the cover, a recognisable star name, or on the brief plot synopsis, whichever appeals.

And then there were those films which were banned after the Video Recordings Act came into effect in 1984 - before my time at EXEL - which saw several films removed from the shelves of rental libraries, and make them valuable collector's items in today's market. So if you were lucky enough before this censorship took place, you might view material in the video nasties which 'they' didn't want you to see, such as: The Evil Dead(5), SS Experiment Love Camp(6), Inferno(7), The Driller Killer(8) etc.

Thanks to the lessening of morality these days we can see most films uncut, and some even appear tame in their content when compared to not just cinema releases but television series which supply copious amounts of nudity and violence.

Other films which couldn't rely on notoriety or awareness relied on outlandish titles, coupled with bold posters and a hyperbolic tagline for their success: The Hunchback Hairball of LA(9), Creepozoids(10), Flesh Gordon Meets the Cosmic Cheerleaders(11), The Slumber Party Massacre 2(12) etc.

And then there were the adult films.

Electric Blue titles were the undisputed champions of our top-shelf range and rented in their abundance by nervous men because yes, very few women watched pornography in those days! Many of these men were clearly embarrassed by their choice of entertainment, while others brazenly brought these films up to the counter - I can recall one particular man bringing a film back complaining that the film juddered upon being paused, rendering the still images unwatchable, and don't misconstrue because I'm not homophobic, but the self-explanatory title was "Yards and Yards of Dick."

Two further anecdotes to bore you with: someone thought Blade Runner(13) was robbed by E.T.(14) in the scoring section at the Academy Awards - protests to p.starling@sky.com; and the quote by Griffin Mill on the cover of The Player(15) video claiming it to be "the best movie ever made" was rubbished by one customer. Does this prove two wrongs don't make a right?

Back to the subject at hand: movie posters. The eighties and nineties saw the hand-drawn poster coming to an inglorious end as it became more common for studio committee's to decide on a singular image to promote their wares, usually globally, which went some way to eliminate unique artistic vision from this form. Photo-shopped floating-heads, montages and franchise imagery have become the norm with a few rare eye-catching posters hitting the billboards, usually referred to as retro style.

I wanted to show a list of twenty favourite posters for you to seek out and view - because for obvious reasons of copyright I cannot reprint any here - but limiting myself to such a small number is quite literally impossible for me, so instead I have chosen to list some of the prominent Poster Artists and Designers along with some of their work, which I feel offers a broader representation of the medium. For your convenience, and if you choose to discover more about movie posters, several of these artists feature in Reel Art Press's "100 Movie Posters

The Essential Collection" by Tony Nourmand, which is an excellent starting point because it covers a mixture of genres and is a beautifully designed book, with brief profiles on the artist, their influences and style .

John Alvin- Blazing Saddles, Young Frankenstein, E.T.: The Extra Terrestrial, The Golden Child, Willow, Beauty and the Beast, The Lion King

Richard Amsel- Chinatown, The Sting, The Last Picture Show, McCabe and Mrs Miller, The Long Goodbye

Anselmo Ballester- The Lady from Shanghai, T-Men, The Big Heat

Saul Bass- The Big Country, Exodus, The Shining, The Man with the Golden Arm, Anatomy of a Murder, Vertigo

Reynold Brown- Attack of the 40ft Woman, Creature From the Black Lagoon, Ben-Hur, Spartacus, Tarantula

Renato Casaro- A Fistful of Dollars, My Name is Nobody, Dracula A.D. 1972, Octopussy, Conan the Barbarian, Flesh and Blood

Tom Chantrell- She, The Brigand of Kandahar, The Plague of the Zombies, One Million Years B.C., Quatermass and the Pit, Dracula Has Risen from the Grave

Renato Fratini- From Russia With Love, This Sporting Life, Carry On-Don't Lose Your Head Captain Clegg, The Phantom of the Opera

Bill Gold- Casablanca, My Fair Lady, The Big Sleep, Bullitt, Magnum Force, Unforgiven, A Clockwork Orange, The Exorcist, City Heat, Platoon

Boris Grinnson- The Big Shot, The Accused, The Lost Weekend, From Russia With Love, The Mummy's Shroud

Al Hirschfeld- Cabin in the Sky, City Lights, The Wizard of Oz

Robert E. MacGinnis- Breakfast at Tiffany's, Thunderball, Live and Let Die, Arabesque, Barbarella

Bob Peak- Every Which Way But Loose, Rollerball, Superman, Star Trek The Motion Picture, Excaliber West Side Story

Rene Peron- From Here to Eternity, Jour de Fete, King Kong, The Caine Mutiny

Sandro Simeoni- La Dolce Vita, Vertigo, L'Avventua, Accattone, A Fistful of Dollars

Georgi and Vladimir Stenberg- October, Man with the Movie Camera, Moulin Rouge, The Eleventh Year, The General, The Girl with the Hat-Box

Drew Struzan- The Thing, The Goonies, Big Trouble in Little China, Masters of the Universe, Indiana Jones and the Last Crusade, Hook

Alberto Vargas- Ladies they Talk About, The Sin of Nora Moran

Bronislaw Zelek- The Birds, The Hunger, Silence, There is such a Lad, The Anxiety, Cartouche

(1) Allan Quartermain and the Lost City of Gold, 1986, directed by Gary Nelson, starring Richard Chamberlain, Sharon Stone, James Earl Jones and Henry Silva. Chamberlain and Stone didn't get along in the first film(King Soloman's Mines), yet still returned for this sequel.
(2) Sahara, 1983, directed by Andrew V McLaglen, starring Brooke Shields, Lambert Wilson and Horst Buchholz. Poster tagline: "She challenged the desert. Its men, their passions and ignited a bold adventure." The poster by Drew Struzan successfully makes this film look like terrific fun, sadly it's a letdown.
(3) Caribe, 1987, directed by Michael Kennedy, starring John Savage, Kara Glover and Stephen McHattie. The video cover had a tropical image in blues, very alluring and sultry, perfect for the impressed renter.

(4) Eye of the Eagle II: Inside the Enemy, 1989, directed by Carl Franklin, starring Todd Field, Andy Wood and Ken Jacobson. Video cover tagline: "Love, revenge and blood-seeking bullets in the killing fields of Vietnam."

(5) The Evil Dead, 1981, directed by Sam Raimi, starring Bruce Campbell, Ellen Sandweis, Betsy Baker etc. Adding a recommendation on the poster from Stephen King certainly did the film no harm: "...The most ferociously original horror film of the year..."

(6) SS Experiment Love Camp, 1976, directed by Segio Gerrone, starring Mircha Carven, Paola Corazzi and Giorgio Cerioni. Poster tagline: "Sex experiments in pursuit of a better tomorrow."

(7) Inferno, 1980, directed by Dario Argento, starring Leigh McCloskey, Irene Miracle and Eleonora Giorgi. Featuring a score by Keith Emerson of Emerson, Lake & Palmer fame.

(8) The Driller Killer, 1979, directed by and starring Abel Ferrara, co-starring Carolyn Marz and Baybi Day. Poster tagline: "There are those who kill violently."

(9) The Hunchback Hairball of LA, 1989, directed by Jeremy Kagan, starring and written by Allan Katz(as hirsute Bob Maloogaloogaloogaloogaloogalooga), co-starring Corey Parker and Cindy Williams. Original title: Big Man on Campus.

(10) Creepozoids, 1987, directed by David DeCoteau, starring Linnea Quigley, Ken Abraham and Michael Aranda. On a personal note, I can only recall this film due to the fact that the back of the VHS sleeve featured an attractive female rearview naked in the shower - and who said I have one track mind?

(11) Flesh Gordon Meets the Cosmic Cheerleaders, 1990, directed by Howard Ziehm, starring Vince Murdocco, Robyn Kelly and Tony Travis. A belated sequel to 1974's Flesh Gordon, and featuring stop-motion by Jim Towler(Batman Returns/Hellboy).

(12) Slumber Party Massacre 2, 1987, directed by Deborah Brock, starring Crystal Bernard, Jennifer Rhodes and Kimberley McArthur. Poster tagline: "The party begins when the lights go out."

(13) Blade Runner, 1982, directed by Ridley Scott, starring Harrison Ford, Rutger Hauer, Sean Young and Daryl Hannah. Based on Philip K. Dicks novel: Do Androids Dream Of Electric Sheep?

(14) E.T.: The Extra Terrestrial, 1982, directed by Steven Spielberg.

(15) The Player, 1992, directed by Robert Altman, starring Tim Robbins, Greta Scacchi, Fred Ward, Whoopi Goldberg and an ensemble cast featuring Bruce Willis, Julia Roberts, Sydney Pollack, Richard E. Grant, James Coburn, and Cher, to name but a few.

CHAPTER ELEVEN

WANDERING Z'DAR - The Face(or chin) Speaks

Al is our new director after the studio fired The Konch but everyone knows its Sly's show anyway so I don't see much difference. Yeah, he and Kurt might get equal-billing but it's been Sly who has held us all together when those around him have been hopelessly flailing. I call Sly the Big Guy because he's the real-deal Hollywood star despite his huge ego. I'm a couple of inches taller than him and broader too but truth is everyone looks up to him, even a rising star like me. Yeah, this Hollywood show is gonna be my big break into the mainstream alright, not that I'm complaining, I ain't gonna forget my roots, I love the little movies too but this is gonna be huge.

Man, I love movies, always have, always will.

Some guys in the business...well, maybe its cause'a the size of this show, like the fella whose been complaining about it being the worst prepared and organised production he's worked on, well, guys like that don't appreciate how lucky we are.

Living the dream, that's what we're doing. Pretending to be someone else for the entertainment of others, the fans. Yeah, even a guy like me gotta fan club now, because of Matt Cordell[1] and you know something, I think it's just great. What better way can there be for regular folks to show their appreciation for this work?

How many jobs do you find where a Teamster chauffeurs you to work on a Monday morning so you can sit and bask in the sunshine of South Hills, just off Interstate 210 outside Irwindale, thats California, shooting the breeze while waiting for Sly, that's Sylvester Stallone to you, and the director to organise the scene?

Not too many, you can bet your bottom dollar!

Heh: Last night me and some of the stunt guys went to the nearest fleapit and caught Lock-Up[2] released a few weeks back. Its Sly's latest, and I was thanking my lucky stars for the extra paydays on account of these additional scenes, and besides, I ain't nothing better to do at the moment than hang with Stallone, and guess what, the Big Guy himself sits right behind me and says, joking like: "You better like this movie or you're fired!" He must'a seen this movie like a hundred times already but he decides to come hang with us, shoot some pool and down a few beers afterwards too. Now that's one helluva a great guy!

It's like I already said: living the dream.

I'm thirty-nine years old, man, so I guess it's about time I started living the dream in this business although I've only been in it since '84. But, hey, look, not everyone can be Van Damme and have two huge movies out in a year to kickstart your career: Cyborg(3) and Kickboxer(4), but who knows, I gotta couple'a aces up my sleeve.

An episode of Moonlighting(5) was one if my very first gigs. I played the part of a police officer, heh, can't imagine why, seeing I used to be a Chicago cop, so that wasn't much of a stretch.

When I graduated outta Proviso West High School, that's Hillside for anyone who is wondering, I went to Arizona State University and got myself a BFA, so there wasn't any real inclination towards law-enforcement at the time. Heck, far from it in some of the things I done, and I done plenty.

Heh: Nova Express. We were once the opening act to The Who. Can you believe that? Our little rock group opened for the big guns. So I can sing, play guitar and keyboards, you name it. In fact one-time I was freelance for a variety of Ad Agencies. Jingle-writer, you might say, for commercials and stuff. That was all cool. I was watching Batman(6) a few months back and thought Jeez, I knew Danny Elfman back when he was an actor while also performing with Oingo Boingo, his band, so if he can do both why can't I?

You might say the entertainment business is in my every fibre, the exterior of which was utilised by the Chippendales. Yeah, you got it, the male strippers. I was only with them for a while on account of my body, of course, because I don't have to work too hard to get into shape, not like some of the blowhards around these days. Brion(James, actor in Tango & Cash(7), Blade Runner(8) etc.) told me that in his last film the "preening star", his words, was constantly pumping iron, and I seen that film a few months back(9) and he definitely looks in shape, but us action actors gotta be at our best because it don't last forever, even Sly is gonna lose the bulk someday, I figure.

But it's my face what sells me. In point of fact the name of my character in this show is Face. Plain name but colourful guy. I dish out the pain to Sly and Kurt, although Kurt must feel worse right now after his last film(10) tanked at the box office, but that ain't none of my business. Kurt ain't here today, he's gone onto his next project I guess, so me and the guys are filming with Sly and, whisper this, 'cause rumour has it Jack Palance(Shane(11), Dracula(12), City Slickers(13) etc) might be filming his first shot in the film today, but I ain't holding my breath just in case it's a load of baloney. Pretty sure he would be here by now. Palance is a legend and, I might add, another guy with a great face and physical presence, a bit like Rondo Hatton(as 'The Creeper'in The Pearl of Death(14), plus many more roles) who had a glandular condition which enlarged his face and hands.

    Doctors say I got something called Cherubism. Cute name but kinda makes me look a bit sinister, although I got over it and its proven an asset in this business. "We need a tall, hulking, menacing kinda guy who looks like he can beat the heck outta all-comers, better give Robert Z'Dar a call!" At least that's what I image takes places. All it is is I got an abnormally wide jaw, gives me a kinda baby-looking face yet dangerous with it, if you know what I mean. Like I said already, it got me here and it got me the role in Maniac Cop and I got another film out this year(Young Rebels(15), directed by Amir Shervan(also Killing American Style(16), and Samurai Cop(17)) and co-starring Aldo Ray(Blood Red(18), co-starring Eric Roberts who was directed by Andrey Konchalovskiy in Runaway Train(19) - fewer than six-degrees of separation going on here!))

    So you see, I ain't complaining. Who would?

    I'm sitting in the sunshine right now, Cola in my hand, shooting the breeze with the guy supposedly riding in the truck with me while we watch and wait. That's what movies this size are about, I guess: endless waiting around for the DoP to get his set-up ready. Fascinating to watch, for me, at least, 'cause I really dig all this stuff. Fake cop cars just rolled, a helicopter overhead, and now there's Sly and the director- heck, it's difficult when someone gets fired and another guy takes his place. Okay, so most of the pictures in the can and has been edited ahead of our December 22nd release date, but this is the middle of September! No wonder everyone is frantic. Just pleased I'm up on this ridge, it's a safe enough distance away to be outta the firing line yet near enough to catch some of the chatter, and some of it ain't good. You gotta feel for this guy, Albert Magnoli(wrote and directed Prince's Purple Rain(20)), taking over someone else's project because the studio ain't happy.

Perhaps this sorta stuff happens all the time on big Hollywood productions, who knows, but it still leaves a bad taste in the mouth when you can feel the unrest, getting to this stage. And don't the critics just love it, claiming it doesn't bode well for the box office. Maybe they're right, only time can tell.(It grossed $63million US, $90million rest of the world, so it was a moderate hit for its year but much less than the takings of the other big buddy action comedy of the year: Lethal Weapon 2(21)).

Heh: On Maniac Cop we shot and released the film in the same time it takes the big guns to shoot retakes and for less money too. So it wasn't a massive hit but it generated enough interest that we're doing a sequel(22), so who knows, maybe if that turns out well I gotta series on my hands(23).

I have so much gratitude for Lustig and the guys at Shapiro(Glickenhaus Entertainment, who produced and released Maniac Cop) for having faith enough in me to cast me in the title role. I play a cop, yeah, another one, only this guy Matt he works for the NYPD and is dead! It's a brilliant concept. There am I, hacking people to death while all others blunder about pointing the finger in completely the wrong direction. It's gonna end up a classic someday, mark my word.

We all gotta start somewhere, don't we?

Look at guys from the past like Robert Mitchum(24), Richard Widmark(25), and Kirk Douglas(26). They all had to start and end somewhere and none were what you might call classically handsome, yet they each possessed a certain something which made them rise above the rest. They had charisma and a face you remembered, just like the one I got.

Directors and ladies want me to get my shirt off in every picture now, how can that possibly be a bad thing? They can see beyond the mask so who knows how far I can go.

I've had so much fun on this show and made lots of new friends - or contacts in the business, if you wanna be cynical about it. Sure theres lots'a testosterone on the set, why wouldn't there be with Sly, Kurt, Brion, myself and the other tough prison guys in the same room? Dog eat dog, scenery chewing, jostling for position are part and parcel of this business anyway. It's not like we are making Bond(27), or Indiana Jones(28) where it's mostly smooth operators, and that Kevin Costner(29) is too clean-cut to do what we do! Naa- we gotta he rough around the edges, dangerous, to get ahead in this fast-paced world of action movies, although it ain't moving fast right now.

The waiting around, yeah, I mentioned it already. Ah, it's their money to burn, I guess, and I'm getting paid so whose moaning? Other guys, that's who. My glass is half full. This whole atmosphere is something else altogether and a person can only really understand what I mean until you've been here yourself. There's the intensity of focus, the excited anticipation, professionalism like you can't imagine- followed by the satisfaction of the end product, which you guys get to see. Gotta be better than taking out the trash, not that there's anything wrong with that, you know? Every job is significant. I mean, I may be a B-movie actor for the rest of my life but we all have to earn a living and I choose this line of work.

We all gotta start somewhere and there's a place for everyone. So what that I'm not the star of this show, you would definitely notice if I weren't around. I can only bring myself to the job because that's all I got. I carry out this work with pride, I enjoy it, and it's kinda like public service insofar as we are public-facing, only sometimes its twenty-feet tall. My personality can rise above the perceptions people have of us in this job, and I sure ain't gonna change my beliefs or standards for nobody and why should I? You wouldn't.

(1) Maniac Cop,1988, directed by William Lustig, starring Tom Atkins, Bruce Campbell and Richard Roundtree. Poster tagline: "You have the right to remain silent...forever."
(2) Lock-Up, 1989, directed by John Flynn(Out for Justice, 1991), starring Sylvester Stallone, Donald Sutherland, John Amos and Sonny Landham. Dialogue quote: "This is hell, and I'm going to give you the guided tour."
(3) Cyborg, 1989, directed by Albert Pyun, starring Jean Claude van Damme, Deborah Richter and Vincent Klyn. Reviewer Dan Scapperotti, from the July 1989 edition of Cinefantastique magazine: "Yet another post-apocalyptic excuse for senseless violence, this is a grim, ultimately boring tale...and a distinct lack of originality make this a prime candidate for the video junk pile." He enjoyed it, then!
(4) Kickboxer, 1989, directed by Mark DiSalle and David Worth, starring Jean Claude van Damme, Dennis Alexio and Dennis Chan. Poster tagline: "An ancient sport becomes a deadly game."

(5) Moonlighting, television series, 1985-1989, starring Cybill Shepherd and Bruce Willis. Both its stars won Best Leading Actor Emmy's in 1987.

(6) Batman, 1989, directed by Tim Burton, starring Michael Keaton, Jack Nicholson, Jack Palance and Kim Basinger. Dialogue quote: "Tell me something, my friend: you ever dance with the devil in the pale moonlight?" Took over $400million at the Worldwide box office on a budget under $40million.

(7) Tango & Cash, 1989, directed by Andrey Konchalovskiy, starring Sylvester Stallone, Kurt Russell, Jack Palance, Teri Hatcher and Robert Z'Dar. Synth-score by popular 80's composer Harold Faltermeyer,, known for Fletch, The Running Man, his Grammy winner for Best song(Top Gun) and score (Beverly Hills Cop).

(8) Blade Runner, 1982, directed by Ridley Scott.

(9) Red Scorpion, 1988, directed by Joseph Zito, starring Dolph Lundgren, M. Emmett Walsh, Al White and Brion James. Released in the US in 1989, and on VHS in the UK in 1990. Poster tagline: "They think he's a machine. They think they can control him. Think again."

(10) Winter People, 1989, directed by Ted Kotcheff, starring Kurt Russell, Kelly McGillis and Lloyd Bridges. Poster tagline: "A passion so strong it kills."

(11) Shane, 1953, directed by George Stevens, starring Alan Ladd, Jean Arthur, Van Heflin and Jack Palance. Oscar nominated co-star Brandon De Wilde, born in 1942, was killed in a car accident aged just 30.

(12) Dracula, 1974, directed by Dan Curtis, starring Jack Palance, Simon Ward and Nigel Davenport. An X-rated TV movie.

(13) City Slickers, 1991, directed by Ron Underwood, starring Billy Crystal, Jack Palance, Daniel Stern and Bruno Kirby. An Oscar winning performance from Palance in a supporting role.

(14) The Pearl of Death, 1944, directed by Roy William Neill, starring Basil Rathbone, Nigel Bruce, Dennis Hoey and Rondo Hatton. The ninth Sherlock Holmes film starring the Rathbone/Bruce duo. Rondo Hatton's first appearance as The Creeper.

(15) Young Rebels, 1989, directed by Amir Shervan, starring John Greene, Aldo Ray, Robert Z'Dar and Tadashi Yamashita. Poster tagline: "When the young gets tough, the tough gets going!"

(16) Killing American Style, 1990, directed by Amir Shervan, starring Harold Diamond, Jim Brown and Robert Z'Dar. Poster tagline: "There are all kinds of killings, the best are American style."

(17) Samurai Cop, 1991, directed by Amir Shervan, starring Mathew Karedas, Mark Frazer and Robert Z'Dar. Poster tagline: "You have the right to remain silent...dead silent."

(18) Blood Red, 1989, directed by Peter Masterson, starring Eric Roberts, Giancarlo Giannini, Dennis Hopper, Burt(Rocky)Young and Aldo Ray.   Filmed in 1986, this is one of the first films for actress Julia Roberts.

(19) Runaway Train, 1985, directed by Andrey Konchalovskiy, starring Jon Voigt, Eric Roberts and Rebecca De Mornay. Poster tagline: "Desperate, and determined to survive."

(20) Purple Rain, 1984, directed by Albert Magnoli and starring Prince. Oscar and Grammy winning score by Prince.

(21) Lethal Weapon 2, 1989, directed by Richard Donner, starring Mel Gibson, Danny Glover, Patsy Kensit, Joe Pesci and Joss Ackland. Dialogue quote: "I'm too old for this shit."

(22) Maniac Cop 2, 1990, directed by William Lustig, starring Robert Z'Dar, Robert Davi and Bruce Campbell. Not entirely unique poster tagline: "You have the right to remain silent...forever."

(23) Maniac Cop 3: Badge of Honour, 1993, directed by William Lustig, starring Robert Z'Dar, Robert Davi and Caitlin Dulaney. Taglines: "The wrong arm of the law is back." "You can't keep a good corpse down."

(24) Jack Spanner Private Eye, 1989, directed by Lee H. Katzin, starring Robert Mitchum, Ernest Borgnine, John Mitchum and James Mitchum. A private detective teams up with his brother to aid an old adversary, nothing like keeping it in the family!

(25) Cold Sassy Tree, 1989, directed by Joan Tewksbury, starring Faye Dunaway, Richard Widmark and Frances Fisher. Just three weeks after being widowed a woman remarries: scandalous!

(26) Inherit the Wind, 1988, directed by David Greene, starring Kirk Douglas, Jason Robards, Darren McGaving and Jean Simmons. TV movie remake and winner of three Emmys.

(27) Licence to Kill, 1989, directed by John Glen, starring Timothy Dalton, Robert Davi, Carey Lowell, Talisa Soto, Benicio del Toro and Anthony Zerbe. Poster tagline: "James Bond is out on his own and out for revenge."

(28) Indiana Jones and the Last Crusade, 1989, directed by Steven Spielberg, starring Harrison Ford, Sean Connery, Alison Doody, Julian Glover, Denholm Elliott and John Rhys-Davies. Poster tagline: "Have the adventure of your life keeping up with he Joneses."

(29) Field of Dreams, 1989, directed by Phil Alden Robinson, starring Kevin Costner, James Earl Jones, Burt Lancaster, Ray Liotta and Amy Madigan. Dialogue quote: "If you build it, he will come."

So is the point of this chapter to highlight the fact a person doesn't need to be a megastar celebrity whose face is always splashed over trashy tabloids or periodicals which promote salacious activity? Am I saying that every person however far down the credits list has some value, some worth, and can indeed be the star of their own show without selling-put? Am I perhaps trying to highlight the fact that without these characters on the fringes our movie experiences would be lessened? Or am I trying to say that I am happy to be a minor character in life because I am enjoying creating my art, which is writing? Am I saying that I am enjoying the 'doing' instead of just 'saying?' I don't know, but if you are looking for the cynical then maybe you can add more prosaic psycho-analysis to my words and undermine 'worth.' Just a thought.

CHAPTER TWELVE

1990: GONE IN TWENTY MINUTES - PASSING MY DRIVING TEST

Arriving promptly at the Norwich City Driving Test Centre at a quarter past nine in the morning with my instructor, Anna Mick, in the passenger seat of the duel-control Nissan Micra - I think it was red - there was a family of butterflies procreating in my stomach, making me feel grateful I chose to forgo breakfast that morning. I was nervous irrespective of the fact this would be my fifth test - I truly believed I had driven better on the third attempt, but what did I know! - and this malarkey was becoming expensive so I certainly wanted to pass sooner rather than later, although giving up never entered my thoughts because I knew I desired to be able to drive. The one thing I had prepared to such an extent that I was one-hundred percent confident of passing was the theory test, which is much different by the standards of today, with just a handful of questions lasting just a couple of minutes after the practical test and not a whole separate thing.

I always have lacked self-confidence and desired praise, although when given a boost of esteem I use humour as a defence to brush it off. At school I seem to recall a succession of teachers knocking down my answers to questions, mocking with their arrogance, unaware of many social skills in the nineteen-eighties which are requirements today, so as to not ridicule the emotionally fragile, or bully those children more easily manipulated. I found the expected teaching patterns restrictive to creativity. It was as if they wanted to drain the self to comply with the structure of an almost dictated, fated life. Anyone with different, unique characteristics, or those whose will was strong, were shunned in favour of the child who followed the parrot fashion tuition without asking deeper, more meaningful or thoughtful questions.

So I suppose this suppression of confidence and fearfulness of failure resulted in my nervousness despite this being test number five. I tend to over-think and over-analyse an outcome which is inevitably never as fatal as the one imagined - with this lack of confidence comes the aforementioned humour defence mechanism.

Back in the eighties or early nineties I was probably still acquiring the ammunition for my mechanism, so at this time my unattuned naiveness must have come across as a bit of odd behaviour.

The Examiner for this fifth test fit the usual prototype fit of these people: conservatively dressed, bland, emotionless, bored, with the equally unexciting name Robert Kent[1] to boot. Yes, I can understand certain jobs require seriousness and composure but can these jobs not serve a personality rather than force a suppression of it? Oh well, we cannot all be perfect like me, I suppose!

Little did I know at the time when I shook this man's hand in greeting that his stoicism was hiding a singular mind whirling with the thoughts of what was meticulously planned for the following twenty minutes.

"In your own time." The Examiner said monotonously, looking at his watch with what I mistook as casual boredom - I was, after all, the first in an endless line of students hoping to impress today, so who could blame him.

Telling myself to focus, I put my foot on the clutch and ensured we were in neutral before turning the key in the ignition of the car as I had done a hundred times before, and its engine encouragingly fired up first time: a good start, one might declare. Next it was mirror, signal and manoeuvre in that order and we were steadily away the short distance across the carpark of the test centre to the first set of traffic lights, which would eject us onto the inner ring-road of Norwich - if I may be allowed at this juncture I would like to point out a well-known fact that many motorists nowadays feel there is no need to observe the mirror, signal, manoeuvre rule in that order, if at all: just saying!

Luckily for me I was taking my driving test just after the peak of rush hour so the traffic had subsided quite considerably, making it a smooth departure through the traffic lights, turning left where I was a couple of car lengths behind a gleaming red Maserati[2] which looked new and expense, so best not get too close, hey?

My passenger sighs almost in relief that we had made the turn without incident. I, on the other hand, was having a good feeling about that morning, conscious of the fact I was relaxed, doing everything by the book while over-doing the awareness of my surroundings routine, without realising the Examiner was more interested in the unmarked white van in his wing mirror.

"Take a right at the next set of traffic lights." The Examiner said in his droning monotone.

Ahead was the set of Old Catton lights with their filtering system where turning right for a first-timer can seem daunting, but as luck would have it the Maserati too was going that way so I followed him easily and no waiting was required: yes, this was definitely going to be my lucky day!

We were now off the Norwich ring road and amongst a maze of roadway, houses and small business premises where the speed is limited to thirty and the only obstacles are from side roads or oncoming traffic, with the road narrowing where vehicles park up to the left and right. A wave of confidence had uncharacteristically overcome my very fibres, making me relax and smile, enjoying the journey and trying to anticipate every eventuality, deploying all my driving knowledge to the best if my ability.

My Examiner was checking his wing mirror before casually glancing at his watch, unintentionally making me aware of the piece of paper in his hand. He was undoubtedly preparing for one of the trio of staples during the driver test: emergency stop, three-point turn, and parallel parking. Owing to the giveaway sign of the paper, and despite the close proximity of the van behind us, I was willing to bet that he would be requesting an emergency stop any time soon.

"When I tap on the dash," the Examiner announced, not wholly unexpectedly, "I shall require you to safely execute an emergency stop."

I nodded my understanding while trying the best I could to maintain my cool, a sixth sense kicking in which would anticipate his instruction on the button.

The road was an incline, houses one side, a school playing field the other, with cars parked at intervals thus eliminating two-way traffic, meaning I had to be watchful not only for the road ahead with the red Maserati not three car lengths up front, as well as the van behind, but for anyone who might pull out, especially the shiny British racing green classic Darracq(3), who was doing so without signalling.

In a blur of motion the Examiner slapped the paper atop the dashboard and I just as quickly applied the brakes, coming to a controlled stop with, bizarrely, the Maserati copying my manoeuvre. Thankfully for me the driver of the white van was equally alert to my braking - no mobile phone distractions in those days! - and was able to come to a stop a safe car length behind me. Maybe he was in some psychic connection with me and knew I was on my test, I only hoped he was transporting nothing breakable.

It was while I was pulling the handbrake on and putting the little car into first gear to continue onward that it occurred to me to subconsciously question why the Maserati could possibly be waiting in front of us. Then I became aware of the commotion behind from looking in the rearview mirror: two people, both sporting black balaclava's, were ushering the driver of the van out of his vehicle by gunpoint - in the nineteen-eighties this was not a normal occurrence. Upon turning to the Examiner in order to ascertain if he was aware of what was transpiring, he smiled at me wryly between checking the time on his watch.

"Don't concern yourself, Mister Starling." He said in a reassuringly calm and casual tone of voice, eliminating the drone. "You shall be back at the testing centre with a pass in the allotted time."

Exactly sixty seconds after I had braked I could see the rear doors of the van being opened but was unable to see what was going on, until the doors shut and two people in balaclava's strode towards us and got into the rear of the Micra as if it was the most natural thing in the world, dropping a bag presumably filled with swag on the seat between them both.

From then on I was to be a participant in a heist, something which was most definitely an entirely new thing for me and it would be a gross understatement to claim I was mildly perplexed by this sudden turn of events, although I had not failed to notice the Examiner had pronounced my success in passing this, my fifth, driving test: splendiferous, I might very well have thought at time had other words not been at the forefront of my mind.

"Let's get outta here!" One of our newly acquired backseat passengers ordered, using the Hollywood cliche said in almost every film ever made in one form or another, who I shall refer to hereon as Loudmouth, simply because he was just that.

"Proceed, Mister Starling." The Examiner said much more calmly.

Releasing the handbrake I applied acceleration and promptly, in my newly received zeal, stalled the engine, much to the sweary chagrin of Loudmouth. Second time lucky and we successfully pulled forward, the Maserati, quite obviously their accomplices in this heist, matching us only without the stall

We wove our way up the incline in our getaway car leaving the white van blocking the road behind us. It was with the supremely satisfying knowledge that no matter how many mistakes I should make, and as long as I stayed alive, I am soon to be the proud owner of a Full British Drivers Licence.

The Examiner looked in his wing mirror and smiled while the two backseat passengers turned in their seat. I looked in the rearview mirror to see what was peaking the interest to see a lovely yellow Ferrari(4) was behind us. They were yet more accomplices in this heist and undoubtedly diversions should the police arrive - who would suspect that the criminals and their loot was in a slow learner drivers car?

Low-and-behold the inevitable police siren blared loudly amongst the houses which engulfed us, and it was now only been two-and-a-half minutes since the heist took place, and the since the van driver obviously sounded the alert, indicating whatever is in the swag bag between my two backseat passengers is of extremely high value.

"Excuse me, Mister Starling," the Examiner says politely, "and my apologies, but if you please continue steering I should wish to take over the rest of the controls."

This was less a request, more a statement, so immediately I relaxed my feet when the Examiner took control.

"We need to turn right!" Loudmouth positively screamed from the back, much to the Examiner's obvious irritation. "Move it!"

An unmarked police BMW(5) burst out of nowhere from the left-hand exit of the roundabout fifty yards ahead, while the rotating blue light of the Ford(6) police-car which was pursuing the Ferrari came into view, its distinctive Nee-Naw announcement synonymous with mid-eighties police dramas.

"Go! Go!" Belched Loudmouth, the Speed Crazed(7) idiot.

"Now, Mister Starling," come's the more assured calmness of the Examiner, "if you can please indicate and turn right ahead as naturally as possible."

Like a natural born Driver(8) I executed the manoeuvre in a pure fluid motion, wth help from the Examiner, of course, without so much as raising suspicion from the two police vehicles, whose pursuit of The Fast and the Furious(9) distraction sports cars continued unabated.

A cheer of exaltation came from the backseat passengers and I, too, could not help but raise a smile of my own, enjoying The Wild Ride(10) I was experiencing during what appeared to be the end of a successful heist.

But even though we were no longer being accompanied by the two cars distracting the police from our getaway vehicle, we weren't out if the woods yet.

"Watch it!" Shouted Loudmouth.

I swerved to avoid an equally fast and unforgiving Taxi(11) coming at us from the opposite direction, the Examiner expertly applying the brakes just in the nick of time, and I felt that my reflexes were sharp and, most importantly, that I was alert enough to avoid a collision.

"Not far now." The Examiner said, erringly calm.

"Thank flip." Loudmouth grumbled.

"Calm down, Hooper(12), it's almost done." The female backseat passenger said with a husky, commanding voice.

After a further two blocks the Examiner told me to make a right turn into a housing estate, which I did, and when we were pointed at a red garage door he pulled a remote control device from out of his pocket and the door arose in front of us. Inside the garage was a motor bike, two helmets and a rucksack.

We drove inside and once stationery the two backseat passengers climbed out with their swag bag. Both Loudmouth and the woman stripped off, much to the pleasure of my nineteen year old one-track mind because the woman's body was curvaceous. Soon they had their leathers on, Loudmouth putting on the black helmet, the woman The Green Helmet(13), and they were on the bike and Gone In Sixty Seconds(14).

The remainder of my drive was mundane by comparison but at least it wasn't the usual uneventful driving test most people experience, so I shouldn't really complain!

(1) Blonde Comet, 1941, directed by William Beaudine, starring Robert Kent, Virginia Vale and Barney Oldfield. The dramatic French poster by artist Albert Jorio features his rendering of dirt track racers.

(2) Fangio, 1950, directed by R. Vinoly Barreto, starring Juan Manuel Fangio, Armando Bo, Miguel Gomez Bao and Yvonne de Lys. An Argentinian film with a poster by RAF which showcases Fangio himself and his Maserati 4CLT.
(3) Genevieve, 1953, directed by Henry Cornelius, starring Dinah Sheridan, John Gregson, Kay Kendall and Kenneth More. British artist Eric Pulford colourfully depicts the Darracq on its poster.
(4) L'Homme a la Ferrari, 1966, directed by Dino Risi, starring Ann-Margaret, Vittorio Gassman and Eleanor Parker. (Italian made, original title: Il Tigre). French poster artist Oussenka creates a striking image with its star and a Ferrari as a centrepiece.
(5) The Last Run, 1971, directed by Richard Fleischer, starring George C Scott, Tony Musante and Trish van Devere. The American poster features a painted montage including a BMW 503.
(6) Ghost of Dragstrip Hollow, 1959, directed by William Hole, starring Judy Fair, Martin Braddock and Russ Bender. The terrific American poster features a Ford hot-rod.
(7) Speed Crazed, 1926, directed by Duke Warne, starring Billy Sullivan and Andree Tourneur. The inspirational Belgian poster, with its title 180 a l'Heure, perfectly captures the feel of high speed.
(8) Driver, 1978, directed by Walter Hill, starring Ryan O'Neal, Bruce Dern and Isabelle Adjani. The bold American poster by Brian Bysouth includes the tagline: "A game... A challenge... A chase to the death!"
(9) The Fast and the Furious1954, directed by and starring John Ireland, co-starring Dorothy Malone. (In 2001 the Rob Cohen directed exploitation B-movie of the same name, The Fast and the Furious, starring newcomer Paul Walker alongside Vin Diesel, launched a box office guzzling franchise.)
(10) The Wild Ride, 1960, directed by Harvey Berman, starring Jack Nicholson and Georgianna Carter. Poster tagline: "From roaring hot rods...to the racing big time."
(11) Taxi, 1953, directed by Gregory Ratoff, starring Dan Dailey and Constance Smith(also a same-titled 1998 French film directed by Gerard Pires, starring Samy Naceri, Frederic Diefenthal, Marion Cotillard, which began its own franchise and was itself loosely remade in 2004 by Tim Story and starred Queen Latifah and Jimmy Fallon).
(12) Hooper, 1978, directed by Hal Needham, starring Burt Reynolds, Jan-Micheal Vincent, Sally Field and Brian Keith. A spectacular

American poster by Brian Bysouth showcases the leaping Pontiac Firebird Trans-Am.
(13) The Green Helmet, 1961, directed by Michael Forlone, starring Bill Travers, Ed Begley, Sidney(Carry On)James and Ursula Jeans. Poster tagline: "The men who love speed and the girls who love them!"
(14) Gone in Sixty Seconds, 1974, directed by and starring HB Halicki, co-starring Marion Busia(remade in 2000 by Dominic Sena, starring Nicholas Cage, Angelina Jolie, Giovanni Ribisi).

My real driving tests were unfortunately never this exciting and it took me five attempts before finally passing, but as I never intended to be a boy-racer and have never had an unhealthy predilection for car's, it didn't matter how long it took just that I did eventually pass. Being able to drive, as those who do so know, opens up a world of possibilities, but most importantly to teenagers it gives a real sense of freedom from home. There really is something special about jumping into your car and taking a spontaneous drive to wherever you might feel, although now the steep cost of petrol make this a bit more prohibitive, of course. I have journeyed many miles throughout England, but the longest drive took me from Norfolk o the Dordogne region of France, a brilliant journey into a foreign country which everyone should try at least once.

CHAPTER THIRTEEN

TWO BECOME ONE...
AND ALL THOSE OTHER ROMANTIC CLICHES

The year was 1993 and if memory serves me correctly - which my wife tells me on this occasion is does - it was a Saturday evening sojourn to SuperSkate in Norwich with friends, which I know is hard to believe but back then I did actually have friends and, yes, shock horror, a social life! The quartet of suspects consisted of myself, - No! - Brian, Clarissa, and someone who will be my future wife and when I remember her name I will let you know.

By process of elimination the season was summer, so I was undoubtedly wearing what I deemed fashionable at the time: probably stone-washed jeans, a white shirt worn with Patrick Swayze casualness, and white trainers. I wasn't as vain as the budgerigar who admires himself in the mirror, which may come as some surprise to those of you who think you know me, but I would definitely have been smartly presentable. In point of fact, and while we, or should I say I, am on the subject of preening, I should like to shed light upon and dispel assumptions: I am not vain! At least not in the way vanity is portrayed in the media and projected by society. Working in a customer facing job I truly believe I should always resemble a tidy, presentable, person. Smart and groomed. Maybe, just maybe, I am somewhat fastidious with my regime to achieve this goal but some men go to greater lengths than I, and they know who they are because their shelves contain more moisturiser than he women in their lives. But in no way whatsoever am I under any delusion that my preening and mirror-checking is to reassert my sense of self-beauty. I know my limits and I am my own limitation - if that makes sense, to quote a phrase overused by a work colleague. I try my best with the appeal I may or may not have, and even though my younger self of 1993 might not look forward to the prospect of a slightly wrinkled brow, creases about the eyes, and grey hair or any of the numerous quirks which middle-age has to offer, he would not have dwelled upon such uncontrollable things.

Anyway, I believe I have digressed for long enough so after checking myself in the mirror on that Saturday evening one more time, and now, to ensure my handsome visage hasn't altered since I started writing this, I shall continue onward with my story.

So it's summertime, Saturday evening, I have completed my ablutions and I am dressed less like a fashion-sheep but more as an individual - I never really cared if I didn't fit in, after all, who wants to conform?

I departed the house after bidding adieu to my folks and it was while walking along our back path, I distinctly recall feeling buoyant, jolly, and as if Love Is All Around Me(1), if that's not too soppy an admission. My spirit was elated, floating like a....shadowy figure in the trees before me?!

Not only did the hairs on the back of my neck spring to life but so did those on the palms of my hands. This shadowy spirit was cloaked in the shadows of the fur-tree cloaked in shadow, in an eerily way of shadowy spookiness.

"I am the ghost of summer." The eerie female voice rasped and I realised immediately she was Mrs Fuller, a woman who has unjustifiably bore the brunt of my youthful disrespect and sarcasm since as far back as I can recall. Here she was, now, haunting me yet undead! "Tonight, you shall be visited by three ghosts at unspecified intervals," she proclaimed before vanishing into the cloak of shadows - which I may have mentioned before; have I also said I am sarcastic, facetious, pedantic and handsome.

Believing Mrs Fuller had finally gone insane from the constant incursions into her garden when we fetched the football invariably kicked there, or tennis ball lobbed, I dismissed this extremely farfetched encounter with her, after all, what the Dickens had she been rambling on about see what I did there?

I think Brian drove, so I only had to walk onto the carpark at Littlewood Lane, adjacent my house, to reach his white Nissan Micra. My car at this time in my life was probably a red Vauxhall Avenger, itself passed on to me from Dad when he changed motor, more about the fate of this vehicle shall follow later.

After collecting the girls from Leeds Way in Horning, Brian drove us to Super Skate, which was situated off the Norwich inner ring-road not far from the Driving Test Centre, and as of this writing is now called Funky's Rollerskating and Adventure Play. Quite frankly its a mystery why we patronised this venue because, to put it kindly, I was and still am a very poor roller-skater. Perhaps it was a fashionable establishment at the time because my friends and I weren't your average beer swilling pub-goers, or night-clubbers either - in fact, alcohol was bottom of our list for a fun time: why waste money on pointless inebriation, and shall mention alcohol and its influence on my life later if I can be bothered to drag myself out of my drunken stupor. Most probably I first went to Super Skate with my friends David and Ivan because Ivan could skate, and he was a mean dancer too, the best of all of us, he displayed a totally unselfconscious routine and people would gravitate toward him just to join in. It was brilliant to watch and I definitely wished I had half his courage. I would move around awkwardly, legs stiff, lacking any grace whatsoever on the rink or dance-floor - I'm not convinced enjoyment is about the taking part because I was unbelievably self-conscious of how stupid I looked.

My things at the time were tennis, snooker, karate and work, the latter being my prime social height. I still feel awkward at gatherings, not that you can probably tell; and my 1993 self definitely lacked confidence around the opposite sex, too. I'm not complaining, though, because so far I've Had The Time if My Life(2) with ups and downs, and apart from those few foibles I am practically perfect in every way!

Are you still with me...?

So: Super Skate. From memory, there was a large foyer where you temporarily traded our shoes for skates after paying entry, then you could either go straight to the large rink or the raised bar/eating area with seating which overlooked the skaters. There was a mixture of quality on display amongst those on the rink, although to me they all looked good because I was so bad.

I probably offered, in my suave and sophisticated manner, to purchase the first round of drinks - any excuse, eh? And the others did not decline. This trio and I had all attended the same secondary School, Broadland High in Hoveton, but apart from the girls there was a mixture of years. I was the eldest, something which hasn't changed, oddly enough, followed by Brian, then the girls. I certainly knew Brian's paramour better than her best friend because she and I - mostly her - had spoken about him on several prior occasions, and by this point in time they might already be 'going out.'

Of course, we might very well have skated before the first drink but it was after drinking that I needed the lavatory and I was promptly visited by the first ghost described me by Mrs Fuller - there is no pun or hidden meaning to be read between these particular lines - and this would begin the pattern for things to come.

"I am the ghost of life past." Said the voice of an oddly attired man standing next to me at the wash basin, although I use the description 'oddly attired' with caution because he was wearing a fashionable, at the time, shell-suit with white trainers. "Look into the mirror." He superfluously told me because I was already doing so - let me also say I was grateful we weren't at the urinal.

Abruptly I was transported through a swirling, twirling, whirling light-show vortex of time and space to a school. This was Hoveton St. John Middle School. A vivid memory from my not-to-distant past. I was somehow looking upon myself in the playground, which was cringe-worthy enough but I now suffered the embarrassing indignity of watching my eleven year old self kissing Emma Cadamy, my girlfriend at the time, surrounded by a couple of kids whose adult selves I still see to this very day from time to time: Clare and Geoffrey. This was indeed a monumental occasion for me because it was my first proper kiss. Strewth, those were indeed the days of innocence!

Unexpectedly the light-show vortex thing hurled me forward a few years to Hoveton Village Hall and Recreation Ground, and there I was under a Silver Birch with Raylene. We were hidden from the swings, slides, climbing-frame and roundabout, which was a good thing because there was some serious snogging going on. Raylene's was the first female breast I fondled, and her friend Christine would be-

In the blink of an eye I am looking back at myself in the mirror from 1993, sparing you from any unnecessary details, satisfied that I haven't revealed too much - does this constitute some kind of equivalent to a movie forth-wall break?

I smiled reflectively at my reflection thinking: That's Amore(3).

Back to the skating rink I went to show off my basically tragic moves for all to laugh at and mock, although in everyone's defence, nobody was watching me really! Okay, maybe some with pity or embarrassment for me, finding it difficult to avert their eyes however much they wanted to, afraid of missing a fall. But that's enough about me-

Gallantly I purchased a further drink for our companion at the rink-side table, sitting opposite her with no idea where this would lead.

Who was this fair young maiden, I hear you wonder. Pity I cannot recall her name!

Susan.

She seemed quite ill-at-ease much like myself in this environment. Maybe alcohol would make her relax but she didn't consume a drop until we were later married: coincidental, huh? Susan was dressed conservatively, her fresh face unadorned by make-up because she didn't require any - what am I after, you say? - and her hair was dark brown, straight, hanging below the shoulder. She lived in the same village as Clarissa, attending the same schools together. If I recollect accurately, and I think I do, this was possbly our first meeting - she was presently listening to Clarissa rhapsodise over Brian in a manner bordering on OCD - and the first word which she ever said directly to me was a positive sign.

Incidentally, their song, which was requested for him by her and played that night, was UB40's Can't Help Falling In Love(4)

I asked Susan: "I suppose you have to listen to this all the time?" With reference to Clarissa's Brian-fixation.

"Yes." Susan replied.

A good start, one might say.

Anyway, as story needs are calling so was the lavatory and off I headed once more.

"I am the second ghost, blah, blah, blah." A new voice said from beside me, sniggering slightly because I was just finishing up at the urinal! "I represent life present!"

What A Feeling(5) this time when I was torn away from the rink by the vortex to the present - that's 1993 present, for those of you who cannot keep up - and Leeds Way in Horning, the home of Susan, her parents Neville and Shirley, and younger sister Mary. They were sitting in their lounge watching televisions Noel's House Party, chatting amongst themselves. Bizarrely, or not so much if you know Norfolk, our parents knew each before Susan and I became acquainted. My Aunt Hilary, my Dad's sister, is Neville's cousin! Yes, I know its weird, but I shall not dwell upon the details! They had attended some functions when the families paths would cross, so I might even have seen Susan earlier than I knew. Spooky. Do you want to know something else spooky - or just plain coincidental in this small world we live in? Well, my best mate Jason Oxer who I would meet when I joined Tesco years later used to come into Exel Electrical, which is where I worked if you aren't following, in his and my younger days.

Norfolk, eh?

Well, talk about Take My Breath Away(6), in no time at all I was back in Super Skate admiring my...handsome face in the mirror of course, you filthy animal!

Upon my return rink-side Susan and I were the duo of our quartet not skating, and I noticed her drinking glass was no longer full.

"Would you like another drink?" I asked.

"Yes, please." She replied after much cogitation - another characteristic which I would become accustomed to - and adding, in her well-mannered politeness: "If it's okay."

"Everything I Do, I do it For You(7)." Is how I definitely would not have replied because it's stupid and corny!

While we drank together there was an immediate attraction, love-at-first-sight, heavenly choir, static electricity, synergy of thought and spirit and mind. But who can blame her, really, a studly, macho, manly, handsome, witty, charming, wealthy catch like me - do I need to explain my tongue might be in cheek and I may not be entirely serious about said claims?

After probably an awkward silence there is a possibility, although I cannot recall one-hundred percent, that we may very well have conversed, and I may have discovered a few facts on Susan such as: she was studying Secretarial Hospitality at Great Yarmouth College; she liked Kevin Costner - so no hope for me, then; she was tee-total; she had relatives who lived in Ireland; her surviving Nan lived in Anchor Street, Tunstead; and her Dad was a carpenter who had helped build a bungalow next to Stalham Fire Station, which coincidentally is where my Dad was a Retained Firefighter and, equally coincidental, years later when my brother-in-law went in joint-partnership in a new Estate Agency this same property was one of the first they sold.

"When I Fall in Love," Susan said, "it will be Forever(8)."

No, not really she didn't, but I guess by now you have probably realised that, although, who could blame her for falling instantly in love with an amazing fellow such as I?

In point of fact our conversation might very well have been about our mutual obsessive friend, Clarissa, who talked of nothing but Brian. Clarissa lacked confidence in herself which is why she needed the reassurance from others that Brian was attracted to her, and although supremely genuine in pursuit there was a risk of neediness suffocating their relationship before it got off the ground. That said, persistence wasn't futile because they are still together as I write this - no jinxing from me by writing that fact down here!

My drink had gone, having mysteriously evaporated in the glass, which always seems to happen to me.

Yep, you guessed it: toilet break!

There is no need to elaborate on the third visitor while I was saying hello to my little friend, and instead of the swirling, whirling, twirling vortex we were astral-ly elevated Up Where We Belong(9) - I know, I am stretching credibility a tad.

"Show Me Heaven(10)." I desperately asked the woman taking me to the future, forgetting to ask her what, or who, she was doing in the mens toilets.

"No." She replied ominously. "I am going to show you the future."

"Oh really?" I responded sarcastically. "It's good to discover I have a future to look forward to." I added in a touch of knowing post-modern self-awareness. "At least I can say that My Heart Will Go On(11) beating for a few more years." Yes!

"Enough already." My Americanised host admonished.

And so I plopped into existence in what I presumed to be my future because the ghost claimed as much so it must be true, like reading something on Wikipedia or in The Sun newspaper! Here I now was standing across the coast-road between Ingham and Sea Palling where my Vauxhall Avenger was being viewed by my future self, plus Clarissa, Cherry and Susan, and no doubt admiring the delightfully deep groove cut into the surface of the road by the car's collapsed rear suspension.

"This is the first time you take Susan out for a drive." The ghost informed me with a frown. "An inauspicious occasion, is it not?"

"Nobody died!" I state pragmatically.

Suddenly I was sitting alone in the driving seat of a brown Ford Escort Mark II, presumably my replacement for the Avenger. I was parked outside Great Yarmouth College. A super-imposed clock ticked the time by in front of me; minutes turned into hours turned into days at a staggering pace.

"You will wait for Susan to leave college." The ghost tells me with a hint of mocking laughter in her ethereal voice. "She will have forgotten you were picking her up and be home already. This waiting which you shall patiently do will be a recurring theme in your future together."

Before I can sigh with exasperation I am abruptly transported to the ABC Cinema down Prince of Wales Road in Norwich, sat behind myself and Susan who are holding hands - aw, sweet!

"This is the first time you take Susan to the cinema." The ghost tells me, with me expectantly awaiting the mocking punchline. "The film is a love story between a professional assassin and the man responsible for stopping him."

"Sounds romantic." I reply naively.

"Quite." The ghost replies(12).

And there I was transported back to the Super Skate men's toilets, my ghostly adventure over yet the real one was only just beginning as a new chapter took over in my life, and became my life, because It Had To Be(Sue) You(13)who would be that future - fine, pass the sick bucket!

(1) Four Weddings and a Funeral 1994, directed by Mike Newell, starring High Grant, Andie MacDowell, Simon Callow, John Hannah and Kristin Scott Thomas. "Love Is All Around Me" by Wet Wet Wet claimed the No.1 spot in the UK charts for 15 weeks.
(2) Dirty Dancing, 1987, directed by Emile Ardolino, starring Patrick Swayze, Jennifer Grey, Jerry Orbach and Cynthia Rhodes. "I've Had, The Time of My Life" by Bill Medley and Jennifer Warnes peaked at No.6 in the UK charts.
(3) Moonstruck, 1987, directed by Norman Jewison, starring Cher, Nicholas Cage and Olympia Dukakis. "That's Amore" by Dean Martin was originally released in 1953 and was subsequently Oscar Nominated.
(4) Sliver, 1993, directed by Philip Noyce, starring Sharon Stone, Tom Berenger and William Baldwin. "Can't Help Falling in Love" by UB40 reached No.1 in the UK singles chart.
(5) Flashdance, 1983, directed by Adrian Lyne, starring Jennifer Beals, Michael Nouri, Lilla Scala and Sunny Johnson.
"Flashdance...What A Feeling" by Irene Cara won the Best Original Song Oscar.

(6) Top Gun, 1986, directed by Tony Scott, starring Tom Cruise, Anthony Edwards, Kelly McGillis, Tom Skerritt and Val Kilmer. "Take My Breath Away" by Berlin reached No.1 on the UK singles chart.
(7) Robin Hood Prince of Thieves, 1991, directed by Kevin Reynolds, starring Kevin Costner, Mary Elizabeth Mastrantonio, Morgan Freeman and Christian Slater. "Everything I Do(I Do it For You)" by Bryan Adams spent 16 weeks at No.1 in the UK charts.
(8) Sleepless in Seattle, 1993, directed by Nora Ephron, starring Tom Hanks, Meg Ryan, Ross Malinger, Victor Garber, Bill Pullman and Rita Wilson. "When I fall in Love" was sung by Celine Dion and Clive Griffin for the film.
(9) An Officer and a Gentleman, 1982, directed by Taylor Hackford, starring Richard Gere, Debra Winger, Louis Gossett Jnr, David Keith and Robert Loggia. "Up Where We Belong" by Joe Cocker and Jennifer Warnes reached No.7 in the UK singles chart.
(10) Days of Thunder, 1990, directed by Tony Scott, starring Tom Cruise, Nicole Kidman, Robert Duvall, Randy Quaid, Cary Elwes and Michael Rooker. "Show Me Heaven" by Maria McKee spent 4 weeks at No.1 in the UK singles chart.
(11) Titanic, 1997, directed by James Cameron, starring Kate Winslet, Leonardo DiCaprio, Gloria Stewart, Billy Zane, Bill Paxton, Kathy Bates etc. "My Heart Will Go On" by Celine Dion reached No.1 in the UK singles chart.
(12) The film was In The Line Of Fire, directed by Wolfgang Peterson, starring Clint Eastwood and John Malkovich. A thriller which can only be interpreted as romantic if one clutches at straws desperately.
(13) When Harry Met Sally..., 1989, directed by Rob Reiner, starring Meg Ryan, Billy Crystal, Carrie Fisher and Bruno Kirby. "It Had To Be You" was sung by Frank Sinatra in the film.

I chose songs as a focal point for the use of music in films, whereas originally I wanted to write about score's themselves. I wanted to mention John Williams, Ennio Morricone, Lalo Schifrin, Max Steiner, Erich Wolfgang Korngold, Bernard Herrmann, Hans Zimmer etcetera etcetera...but I couldn't find a suitably defining story or moment when I realised I loved the music from film. Maybe it began with John Williams(Superman/Star Wars) and John Barry(James Bond), evolving with the music of Jerry Goldsmith and James Horner, gaining greater scope of style with Ennio Morricone and Lalo Schifrin, but there are so many great scores and composers I didn't want to miss any out - Jerry Fielding, Elmer Bernstein, Danny Elfman, Ron Goodwin. You can understand my problem when there are so many fantastic themes and soundtracks for fans to choose from, that I found it better and appropriate to settle upon a few hit songs from movies. Maybe next time I will talk soundtracks.

CHAPTER FOURTEEN

KASSIOPI
FIRST FLIGHT HOLIDAY

The majestic endless expanse of the sparkling Ionian Sea glistened in the shimmering late afternoon sunshine. Airplane noise as we slowly, laboriously, descended was remarkably disconcerting for a first-time flier: were the engines in fact struggling, was the fuselage really straining against the forces of gravity, is the loudly rushing wind tearing the wings off? I don't doubt that these stresses upon our environment were more imagined than real, heightened in my mind's eye, but that notwithstanding the rattling whine was a clear and present concern, nonetheless. We were coming in for our landing at Corfu International Airport which is a single runway in the Kerkyra town peninsula on the island, yet the Sea was rushing at us within what seemed like touching distance, like I could reach out and run my finger across the beautiful surface without a stretch of sinews, and I was sure there was no visible land. Had the pilot made an error of judgement in speed and distance and failed to inform us? Were we about to become tumbling wreckage churning up the surface of the blue Ionian water, a disaster statistic mourned for five minutes in the British press? Where was this land we were supposed to be, you know, landing upon?

When finally we did see land it seemed frighteningly instantaneous, followed rapidly by our touchdown and there was once more a disconcerting melee of sounds from presumably the air-brakes, throttling engine, tires on macadam and the plane itself bellowing relief - I'm no expert on all devices which come into play during an airplane landing, but I do know it takes many things to bring to a stop a 100,000kg behemoth as it hurtles along the runway full of people and luggage.

Of course everything was fine, despite the sharp braking, the now visible land seeming to run fast by us until slowly, steadily, the airplane stopped. Our three hour flight had gone without incident, no uncomfortable air turbulence, a distractingly average yet welcome meal, and now here were the passenger boarding stairs systematically rolled to our airplane and voila, or at least the native Greek equivalent to voila, we had indeed arrived on Corfu, yay!

Coming from the not-so-sunny England to this southern part of European the glorious heat hits one instantly and sweat breaks out all over the skin from pores previously untapped, yet the air itself is noticeably different, less oppressive than our own - more akin to 2017's air - and produces a bearable climate than the so-called heatwaves which some English people in the twentieth century complain about.

While I am on the topic of the UK's obsession with our weather, I have noticed the inability of many people to look out their window to decide what the day may bring, instead they rely upon the so-called knowledgeable Forecasters, or worse still, their mobile phone. Maybe it's just another one of those innumerable things which us human's like to blame others on, because in this day and age we seem unable to cope by ourselves or use our common sense, a thing long gone, an antique to this new Health and Safety political correctness! There is also the surprise element of the weather, too. Oh good grief, it is raining/sunny/windy, like it's something unusual to receive weather in our country! And then there are the people who come into Tesco- and you will know who you are - and say "it's really bad outside" without fully realising that if the weather actually was "really bad" you probably would not have been able to get out of your house.

Anyway, enough of the condescending rant, back to the past- and Corfu.

Susan and I retrieved our luggage with only a short wait for it to get from the airplane to the conveyor belt, before we joined a huddle of people awaiting the coach which would transport us to our destination, an exciting yet nervous first-time experience.

The journey from Airport to Destination was theoretically just a mere 22-miles on the most direct road, but because we made several drop-offs on route it took much longer - incidentally, the 22-miles is estimated to take just over one hour, which gives you an idea of the road quality itself, because those miles on a good road might take no more than half-an-hour. A very positive result of this detouring was seeing the lushly coloured island, the variety of resorts, the clear waters and splendiferous views - I shall leave the greater details for later.

When daylight began to fade into beautiful purple twilight the in-coach CRT(that's Cathode Ray Tube, for those of you not in the know) 15-inch television/VHS(Video Home System) combination unit was put on by our driver, and we were treated to classic Only Fools And Horses. I truly believe this wasn't just to prevent us from becoming restless but also as distraction against the scary view of the treacherous mountain road with its plummeting edge we were eerily close to!

It was late evening and dark when we arrived at Kassiopi and our hotel, with the driver bidding us a good holiday when he left us curb-side with our luggage. We were expected, so our keys were promptly given to us and it was relief, and not a small amount excitement, that our journeying was over and our fortnight here beckoned. We were both tired - did we admire the view out of our second-floor hotel balcony overlooking the Sea, I cannot recall - so we probably went straight to bed...

But I know that when I opened our window-slats and stepped onto our second-storey balcony as the morning sunshine rose over the land and sea the view across the small harbour, with its meagre amount of orange and pink buildings and concrete, was worth drinking in for many minutes while realisation that we had made the perfect choice of destination began to sink in slowly. Picture postcard perfect is how I would describe it. The small boats at rest upon the quaint horseshoe-shaped bay; the calm blue water with a further smattering of craft lazily going about their business; a few wandering people; and the mainland of Greece shimmering far off across the Ionian Sea.

The morning was delightfully warm, calling for shorts, t-shirt and flip-flops, and after enjoying complimentary breakfast of croissants, yogurt, cereal or full English, in the hotel restaurant served with either fresh orange juice or coffee, we investigated our new surroundings.

Eastwards from our hotel, past the white-washed adjoining apartment, between the outdoor seating of a waterfront restaurant, the cracked concrete surface rose steadily with the cliff-edge and became cobbled with rock and stone, weather-worn trees and hardy foliage dotted along the well-trodden unmade path. Small cats, Greek cats, with spindly legs and affection to spare enjoyed our company as we walked onward, meeting nobody in this gloriously quiet location until we came upon the beach of shingle where occupied, and unoccupied, deck beds faced the water. One could stand and drink in this scene of the great expanse of Sea lapping gently, translucently, against the shore and rocks, with the beach itself a cove in the cliffs, sun shining brightly, gloriously, in a clear blue sky.

Thankfully ours were not the only untanned skins but the over the days the sunshine, warm wind and exotic air will leave us with a bronzed complexion.

Exploring near the cove revealed wonderful rock-pools, more views of the island and its vegetation, the occasionally appearance of wildlife indigenous to the island of Corfu, as well as dwellings dotted on the mountainside.

Wandering back to the main town our thirsty work in the heat meant a stop at a bar for a refreshing iced drink, taking stock of these foreign sights and sounds of our base for the next fortnight, relaxing and reading and thinking how fortunate we are to be able to come here - I am not a person who takes anything for granted, it's important to enjoy every experience and appreciate how lucky we are to be who we are, because these luxuries don't belong to everyone.

Passing our hotel in the opposite direction we walked up the inclining main street which was more commercialised but by no means overcrowded or tacky, making the walk more pleasurable without any hustle and bustle faced in the more touristy holiday destinations. There was boat-hire and excursions, scuba-diving excursions, restaurants offering a diverse range of entertainments, plus the requisite gift shops, but one felt under no pressure. The architecture was classic Greek/Mediterranean in feel and appearance, with older ruins visible on the lower slopes of the mountain which is behind
Kassiopi.

There was also the likelihood that we returned to our hotel room, flung open the doors on our balcony and partook in an afternoon siesta before venturing out in the late evening to the restaurant along the main street which we had deemed the setting of first our first meal here. Playing it safe we might very well have consumed familiar food this first night, choosing to be more adventurous as the holiday continued, while washing our meal down with a drop Ouzo accompanied by a glass of water for myself, peach schnapps for Susan, winding up our first evening with a walk along the moonlit waterfront. Splendiferous.

It was a dark, dank claustrophobia I felt when groggily I awoke from what now seemed like a restless, fitful sleep. I was sweating, the environment stuffy. At first I wondered if the island was suffering from a earthquake or other natural disaster, the sensation was alien, certainly nothing which I had experienced in England. I was rolling and bumping amidst a low rumble of sound and I could not move my legs or arms very much, while my skin touched coarse hessian cloth. Lifting my head resulted in a connection with metal. If I hadn't already realised I knew now that I was no longer in the room at my hotel in Kassiopi, instead I was in the boot of a car.

Am I being kidnapped?

Where am I being taken to?

Obviously I was drugged at some point last night which explains why I didn't notice my own abduction, and it also explains why my mouth is parched and I feel out of sorts, not unlike a hangover but with noticeably different side-effects.

The bouncing becomes more uncomfortably rough and I seem to slip sideways across the minimal floor, which perhaps indicates we are leaving the main road. And we are now slowing. And as I write this we are stopping!

Doors creak open and bang shut, another door creaks and the feint glimmer if light pierces the cloth over my eyes and face. A pair of big hands belonging to a man or very butch woman hauls me unceremoniously from the boot and roughly flings me over his/her shoulder. As he and his companion walk they chatter in the local tongue. Up some steps, passing through a wooden door which by shoulder bumps against, and a softer walk presumably across a carpeted floor into a house before I am dumped unceremoniously upon cushions which I discover, when my restraints and hood are removed, are the cushions of a lime green sofa.

Gradually my eyes become accustomed to the light. A familiar face smiles upon me.

"Hello, Mister Starling." The man says in Greek, his voice hoarse from years of smoking and alcohol abuse.

"Good morning, Luciano(1)." I reply fluently in his language, dispensing with any pointless pretense. "I am to finally repay my debt to you, presumably?"

Luciano nods slowly, his teeth pin-sharp white between his lips without nary a sign of nicotine. This is the smile of a shark, his suave nonchalance disarming to those who do not know him from his Sicilian Cosa Nostra ancestry.

"What do you want me to do?" I ask without further ado.

"I need for you to get back what is mine." Luciano states pleasantly, without the requirement of amateurish menace. "A man called Marcel(2) has stolen it from police evidence and has it hidden somewhere in his chateau."

"How did it get out of the police station in the first place?"

"Because Marcel is the Chief of Police."

"Why is there always a corrupt police chief?" I sigh rhetorically. "What has he taken that belongs to you?"

"A bottle of Ouzo." Replies Luciano.

It takes a summoning all my will-power to prevent myself from laughing, and I quickly ask Luciano why the chief of police would take the trouble to steal a bottle of Ouzo from his own station and risk being discovered, when he can walk into any off-licence on Corfu and simply buy himself a bottle.

"Because my bottle of Ouzo is like no other." Luciano states as if it were the most obvious thing in the world - which, of course, it is, really! "Mine is of an exceptionally rare quality, you see. It has diamonds encrusted within the glass."

Now it makes a bit more sense.

"You are smuggling the diamonds." I offer logically. "Marcel somehow discovered as much and had your bottle confiscated. Only thing is he hasn't told anyone else what it really contains. For all intents and purposes it is a plain and simple bottle of Ouzo."

Luciano nods, smiling at my self-discovery of the true facts.

"Presumably Susan," I say, "my girlfriend, is drugged, and I have until she awakens to retrieve your diamond bottle?"

"Oh you are clever." Luciano claps his hands gleefully, looking at his two companions, encouraging them to join in, which of course they do not. "It's just like the good old days, isn't it, Mister Starling?" He indicates the bigger of his two companions. "Merli(3) will drive you to Marcel's chateau, it's not far, and you can proceed as you deem best."

"And how long do I have?" I ask.

"Your girlfriend will awaken in twelve hours-time." Luciano tells me, then faces the other thug. "Marino(4). Get the map of

Marcel's chateau for our friend." Then, addressing me once more: "You don't mind if I leave now, do you, I have other matters to tend?"

Without giving the opportunity to respond, the task has been placed in my hands and Luciano and his loyal bloodhound depart, leaving Merli and I alone in the house somewhere along the coastal road of Corfu, where the sea is visible, not that this narrows things down very much because the coast road is the main road, so I could really he anywhere.

Unrolling what seem to be ancient architects plans for the chateau belonging to the chief of police upon the carpeted floor, I study the general layout. The only real benefit for doing so is that my entry and search of the premises can be expedited more rapidly, because unfortunately the Ouzo bottle could be anywhere and I shall not have unlimited time. The lounge will be a good starting place because it can be directly accessible via the rear French windows, which will be my entry point then it's just a matter of surreptitiously searching the rest of the possibilities.

"Okay." I say to my watchdog, Merli. "Let's get going."

Bright early morning sunshine slung low stings my eyes as we walk from the cottage to Merli's severely undersized yellow Citroen which rock'n'rolls on its axis as we begin negotiating the coast road for approximately one and a half miles, before descending an even more treacherous route downward to a set of Chateau's and Villa's which are nestled almost secretively amongst trees on the coastline. This road is very much off the beaten track, we meet no one, and end at an overgrown communal car-parking area. Half-lane paths branch off from the car-park, permitting minimal access to the properties, all indicated individually with a named post-box on each.

I must admit this would be a lovely place to live if you like privacy and seclusion, the view and scenery are undeniably magnificent. It is a great wonder to me how the chief of police on this island can afford such luxuriously expensive accommodation.

From our ever-so slight elevation we can see Chateau Richet(5)which is my target. The pathway winds down the mountainside amongst trees until it opens into a front lawn area on the property, where a swimming pool glistens in the sunshine, and two figures are barely visible.

"Binoculars." I say to Merli, who retrieves them from the backseat of his car without protesting my impertinence; after all I'm not a shop customer who might rudely form their question with a one word statement instead of asking politely what one requires - yes, you know what I am saying and to whom!

When I bring the binoculars into focus against my eyes everything comes into focus, as one might expect. The two-storey Chateau is quite splendiferous with its rustic Mediterranean orange paint and traditional Greek ornamentation. Upon the front lawn I can see clearly my old nemesis Umberto(6) as he is about to dive into the swimming pool, his hairy fat stomach wobbling as he composes himself for the belly-flop that follows - I should refrain from adding that he is naked because its grotesque, and my readers might read more into my overuse of nudity, like I have an unhealthy fixation on nakedness, or worse still, it's some obsession!

At this point I wonder why the villainess terrorist Umberto is swimming in the pool of the chief of police. Does Marcel know he is here? Is there something more sinister afoot in these parts? Speaking of which, I can now see Umberto's wife Della(7) swimming across the pool - another nail in my coffin if I mention her lack or apparel!

"How soon can you get us a pair of walkie-talkies?" I ask Merli-

-Twenty minutes later I make my way through the property neighbouring Chateau Richet armed with a walkie-talkie after instructing Merli to press the send button if the police chief's guests venture indoors. While I waited the time it took Merli to fetch us the communication devices I observed what seemed to be nobody else on the premises, no obvious surveillance cameras, and a few burglar alarms on the Chateau and other surrounding properties.

Exquisite scents of the European flowers and other flora assail my nostrils with their hints of exotic appeal, and if I were presently a tourist I might have paused to take in this beauty and drink in the spectacular view, but I aren't so I don't. My task is at hand, a debt requires the paying off of, and my focus is fully on this mission Della's nakedness.

I scramble up the neighbour's high dividing wall clumsily, landing in the Chateau's grounds with an ungraceful tumble, but at least I am hidden behind a wooden building containing the hot-tub, from anyone who might be watching. My path is cautiously trodden from thereon as I dash across the rear lawn to the back wall of the Chateau, between a closed, shuttered door, and the open French windows of the patio area with its plush oak table and chairs upon it.

My hearing strains to detect any noises from beyond the French windows which might be of concern while an image of the interior schematic of Chateau Richet replays in my brain. Determining that all is clear I quickly enter the property, taking in the decor and furnishings automatically, eyes and focus settling upon a corner drinks bar - if I were to offer appraisal of the Chateau after the event I should say it was typical 1990's Greek-chic quite tastefully understated but lacking a woman's eye for richness of detail.

While striding I make a visual scan of the bottles on the racking behind the bar before opening the various cupboards below and beneath, expediting my search for the fabled bottle of Ouzo, a desired elixir belonging to crime boss Luciano but presently in the possession of Police Chief Marcel. I find nothing here so proceed swiftly through the entrance foyer, casting a cursory glance out the open front-door whilst doing so, noting that the swimmers are blissfully continuing their morning swim ignorantly aware of my presence, before I enter the kitchen.

It takes less than a minute for me to realise my search of the kitchen has been in vain and I begin to question the logic in continuing, but considering I have next to no time for dwelling upon the possibility of failure I bound silently upstairs and locate Marcel's airy bedroom, no signs if a feminine touch, the curtains wide open letting in the brilliant early morning sunshine.

A crackle from the walkie-talkie alerts me amid rifling through the American-style walk-in wardrobe, which I abruptly cease and desist before striding out the bedroom, bounding down the staircase but I get no further than the foot of the stairs because I am immediately confronted by the menacing presence of two surly gentlemen, Luc(8) and Tom(9). These are the chief of police's personal entourage, while the man himself, Marcel, grins in the doorway behind them - how they are here unnoticed by Merli is something which I shall find out soon enough.

Before I can move further the duo converge. I endeavour to take the smaller of the two, Luc, by surprise with a well-aimed roundhouse to the left side of his temple but the man is too quick, dodges the blow, blocking my forearm like it's nothing to him before twisting his body into mine and before I know what has happened I am laying upon the floor.

So much for my training, I think ruefully.

Before Luc can stamp on me I instinctively role away, right into the path of Tom - this just isn't my lucky day. The big guy lifts me off the ground as if I am nothing more than a sack of spuds before he launches me across the foyer into the lounge, where I thankfully land against the sofa, bouncing off it onto the floor. All this rough and tumble is very disorientating and I am barely on my feet once again when Luc is clamping his hands around my head.

"Wait!" Bellows the voice of Marcel, entering the lounge behind his bulldogs. "Let him go."

Reluctantly, Luc relaxes his grip, not taking his eyes off mine which hold a hint of regret that he is unable to finish his job on me.

"You are Paul Starling," Marcel says, "are you not?"

I nod, not quite sure whether to be pleased by my celebrity or otherwise, even if it is on the point of a break-in!

"Good." Marcel smiles thoughtfully, his mind clearly whirring behind the dark eyes. "Luciano's man on the hill back there will be fine when he recovers, we didn't hurt him, really, just knocked him out, not that I particularly care. I presume, Paul, that you have been employed by Luciano to retrieve the bottle of Ouzo in my possession?"

From this point onwards there is obviously no point in maintaining any pretense so I tell Marcel everything which was agreed between Luciano and myself. I really have nothing to lose in this matter now, my main aim has to be getting back to Susan before she awakens this evening, irrespective of how I achieve this goal.

"Hmm." Is Luciano's response.

The police chief paces across his lounge while we trio watch him, wondering what is going on in his mind, what scheme he is concocting, and most importantly how the results will affect me.

"I cannot let you have the bottle just yet, my friend." Luciano finally says thoughtfully. "It is not located here." He faces me at last. "But I can lead you to its whereabouts if you will do something for me."

"You want me to lure Luciano into a trap." I state. "So you might catch him red-handed."

"You are very perceptive, Paul"

"Thats why they pay me the big bucks." I quip, feeling slightly more relaxed now I know I'm not going to be dumped in the Sea!

"And in return for your cooperation I shall permit you to return to Susan unharmed so you might enjoy the remainder of your holiday."

Irritably, I wonder why it is common knowledge that I am in fact on holiday on Corfu, although it should make sense that the police chief of the island would know of my movements, and maybe thats why they were here so fast after my meeting with the crooked Luciano. Its natural I should feel aggrieved when being played by both sides of the law, though.

"So where can I find this magical elixir?" I ask, drawing blank expressions so I add for good measure: "The Ouzo?" I prompt.

"In one hour from now," Marcel says, "you will be able to locate Luc, here, at the restaurant along Potente(10) Harbour, on the other side of the island, where, for the sake of keeping up pretence to our mutual benefactor, you shall beat the location out of him."

I look more pleased at this notion than Luc does, although I'm not entirely sure the odds are in my favour to do him any serious harm.

"And when I arrive with Luciano to claim the prize," I finish for Marcel, "you and your people will already be there to arrest him."

"And give you your freedom." Marcel adds-

-I feel a not unreasonable amount of satisfaction for successfully departing Chateau Richet of my own volition - not to mention alive! - and although I realise Marcel has instructed me to double-cross Luciano my conscience inexplicably tugs at me.

A newly restored Merli drives us to Potente Harbour, convinced by my tale of what happened to myself, and to him, which makes the beating I give Luc all the more rewarding. How much actual hurt I dealt was maybe negligible to Luc but it felt satisfying enough to me. All this over a bottle of booze. Admittedly it's a diamond encrusted bottle of booze, but that isn't the point.

Upon our arrival at the cottage where my adventure began, which I now notice is called Kalyva Berleano(11), Luciano is already waiting with a duo of bodyguards, or a twin-set of bodyguards, whichever is the correct descriptive for a group of bodyguards, a gaggle, perhaps?

"Well?" Is Luciano's pointedly singular question.

"Marcel is laying a trap." I state bluntly. "But I do have the name of the place where the Ouzo is supposedly being kept: Enzo(12) Pointe Villa. Although I doubt you will find it there of course."

Luciano nods thoughtfully at all this, not a glimmer of surprise registering in his sun-kissed face. This sort of double-crossing must be a regular occurrence to the crime boss and I wonder what his next move is going to be.

"An ambush-" Luciano says. "You have done very well telling me this, Mister Starling, and shall be rewarded for your honesty in due course."

"Thank you." I reply without smiling because who knows what kind of reward awaits me but the man Luciano himself?

"Moritz, Merli." The boss addresses his thugs. "Get all the guns we have hidden in this cottage and contact the boys. Instruct them to meet us near Enzo Pointe Villa, they will know where it is."

"Yes boss." They reply in unison like obedient servants.

Next, Luciano addresses the sole female amongst us: "Gardenia(13), can you fetch the gift for Mister Starling so we can be on our way."

Gardenia too enters the cottage.

"You will appreciate that I cannot take you will us." Luciano states most reasonably. "But also I cannot permit you to leave just at this moment. You are- security, in case anything untoward should happen to my men and I. Also, you will be unable to contact Marcel and warn him of our knowledge. I have seen enough Spaghetti Western's to know how this game is played! Hence you will remain here, sleeping for about an hour while we attend our work. When you awaken, your departure shall be unhindered."

"That sounds reasonable enough." I reply.

"You have no choice in this matter, Mister Starling." Luciano states matter-of-factly.

-Just as Luciano informed me I do indeed sleep for an hour, which affords me just two hours to return to Kassiopi. Yet now a further dilemma presents itself to me because what will be the most capricious thing to go? If I leave now, which I can do because they chose not to restrain me, will Marcel send people after me if he discovers I deceived him? What can I look forward to if I await Luciano's return? Will he really permit me to leave? My only regret at this moment in time is I missed out on all the action which undoubtedly transpired at Enzo Pointe Villa - what a darned anti-climax.

There is a sole unoccupied car in the cottage driveway for me to use, the keys having been left in the ignition for me. Is this a sign that Luciano, the big crime lord, has faith in the information I gave him and is permitting my departure without actually saying as much? But also a loaded gun is on the driver's seat. Is this meant as a defence for me should the chief of police succeed in defeating the crime lord and come here after me?

Before I get the opportunity to act on either possibility a car pulls into the driveway cottage transporting a familiar face: Luciano. He looks pleased, which is certainly a good sign for me. When the car pulls up alongside the one I am contemplating departure in, the crime lord victoriously holds aloft the fabled bottle of Ouzo.

"Thank you, my friend." He says. "All our troubles are taken care of."

I smile, relieved. My debt is now repaid to Luciano's organisation, the Corfu chief of police is off my back, and I can now return to Susan and enjoy the remainder of our holiday - but how to explain her sleeping for twenty-four hours!?

(1) La Polizia ha le Mani Legate(Killer Cop), 1975, directed by Luciano Ercoli, starring Claudio Cassinelli, Arthur Kennedy and Franco Fabrizi. These Italian Poliziotteschi, or crime thrillers, were popular during the 1970's, owing a debt to their American cop movie counterparts in style, but possessing their own substance.
(2) Quelli Della Calibro 38(Colt 38 Special Squad), 1976, directed by Massimo Dallamano, starring Marcel Bozzuffi, Carole Andre and Ivan Rassimov. Director Dellamano was cinematographer on Sergio Leone's first two films in the Dollars trilogy.
(3) Il Cinico, L'Infame, Il Violento(The Cynic, The Rat and the Fist), 1977, directed by Umberyo Lenzi, starring Maurizio Merli, John Saxon and Tomas Milian.
(4) Roma Violenta(Violent Rome), 1975, directed by Marino Girolami, starring Maurizio Merle, Richard Conte and Silvano Tranquilli
(5) L'Instinct de Mort(Mesrine, Part 1), 2008, directed by Jean-Francois Richet, starring Vincent Cassel, Cecile deFrance, Gerard Depardieu etc. This film chronicles the rise of Jacques Mesrine, a gangster who became France's Public Enemy No.1, whose

story continued in L'ennemi public No.1 (Mesrine, Part 2), also released in 2008.

(6) Napoli Violenta(Death Dealers), 1976, directed by Umberto Lenzi, starring Maurizio Merli, John Saxon and Barry Sullivan.

(7) L'uomo Della Strada fa Giustizia(Manhunt in the City), 1975, directed by Umberto Lenzo, starring Henry Silva, Luciana Paluzzi and Silvano Tranquilli

(8) Leon, 1994, directed by Luc Besson, starring Jean Reno, Natalie Portman and Gary Oldman. American release poster tagline: "A perfect assassin. An innocent girl. They have nothing left to lose except each other."

(9) Lola rennt (Run Lola Run), 1998, directed by Tom Twyker, starring Franke Potente, Moritz Bleibtrau and Herbert Vaup. Original German poster tagline: "Every second, of every day, you are faced with a decision that can change your life."

(10) The Bourne Identity, 2002, directed by Doug Liman, starring Matt Damon, Franka Potente, Chris Cooper, Clive Owen, Brian Cox and Julia Stiles. Baded on the first book in Robert Ludlum's Jadon Bourne trilogy.

(11) The Transporter, 2002, directed by Louis Leterrier, starring Jason Statham, Qi Shu and Francois Berleano. Dialogue quote: "Rule number one: never change the deal."

(12) Il cittadino si Ribella(Street Law), 1974, directed by Enzo G. Castellari, starring Franco Nero, Giancarlo Prete and Barbara Bach.

(13) Il Grande Racket(The Big Racket), 1976, directed by Enzo G. Castellari, starring Fabio Testi, Vincent Gardenia and Renzo Palmer.

The first holiday I took abroad to the lovely town of Kassiopi on the Greek island of Corfu was everything I imagined it to be and more. It was indeed like a wonderful adventure of discovery where every experience was new. It might not be the kind of holiday which appeals to the so-called 'average person' but it was our holiday, taken on our terms and not filled with the perceived 'norm' which society seems to dictate. I also deliberately choose to refrain from going into too much detail with what we did, or why, because holidays should be a special time away with memories which belong to us, and our family, not something to be broadcast for all to see, which seems the fashionable thing these days.

It seems these days when people go on holiday they are more obsessed with making their Social Media posts than actually enjoying their holiday.

In recent years, at a tranquil caravan and camping complex amidst trees and nature, I witnessed a couple of retirement age people moaning about the lack of a Wi-fi signal. I was so tempted to ask them if they considered such technology important on their first holidays before the internet was around, but the irony would probably be lost to most people, especially those who need their Wi-fi or mobile phone to function in society without question.

Also, I wonder at the intelligence of people who practically advertise on Social Media to potential burglars that their home is empty for a week or two, because only the truly naive believe their posts are not viewable by the unscrupulous members of society.

Enjoy your holiday. Enjoy family time, and your time. Make your memories and keep them to yourselves rather than trivialising their importance on Social Media.

CHAPTER FIFTEEN

MILLENNIUM COUNTDOWN

Everyone who likes and watches movies has their favourite(or favourites) while composing their own opinion on what, to them, constitutes a good film, and what makes a bad film. There really is no right or wrong in this matter because we are, individually, imbued with such a variation of tastes and opinions the pendulum of opinion can swing forever. This is all very obvious so to simplify my own favourites which change and alter depending upon what mood I am in, I have compiled my list comprising just ten films in order of a random countdown - well, the title of this chapter is self-evident, isn't it?

Favourites alter as we alter, they mature as we mature. What my favourite film might have been when I was twelve years old is much different now, mainly because I have seen more films and expanded my breadth of taste and understanding of this art form. Film is indeed an art if you choose it to be, or a way of wasting two hours or so if that's what you prefer, as I have already suggested above: there really is no right or wrong in this matter. We all gain pleasure differently.

This list has no order of favourite first or last, it is merely a compilation of films which I enjoy and an explanation of why I enjoy them and most are easily accessible to viewers - I enjoy foreign language films, some are exceptional and better than those listed here, but I fully understand and appreciate that subtitles can put some people off and, yes, okay, I realise the hypocritical side of this observation when I have included a silent film amongst them. The following ten films will hopefully inspire you into viewing them for the first, second, or more, time, and to gain further understanding as to why these specific favourites of mine are as good as I say - or not.

Napoleon
1927 Abel Gance- Albert Deudonne, Andree Standard, Adrien Caillard, Luois Sance etc.

This is truly revolutionary epic cinema at its very best - and silent too. The BFI and film historian Robert Brownlow recently restored this long-thought forgotten masterpiece and what a terrific job they have done. At five and a half hours running time, with a new score by Carl Davis in which he utilises many well-known classical pieces as well as his own original material, this never fails to capture the imagination. Ninety years after filming, Napoleon almost has a documentary feel about it. The images on the screen look real, the acting feels real, as if Gance were there in the early eighteen-hundreds to film the actual events as they transpired. There is a very intimate feel to the story, yet the bigger moments are truly epic, filled with much-imitated imagery, stylish and innovative for its time

I watched this film in four viewings, as per the 4-Act structuring of the Blu-ray, like one might watch a multi-part television adaption, and this did nothing to diminish the feeling of something truly worthwhile. But don't take my word for it:

"A masterpiece of cinematic invention." - Stanley Kubrick.
"A genuine sensation." - Martin Scorsese.

Casablanca
1942 Michael Curtiz- Humphrey Bogart, Ingrid Bergman, Paul Henried, Claude Rains, Peter Lorre, Sidney Greenstreet, Conrad Veidt, Dooley Wilson - the list of actors and actresses playing memorable characters could go on.

I don't really need to explain how good this film is because its status has already been assured and you have already heard its virtues extolled, but just in case you have never seen it...

Casablanca is a wartime espionage tragic romance noir ensemble comedy adventure propaganda thriller with musical interludes, somehow woven together from a script which, at the time, was constantly being rewritten after its humble beginnings as a stage play, and starring actors who are now associated fully with these roles yet were not the first choice of a studio head whose constant interference threatened to derail the entire production, and upturn an entire hill of beans. This film could very have turned out to be just another wartime potboiler like many others during the early forties, but Casablanca truly transcends its fairly constrained boundaries and leaps out at you with its plethora of now classic scenes, that repeated viewings reap great benefits because its near impossible to pinpoint which iconic scene to extoll the virtues of.

Don't take my word for how good this film is, play it yourself, Sam, play Casablanca!

Ben-Hur
1959 William Wyler- Charlton Heston, Stephen Boyd, Jack Hawkins, Haya Harareet, Hugh Griffith

The ultimate EPIC SPECTACULAR with so many HUGE scenes and powerful moments filling out every frame, compelling acting, beautifully filmed sets and locations, there just aren't enough AMAZING superlatives to fully compliment the SCOPE of this movie. There are many reasons why "they don't make them like they used to" and this is a prime example. BIG SCREEN splendour and TERRIFIC plotting don't come much LARGER than this. I don't feel it is necessary to explain why I ENJOY this film as much as I DO, but for me, everything I love about the BIBLICAL tales on the silver screen is woven into this single film.

Once Upon a Time in the West
1968 Sergio Leone - Claudia Cardinale, Henry Fonda, Charles Bronson, Jason Robards and Gabrielle Ferzetti.

Like all films which transcend the simple act of sitting and wiling away time, this one will be viewed differently to me than by yourself - if you have already seen it, of course. Some movies are easily forgotten and thus more readily categorised. This classic late-entry to the classic western pantheon is not one which a person can easily dismiss based on the genre it represents - the western genre has had more filmed hours, be it movie or television time, than any other genre - but it certainly requires appreciation of said genres histrionics, awareness of film-making techniques and storytelling to fully understand how good it is.

The first time I saw Once Upon a Time in the West was on television way back when and I found it ponderous, dull and tedious. What was all the fuss about? Long, laborious scenes where nothing happens and what about the beginning, which seemed to stretch out for an inordinate amount of time: why? Get to the action already! This is not A Fistful of Dollars!

This film is proof-positive to my maturing understanding of movies.

The first ten minute sequence which is very minimalistic sets the tone for a film about the changing face of our world which still goes on today. Every nuance in this build-up is heightened and amplified, the viewer is drawn into it, is forced to focus upon it, so that as the entire story unfolds we become part of this story with whichever character we can relate...and that's just the opening!

But it's not as simple as this. There is more going on.

The photography captured by cinematographer Tonino Delli Colli is familiar to us from other westerns, landscapes we have seen before, but somehow there is something new and iconic drawn from it, helped no doubt by the exemplary score from The Maestro Ennio Morricone and the editing of Nino Baragli, while the Sound Department are attuned to this vision like we haven't heard before - which is bizarre because there have been many so-called Spaghetti Westerns preceding this one which have utilised creative sound effects and music to heighten their narrative.

Harmonica upon first sight seems like a shallow heartless killer until we learn his true motives.

Frank's remorse is backed by self-awareness his gunslinging talents are becoming obsolete in an increasingly mechanised world.

Cheyenne enters the story as a ruthless outlaw but moves beyond his perceived histrionics into selfless heroism.

Morton is fuelled by money but his affliction and greed hide his faceless regrets, his desire to reach the ocean.

Jill McBain is the epicentre of the story, stabilising and focusing the trio of macho killers into becoming more self-aware, while herself never really altering throughout the picture despite everything she has to face - she is strength and stability amid the chaos.

It is all of these elements and more besides which together create an artistic whole where no amount of superlatives entirely do it justice: watch it, ponder it, debate it watch it again because you will inevitably have missed something.

Double Indemnity
1944 Billy Wilder- Fred MacMurray, Barbara Stanwyck and Edward G Robinson

A man is fed false promises by a femme fatale should he do her bidding.

The above synopsis could indicate the storyline of any Film Noir but from the screenplay by Billy Wilder and Raymond Chandler, based on a crime novel by James M Cain, this movie rises way above most others of its type.

Here's the basic plot:

Insurance salesman Walter Neff(MacMurray) is lured into and affair with Phyllis Dietrichson(Stanwyck) while renewing her husband's life insurance policy. She persuades Walter to murder her husband while he also devises a scheme to receive twice the money claimed on a Double Indemnity clause. When Mr Dietrichson is found dead the police accept it as an accident. Insurance Claims manager Barton Keyes(Robinson), who is also Walter's friend, believes it was murder and is determined to unravel the truth as Walter's world gradually falls apart around it.

Brilliant performances all around, a tightly woven script with sparkling dialogue dripping with cynicism and dark humour, while tension-filled throughout, this epitomises everything which Film Noir should be. A must see movie for anyone with even the slightest interest in the form.

Dirty Harry
1971 Don Siegel - Clint Eastwood, Andrew Robinson, Harry Guardino, Reni Santoni, John Mitchum and John Vernon.

One man stands up for what he believes is the right path in the face of bureaucratic opposition. Or a cop breaks his oath to go above the law. Or one man uses the law to satisfy his own sadist ways. Or sadism and violence blurs good and bad. Or bad people begat bad people.

Whatever your views on this film it cannot be denied that it now holds iconic status and has transcended its own controversy - in fact, now, in the 21st Century, the violence and morals are somewhat old-hat. Is it fascist heaven? Is it an allegory to the unrest felt by the Vietnam War? Is it a cornucopia of quotable lines, seventies cool, and swift justice?

For me Clint Eastwood is at the peak of his acting career here and becomes the icon we know, settling into this particular role which he will repeat in many films to come - and not just the four other Dirty Harry films which followed over the next seventeen years, spanning different socio-political changes(police corruption(Magnum Force, 1973) anarchy(The Enforcer, 1976) revenge(Sudden Impact, 1983) media grabbing(The Dead Pool, 1988) and the Eastwood film which could almost be Dirty Harry long after retirement but isn't,(Gran Torino, 2008), about tolerance)while also painting a diverse picture through two decades of cinematic upheavals. This film still has relevance today, maybe more so now. It resonates with blatant anger at a system which seems designed to protect the criminal and although people in real-life should not take the law into their own hands, it is extremely satisfying to see this achieved in fiction, as perhaps fulfilling certain audience proclivities.

Like all good movies which deserve multiple viewings, Dirty Harry, for me, never loses its appeal, offering up a world view in context equally now as with the '70's.

North by NorthWest
1959 Alfred Hitchcock- Cary Grant, Eva Marie Saint, James Mason, Martin Landau and Leo G. Carroll.

It's very difficult to choose one Hitchcock film over all the others without creating a problem: I should've picked Vertigo, Psycho, Rear Window, Strangers on a Train, The Man Who Knew Too Much, Blackmail, Secret Agent etcetera. But I have chosen to include this one because I believe it epitomises all aspects of those elements which make Hitchcock films stand head and shoulders above so many others - even his lesser films are better than the output of many other directors.

Cary Grant is on top form as Roger O. Thornhill who, through a case of mistaken identity, becomes a component in international espionage. The plot involves foreign criminals looking to destabilise Western society, sinister henchmen out to kill Thornhill, CIA agents looking to exploit the situation despite the risk of death to an innocent man, and a femme fatale whose loyalties are tested to their very limits.

Everyone on- and off-screen are at the top of their game here, from Ernest Lehman's witty script, Bernard Herrmann's exciting score, Robert Burk's vibrant cinematography, the brilliant editing by George Tomasini, and everyone else.

In other words this film is utterly brilliant and if you haven't seen it yet watch it next, and if you have seen it then you know exactly where I am coming from.

12 Angry Men
1957 Sidney Lumet- Henry Fonda, Lee J Cobb, Martin Balsam, John Fielder, EG Marshall, Jack Klugman, Edward Binns, Jack Warden, Joseph Sweeney, Ed Begley, George Voskovec, Robert Webber

How is it possible for a film set essentially in a single room to ratchet up the tension and suspense to such a nail-biting degree where the audience is sweating almost as much as the cast? Also, how is it possible to watch twelve men debating and arguing for ninety-minutes and be thoroughly enthralled throughout? Well, this is exactly what the director has been able to achieve and then some in this story about questioning what on the surface even appear to be the most damning facts.

A jury are sent to pass sentence on a young man for apparently murdering his father, the evidence has been presented, and all but one member of this jury believes the young man is guilty, and while explaining his reasoning and exposing prejudices of other jury members, the story unfurls in unexpected ways.

Lumet has directed numerous thought-provoking films during his career including The Hill(1965, starring Sean Connery, Harry Andrews, Ian Bannen etc), Dog Day Afternoon(1975, Al Pacino, John Cazale and Penelope Allen) and Network(1976, Faye Dunaway, William Holden, Peter Finch etc), all of which are exceptionally entertaining along with the messages which they convey, but I have chosen this riveting movie because no matter how many times I have watched this plot as it thickens I am constantly amazed by its structure and fluidity of execution. Brilliant.

Raiders of the Lost Ark
1981 Steven Spielberg- Harrison Ford, Paul Freeman, Karen Allen, John Rhys Davies, Denholm Elliott, Ronald Lacey.

This is another film which really needs no explanation for being on this list because it is just such a great, fun adventure film which doesn't pale in the enjoyment I gain from it after numerous viewings, and I have seen it at least once a year since I first saw it on VHS - we hired the film for five days and I saw it five times!

The impact it had on me at a young age is immeasurable: the orchestral score by John Williams created my interest for Film Scores, and my taste has grown and broadened with each new discovery; it's fluid and well-paced story structure made me want to write more myself, although I never wrote an Indy adventure; the consistently evolving films by director Spielberg, and his maturity as a storyteller have been a constant pleasure; while the awe-inspiring poster artwork has me led to appreciate this particular medium. A much imitated film and never bettered, even from the follow-up Indy adventures, because of the raw, rough feel which Raiders has in abundance.

This film works on so many levels and if you haven't already seen it, then why not?

You may have noticed that there are only nine films above, well, I couldn't decide on the tenth. You might also think from the list that I don't like films made in the last thirty-six years. Maybe I take for granted the fact that you may have seen more films yourself from the past four decades, and fewer before this, if you are just an average filmgoer. I could've included Back to the Future(1985), L.A. Confidential(1997), The Artist(2011), or even La La Land(2017), amongst the films to keep it more contemporary. Yet it would mean excluding The Great Dictator(1940), Network(1976), The Grand Budapest Hotel(2014), Rocky(1976), The Maltese Falcon(1941) or Jason and the Argonauts(1963) from the list, and that just wouldn't do.

All these films are just part of the iceberg, a mere drop in the ocean of possibilities without even mentioning 8 1/2(1963), Throne of Blood(1957), Arietty(2010), or Busanhaeng(2016).

It's not easy, is it? I have also not mentioned...

Better stop there.

CHAPTER SIXTEEN

ELECTRICAL SHOP OF BIBLICAL PROPORTIONS

"What the flip!?" Exclaims Adam(1) upon his arrival for work at TAMS Electrical in the village of Stalton-on-the-Broads, a village situated between Stalham and Sutton in Norfolk. It's a splendiferous Monday morning and he is as punctual as ever, unlike some colleagues who he can but will refrain from mentioning. Adam has been working at this store for as long as he cares to remember and the building is in its usual location at the bottom of the customer carpark, yet the store itself has altered somewhat and causes Adam to rub his eyes in disbelief and pinch himself to ensure he is awake - which he is.

TAMS Electrical in Stalton-on-the-Broads now resembles an ancient Roman Colosseum only approximately half-scale and has weathered two-thousand years of English air like it was built yesterday, which may be the case because when Adam finished his shift on Saturday the building was fine, normal, and modern by 21st Century standards. Hence Adam's surprised exclamation at the head of this chapter, although the store aesthetics, he admits, are an improvement upon the store builds of today and has a curiously symbiotic appearance with the surroundings. He wonders how ecologically friendly this apparition is, maybe the roof, if there is one, is solar-conductive? Only it isn't an apparition nor is it a mirage, this is the real deal right down to the garish TAMS logo erected on its front, incongruous against the sandstone.

"Ah, young Adam." A familiar voice suddenly booms from behind him. "You excel yourself with promptitude."

When Adam turns he is less surprised to see that it is the store manager David(2) standing behind him, but it is the Roman attire and elevated haughtiness which throws him off somewhat, and before Adam can respond his manager is frowning more deeply at him than is usual.

"Where is your uniform, young man?" Is the accusatory demand, a voice which doesn't suffer fools lightly.

Adam regards his clothing in puzzlement because he is wearing the TAMS uniform. Maybe it is dress-up day, Adam thinks, and he missed the message, but this does not explain the nature of the stores transformation.

"I suggest you get a replacement from acquisitions." This order does not need emphasising any more from the store manager.

"Yes, David." Adam replies as apologetically as possible under present circumstances.

"David!" Bellows the manager. "I am the Senator Aurelius(3), bearer of the Seal of British Traders, holder of the Laurel of St.Cohn, cousin to our great Caesar himself! I do not carry the slave name David nor shall I bear it ever, and I encourage you to remember this fact, young Adam of Eve."

Senator Aurelius virtually pirouettes on his heal in anger before beginning to stride away from Adam until he hears the young man sniggering, causing him to stop abruptly in his tracks and faces him once more.

"Your insolence is misplaced, my man!" The Senator veritably seethes with anger now. "Once you have the appropriate attire upon your scrawny frame I expect to find you in my office immediately!"

Continuing onward, Aurelius' mood has swung fully in the emotional cycle of change described by the philosopher Senta(4) in his studies of the human condition, on account of young Adam, whose service to TAMS up to this point has proven exemplary. The kiss he received barely an hour prior to this moment from his wife fades into memory, her love and affection a feeling from the distant past now, thanks to this singular instance. But why? He wonders. Why let it get the better of him? Today is going to be a good day, a glorious day, one of hope and moments devoid of dullness. Aurelius' goblet is half full! He must centre himself. His wife Lucia(5) is learning a calming technique which involves deep breaths while counting to ten, which he tries now while he strides across the courtyard of his store, settling his nerves and forcing a completely fake smile onto his face. His wife is his steady rock, now he must overcome the hard place.

Passing between the magnificently apportioned colonnade entrance to his electrical store - don't question the logic! -   lifts Senator Aurelius' spirits instantly owing to its splendour and opulence, with the powerful Greeting Guard, Agrippa(6), an imposing yet welcoming face at his station by the door. The guard salutes the Senator rigidly, loyal to his boss and protector of his colleagues and the stock.

"Good morning, Agrippa." Senator Aurelius says.

"Good morning, sir." Agrippa replies with a reassuring firmness.

Well-stocked shelves and an efficiently running in store is what the manager would like to witness but even he can see this is not to be the case this morning, and this blood-pressure cannot fail but rise! The night team shall indeed pay dearly for their incompetence. How does it appear to his customers, the people who keep his business alive, customers who enable him to pay reasonable wages to his staff? He must now ensure the day workers double their efforts to ensure healthy sales, resistance to his demands will be futile, fatal to some if they inflame his wrath further.

"Good morning, my Senator." Says Dathan(7), bowing low at the waist in a grovelling fashion perfected by this loyal male succubus.

"It was!" Snaps Aurelius. "Until I arrived here."

"I agree, my Senator," the duty manager laughs weakly, correctly predicting the nature of some of the Senator's wrath. "Which is why night manager Seti(8) is still here working to correct the failings of his people."

Aurelius raises an eyebrow, impressed to discover he isn't completely surrounded by incompetent fools. It is now that the Senator notices a young child being held tightly in Dathan's grip, a scruffy street urchin.

"What is that?" The Senator asks quite calmly, yet with disdain.

Dathan holds the child at arms-length: "I caught this urchin trying to steal a plug."

"I see. The parents of this child were not with it?"

Dathan shakes his head.

Aurelius looks down upon this child of no more than twelve years of age, scowling: "And skipping your schooling, no less. Bring it to my office."

"Yes, Senator." Dathan slithers. "Senator Gracchus(9) is awaiting you in your office."

Gracchus is a name long dismissed by Aurelius, a man from his past who lives beyond Rome and operates similar business enterprises to Senator Aurelius himself. The fact that Gracchus is now a member of the Senate is something new and Aurelius wonders why it has taken today for him to learn this information, is there some infamy afoot, perhaps? The man's presence here alone sets off signals in Aurelius' brain to be cautious, and it will be intriguing to discover what this unscrupulous man desires.

"Today," says Aurelius, "is one filled with myriad challenges."

Without uttering a single word to any of his minions as they salute when he passes them by, Senator Aurelius strides into the back area of the supermarket with Dathan and the street urchin in tow, determined to deal swiftly with the young lad so he might focus his full attention on this new arrival, his mind swirling with conspiracies involving Gracchus and what his presence signifies.

When Senator Aurelius enters the large office which is the equivalent of an entire home to some people, he has to look beyond the desk and chairs to the chez long by the rear window to see Gracchus. The bulky man who seems more obese with the passing of time is wrestling with the beautiful defenceless secretary who is attendant this morning, his wet mouth upon hers, hands groping flesh. At least they are not in the bath, Aurelius thinks with some measure of relief, and he should call his secretary away for her own good but this other matter requires his attention first.

"What is your name?" Aurelius asks the young child who struggles painfully in Dathan's grasp, and when there is no reply forthcoming he strikes the urchin hard across the face. "Well?"

"Ilderim(10)." The child splutters through blood and the tears.

Aurelius walks around the side of his desk and opens a drawer, nodding to Dathan who need not be told what to do: he forcibly places the child's left wrist onto a block of blood-stained dark wood, a basket beneath the overhang. The child shakes his head and begins screaming, horrified his eyes wide with terror.

"Let this be a warning to you." Aurelius says sternly to the child, trying to adopt a more reasonable voice. "Be thankful I take only one hand."

A small axe is in the Senator's hand and he brings it down swiftly, cleanly severing the left-hand from you child's wrist, the pain unbearable and the urchin collapses unconscious to the floor.

"Get this creature out of here." Aurelius tells Dathan, who does as instructed.

In the excitement Gracchus has left the girl on the couch and is watching the brutality, licking saliva from his rosy lips, breathing heavily, red-faced. He smiles at Aurelius when he catches his fellow Senator's attention.

"It's good to see you old friend." Gracchus says fatuously. "How long has it been since Lucius(11) died?" He asks with concealed contempt.

"Two years, Gracchus." Replies Aurelius without concealing his contempt. "And we have not been, nor shall we ever be, friends or countrymen, just Roman's. State your business here then leave, taking your foul stench with you."

"Leave?" Gracchus pretends to be shocked with indignation by the Senator's suggestion. "But you must have many questions, Senator." He emphasises the last word in this statement. "Surely you are wondering when I won a seat on the Senate and why you are only now finding out my wonderful news."

Aurelius stares at the globulous man in front of him, trying to read his intent through the eyes but Gracchus always was a good, conniving trickster, and able to hide his emotions well, particularly when their shared partner Lucius was murdered. He looks at the bloodied axe upon his desk, seductively close, the severed hand in the basket, and he smiles.

"What...do...you...want?" Aurelius asks menacingly.

Gracchus returns the smile with uncertainty, clearly the axe in touching distance is having some effort on his composure.

"The High Senator Petronius(12) has reinstated my position on the board of trade." Gracchus says, talking quickly, satisfied by the reaction he sees behind Aurelius' eyes. "Which is why I am now a Senator. I was instrumental in forging the unification of the trade treaty with Egypt. That was my first success. My next success is going be merging our two businesses into a mutually beneficial conglomerate. Imagine the control we could exhort over the manufacturers of goods and the engineers." He rubs his hands together gleefully at the thought of the untold riches to be had. "We can make money beyond the wildest dreams of even the great Caesar himself, who has decreed this himself, by the way."

While Gracchus has spluttered and dribbled with the excitement from his proposition, Aurelius eventually lowered himself into his chair, listening with growing interest, not because of the suggestion of the merger, but thinking over the possibility of himself taking total control and the phenomenal wealth involved. He breaks into a smile himself, thinking over how to manipulate this man for his own gain without overdoing it. Gracchus is not stupid and will sense deception straight away.

"It seems I have little choice in this matter." Aurelius says disdainfully. "But by the laws of Rome, as decreed by Caesar himself,

I have the right to offer a challenge to determine which one of us has the majority share and decision-making in this venture. So, I suggest a race. My very best charioteer pitted against yours."

Gracchus steeples his fingers atop the desk in front of him, satisfied with this predicted outcome and suitably prepared for it.

"Agreed." Says Gracchus unwaveringly. "When do you propose this take place?"

"One after the hour of noon today. In the courtyard here, at my store."

"At our store, my friend, Senator Aurelius."

Gracchus eases his bulk out of the chair and extends a hand with stubby fingers for Aurelius to take which, out of protocol, to bind their agreement, he shakes. Licking his plump red lips, Gracchus leaves without saying another word.

Before Aurelius can order his thoughts into cohesion there us a resounding knock upon the door.

"Yes!" Aurelius shouts irritably.

The door slowly swings open and Adam is presented before the Senator. This time the young man is more appropriately attired for the era but he stills looks as confused as he did earlier. His arrival promptly reminds Aurelius of their close encounter and this draws forth an idea.

"Can you drive a chariot, my boy?" Aurelius' question is loaded in his favour: how can the boy possibly say no without provoking an outburst of anger?

"I um- I guess so." Adam replies cagily.

"Splendiferous!" The Senator says with unconcealed glee. "In that case I shall require your services in the store courtyard at precisely an hour after noon today. Is that understood, young man?"

Adam nods slowly, realising he has no choice, and is waved away without further ado, leaving the Senator's office.

"Miriam(13)!" Aurelius hollers and without hesitation the secretary appears from the direction of the bed chamber, in better array than earlier. "Heat the coals, my dear. I shall require a bath and favours upon completion of the morning inspection."

With this declaration the Senator departs his office for the shop floor, his spirits only marginally improved upon. Dathan awaits him like an obedient dog, correctly anticipating the routine inspection but

Aurelius is prompt in locating the first of what will turn into many irregularities.

"Why is Semadar(14) dressed that way?" The store manager and Senator asks Dathan, nodding in the direction of the service area.

"I asked her myself, my Senator." Dathan grovels. "And I beg your pardon, but Semedar is sore-ridden after the thrashing which she received yesterday for her lateness. I deemed it a necessity after confronting her about this issue, and seeing the gashes upon her flesh, that she uncover her breasts for today."

Aurelius accepts this excuse and strides onward, observing the shop-floor, shelves, and other things which the layman might miss, only to be intercepted nearby the store entrance.

"My dear Veronica(15)!" Aurelius smiles with ingratiating falseness at the old woman whose custom is as regular as her moaning. "How are you today?"

"Never better." She replies uncharacteristically chirpy.

Aurelius makes eye contact with a carrier of trollies, whom he has never seen before, and beckons the lad to him.

"Whats your name, boy?"

"Verulus(16) sir."

"I haven't seen you here before! Why?"

Dathan clears his throat: "The lad only started this morning, my Senator."

"Oh? What happened to- whatsisname?"

"Pod(17), my Senator." Dathan replies helpfully. "We were forced to return him back to the slave market because of his slovenly ways."

"I see." Senator Aurelius says, turning back to this new lad. "See that you do better than master Pod, young Verulus. You may start by helping this lady, Veronica, our most loyal customer, with her shopping cart."

Verulus nods simply while unable to muster words, bordering on tears, and sets about this new task he has been assigned, helping this lady who, smiling, looks the boy up and down with lascivious approval.

Aurelius and Dathan continue, pace slower, the Senator taking on a conspiratorial air, his head moving closer to his Number One.

"Dathan, my most loyal servant." Aurelius says under his breath. "I need to ask a favour of you which I know you shall perform to your usual professional standards. I wish for you to go forthwith to my Barracks and rouse the First Legion there. I need you to bring them here as covertly as possible before one past noon today, but nobody should suspect their arrival."

"To bring so many men here without causing a stir will be difficult, my Senator." Acknowledges Dathan. "But I shall indeed perform this task to the best of my ability. May I ask why you require their presence here?"

"Your insolent question does not become you, Dathan." Senator Aurelius chastises his main-man. "I have arranged a chariot competition with Gracchus, my old nemesis who would be friend!" He continues to explain to Dathan, softening his attitude so as to get the man's buy-in. "The face of it is a settling of trade deals. Much of the Senate will undoubtedly turn up, they cannot resist such spectacular propaganda. My intention is to overthrow the Senate by force, killing Gracchus and those who support his treachery, then- well, who knows what the fates will bring?"

Dathan remains silent while he digests this extreme proclamation by his boss, wondering what will be in it for him, while also worried about the rashness of the Senator's garrulous decision.

"Well?" Aurelius prompts for a response.

"Yes, my Senator." Dathan replies with slight reservation in his voice. "I shall, of course, do as you ask but- but are you certain this is a wise thing to attempt? Do you not think Gracchus will bring-" Dathan leaves the question hanging because...

"Leave my daughter Portia(18) to me." Snaps Aurelius as quietly as possible, his impatience threatening to bubble over. "Dathan is cunning and shall without doubt bring her in attendance, but I will bring her back unharmed to her true family."

Dathan nods understanding although even a blind person can see he is not entirely convinced by the rationale of Senator Aurelius.

"Excuse me." A raspy voice says. "Are you managers?"

Dathan thanks this interruption for saving him, by the bell one might say, which is an expression un-Roman-like.

"Yes, sir." Smiles Dathan diplomatically.

"Eggs."

"What of them, sir?"

"I want to know where they are." The man says irritably, (it must be noted that shop workers really are treated like scum on occasion, and are asked stupid questions!)

Senator Aurelius strides away, muttering to himself: "Eggs, eggs, my kingdom for some eggs! Can he not see this is no convenience store?"

Makeshift wooden bleachers have been erected one side of the TAMS Electrical courtyard by order of the great Caesar himself, upon which are seated four-dozen members of the Senate with their retainers, plus a half-dozen trade Emissaries from neighbouring regions here for the talks. Senator Gracchus and his wife Portia, Senator Aurelius' daughter, are alongside their magnificently lacquered chariot, its horses pawing - or should that be hoofing? - the ground with anticipation, while his champion driver Nathan(19) struts around his chariot proudly, arrogantly, his young women groupies swaying and sighing romantically.

Senator Aurelius is offering advice and courage to his own charioteer, young Adam. He will need plenty of both! Adam is at least trying to look proud and confident, mimicking his counterpart as best he can after having eventually come to terms with the events which fate has bestowed upon him. He hopes his horses know what they are doing!

Still awaiting the return of Dathan with his Legion of soldiers is causing Senator Aurelius some consternation: he knows without a shadow of a doubt(yes, I know, wrong genre) that Adam has real no chance whatsoever against Nathan, Rome's most lauded charioteer in history. Aurelius' only hope is that Adam doesn't do something utterly stupid, like losing the race on the first turn!

"Do not fail me." Aurelius tells his man with steel-eyed warning, not that threats will help much but he can hope. "You know what rewards face you upon victory, young Adam...glories which you have yet to imagine." The Senator nods in direction of his own seating area where scantily clad maidens await their victor.

Spectators and Senators move from the makeshift circuit into their seats, and the countdown begins, carried out by Mercia(20), the unfortunate person in charge of bringing the official starting board but who forgot to do so.

"One!" Shouts Mercia reaching the end- well, you know, times were hard back then!

The horses and the chariots lurch forward, the expert Nathan deftly controlling his charges, while Adam is visibly shaken by the surprising burst of speed yet remains balanced and is please to still be in the race.

From his place in the bleachers Senator Aurelius can be seen sighing with relief while Gracchus smiles with arrogance tasting sweet victory despite the first corner of the first lap not being reached yet. Out of the corner of one eye Aurelius see's movement within the shop front: it is Atticus(21), leader of his First Legion. Now it is Senator Aurelius' turn to grin. He issued Dathan with instructions to attack during the first lap, and for Atticus to rescue his daughter from the clutches of Gracchus.

A battle-horn sounds. Suddenly a Legion of the finest soldiers in all of Rome resplendent in the colours of the House of Aurelius, armour shining, swords held high, converge upon the courtyard.

The charioteers register the commotion.

Adam steers his horse as best he can, wrestling with the multiple tangle of reins, his foe precariously registering in his periphery, while the noise becomes a deafening roar when suddenly Adam collides with the Wall Of Reality and is abruptly transported into the 21st Century, his Century, bedecked in his TAMS Electrical uniform sans Roman effects, the store returning to its old self, cars in the carpark, people going about their shopping...and he sighs, pleased to be back where life isn't quite so harsh, not quite so strict, where human conditions are slightly better. He thinks he should write down this amazing adventure he has had before it fades from his memory, maybe furnishing a proper ending for himself: so it shall be written; so it shall be done.

(1) The Bible: In the Beginning, 1966, directed by John Huston, starring Michael Parks, Ulla Bergryd, Richard Harris, Ava Gardner, George C Scott, John Huston, Stephen Boyd, Peter O'Toole etc. Poster tagline: "The first adventure story...the first love story...the first murder story...the first suspense story...the first story of faith." Three hour all-star epic based on the first parts of the Book Of Genesis.

(2) Solomon and Sheba, 1959, directed by King Vidor, starring Yul Brynner, Gina Lollobrigida, George Sanders, Marisa Pavan, David

Farrar, John Crawford, Harry Andrews etc. Poster tagline: "The mightiest motion picture ever created." Unfortunately not the mightiest for its original star, Tyrone Power, who died early on during filming.

(3) Gladiator, 2000, directed by Ridley Scott, starring Russell Crowe, Joaquin Phoenix, Oliver Reed, Richard Harris, Connie Nielsen, Derek Jacobi, Djimon Hounsou etc. Dialogue quote: "Are you not entertained? Are you not entertained? Is this not why you are here?"

(4) Land of the Pharaohs, 1955, directed by Howard Hawks, starring Jack Hawkins, Joan Collins, James Robertson Justice, Dewey Martin, Alexis Minotis etc. Poster tagline: "The barbarous love that left Egypt's Great Pyramid as its wondrous landmark."

(5) Demetrius and the Gladiators, 1954, directed by Delmer Daves, starring Victor Mature, Susan Hayward, Michael Rennie, Debra Paget, Anne Bancroft, William Marshall, Ernest Borgnine etc. Dialogue quote: "Men do not kill what they despise...only what they fear."

(6) Cleopatra, 1963, directed by Joseph L Mankiewicz, starring Elizabeth Taylor, Richard Burton, Rex Harrison, Pamela Brown, George Cole, Hume Cronyn, Andrew Kier, Martin Landau, Roddy McDowall etc. A huge epic which has had enough written about it to make a further epic!

(7) The Ten Commandments, 1956, directed by Cecil B DeMille, starring Charlton Heston, Yul Brynner, Anne Baxter, Edward G. Robinson, Yvonne De Carlo, Debra Paget, John Derek, Judith Anderson etc. dialogue quote: "So it shall be written. So it shall be done."

(8) Exodus Gods and Kings, 2014, directed by Ridley Scott, starring Christian Bale, Joel Edgerton, Ben Kingsley, Sigourney Weaver, John Turturro, Aaron Paul, Hiam Abbass etc. "Follow me and you will be free. Stay and you shall perish."

(9) Spartacus, 1960, directed by Stanley Kubrick, starring Kirk Douglas, Laurence Olivier, Jean Simmons, Charles Laughton, Peter Ustinov, John Gavin, Tony Curtis etc. From 1960's The Illustrated Story of the Spartacus Motion Picture Production: "Mercurial, restless, inquisitive, Kirk Douglas is interested in every detail of movie-making. Driving everyone hard-himself hardest-he is known as 'the mixmaster'. His vitality, a hallmark on-screen, is key feature off-screen as well." This is Dalton Trumbo's first credited script since

his blacklisting during the HUAC witch-hunt, championed by Kirk Douglas after the studio objected and Kubrick said he would take credit for the script.

(10) Ben-Hur, 1959, directed by William Wyler, starring Charlton Heston, Stephen Boyd, Jack Hawkins, Hara Harareet, Finlay Currie, Martha Scott etc. Won 11 Oscars from 12 nominations.

(11) King of Kings, 1961, directed by Nicholas Ray, starring Jeffrey Hunter, Siobhan McKenna, Viveca Lindfors, Hurd Hatfield, Ron Randall, Harry Guardino, Rip Torn etc. Poster tagline: "A story of the Christ and the inspiration of His spoken words."

(12) Quo Vadis, 1951, directed by Mervyn LeRoy, starring Robert Taylor, Deborah Kerr, Peter Ustinov, Leo Genn, Patricia Laffan, Finlay Currie etc. Dialogue quote: "It is not good enough to live well, one must die well."

(13) The Robe, 1953, directed by Henry Koster, starring Richard Burton, Jean Simmons, Victor Mature, Michael Rennie, Dean Jagger, Torin Thatcher, Richard Boone etc. Poster tagline: "The first Motion Picture in CINEMASCOPE. The modern miracle you see without glasses."

(14) Samson and Delilah, 1949, directed by Cecil B DeMille, starring Hedy Lemarr, Victor Mature, George Sanders, Angela Lansbury, Henry Wilcoxon etc. Poster tagline: "A story as timeless and tumultuous as the violent age it spreads before you."

(15) The Greatest Story Ever Told, 1965, directed byGeorge Stevens, starring Max von Sydow, Dorothy McGuire, Charlton Heston, Caroll Baker, Victor Buono, Martin Landau, John Wayne etc. Nominated for 5 Oscars.

(16) The Fall of the Roman Empire, 1964, directed by Anthony Mann, starring Sophia Loren, Stephen Boyd, Alec Guiness, James Mason, Christopher Plummer, Anthony Quayle etc. End narration: "This was the beginning of the fall of the Roman Empire. A great civilisation is not conquered from without, until it has destroyed itself from within."

(17) Carry on Cleo, 1964, directed by Gerald Thomas, starring Sid James, Kenneth Williams, Amanda Barrie, Charles Hawtry, Joan Sims, Kenneth Connor, Jim Dale etc. Poster tagline: "The funniest film since 54 BC."

(18) Julius Caesar, 1953, directed by Joseph L Mankiewicz, starring Louis Calhern, Marlon Brando, James Mason, John Gielgud, Edmond

O'Brien, Deborah Kerr, Greer Garson etc. Dialogue quote: "Friends, Roman's, countrymen, lend me your ears."

(19) David and Bathsheba, 1951, directed by Henry King, starring Gregory Peck, Susan Hayward, Raymond Massey, Kieron Moore, James Robertson Justice, Jayne Meadows etc. From Film Review, 1952, by F. Maurice Speed: "Spectacular yet always personal, magnificent yet subtle, with a grand performance from Peck."

(20) The Sign of the Cross, 1932, directed by Cecil B DeMille, starring Fredric March, Claudette Colbert, Charles Laughton, Elissa Landi, Ian Keith etc. Dialogue quote: "My head is splitting...the wine last night...the music...the delicious debauchery."

(21) Pompeii, 2014, directed by Paul WS Anderson, starring Kit Harrington, Kiefer Sutherland, Emily Browning, Adewale Akinnuoye-Agbaje, Carrie-Anne Moss etc. Poster quote: "No warning. No escape."

The films mentioned are just the (mammoth) tip of the epical iceberg when it comes to historical epics and I have only focused on those which tell stories before 100AD(I think), and there are many more, based on fact or fiction, varying wildly in substance and quality. It is to our benefit - the cinema-goer - that we are fortunate the major Hollywood studios made larger, longer, broader of scope films to compete with distractions such as television where screen size is limited. We are able to enjoy these stories of epic proportions, usually with a Who's-Who star cast, thanks mostly to the increasing quantity of the tube in homes, plus other alternative leisure activities to keep customers out of cinemas, and although few of these films are worth more than a single viewing because some unfortunately lack deeper artistic merit, in most the production design, costumes and art direction are worth it alone.

These epic tales have been remade with the benefit of modern CGI and a few are listed among them, but they often achieve lesser success with their story-telling, particularly those which are of a Biblical nature because they have lost relevance with the youthful audience of today whose religions are hand-held technology, gaming, football, and Comic Book movies. But fortunately this new technology allows the studios to remaster the classic biblical epics into higher-definition where they are resplendent and vibrant and shall themselves never be forgotten in history.

CHAPTER SEVENTEEN

NAKED BABES IN BEACH TOWN

It can be a major step from sunbathing nude on a relatively secluded beach with like-minded people to attending a resort dedicated fully to naturism. A beach is often less crowded and usually less accessible to the casual bather, or voyeur, while the resort means being surrounded by hundreds of other naked people with nothing but their social status and standing hidden from view.

How my wife agreed to going on holiday to the naturist colony of Cap d'Agde is something which only she can explain: "I can relax more because no one I know will be there." Simple.

This is the summer of 2001.

Cap d'Agde is a very pretty picturesque harbour town on the south coast of France, which bustles with people but isn't too large a town to be overcrowded with tourist's, and it just so happens to have the world's largest naturist resort nestled on the coastline right beside it. Here you can spend the day and night, 24/7, without clothing in a safe environment - that is without fear of being arrested due to improper exposure.

Splendiferous.

Admittedly we were not entirely sure what naturist colony life was going to be like until we got there, probably owing to the salacious media prejudices one witnesses, so we were gambling a week here. Yet, in hindsight, if we did decide that communal naturist mingling wasn't for us we did have the advantage of a third-floor terrace apartment to stay in if we chose, which was bestowed with sunshine most of the day, where we could spend our time. Prior to this holiday, though, we discovered friendliness prevailed during our beach experiences, so there really was nothing to concern us: on one particularly windy sunbathing occasion a family asked if we would like to join them with benefit of their breakers, which we did, and had a lovely chat with them too - you cannot envision such an occurrence taking place on a 'clothed' beach.

We went in June and lucky for us when our plane touched down at Montpelier Airport the sun was shining, leaving behind us a cloudy, wet, and cold England.

We boarded the bus(1) with the other travellers heading to the same resort for a lovely forty mile journey along the coastal road of southern France, where the beautiful scenery of somewhere new offered a diverse range of sun-kissed grass, Mediterranean properties and Suburbia(2), bright and varied flowers with the occasional view of the sea. When visiting someplace new we tend to view things with multilayered interest irrespective of what part of the world we are in, this new experience is what a holiday should be about because it is a unique experience, whether positive or negative, and taking us away from the daily routine we tend to absorb more, and are frequently aware of more in this new environment because, after all, that should be part of the goal for leaving behind the familiar for a while.

Arrival at the naturist complex of Cap d'Agde is much the same as that at 'clothed' resorts - although this is certainly no Butlins! - and the temperature and humidity could not have been more perfect for us, the clear blue skies and sunshine of the region were definitely smiling upon the newcomers.

Our holiday representative showed us to our apartment, the walk affording us a view of the small resort harbour, its hotels and the horseshoe shaped main resort complex(3).

When we were unpacked and unclothed and familiar with our apartments facilities, we decided to go for a self-tour of the resort to get our bearings, with our first destination being the beach itself which was a thirty-second walk away, and what a delightful sandy beach it was, the sea gently lapping against the shore, while on the horizon were boats and nothing else but the great expanse of blue water itself.

We learned quickly that footwear is a definite requirement during the hottest parts of the day because even the sand was uncomfortably hot on the soles(4). The sandy beach(5) is narrow and long, ending at a jetty, the warm Mediterranean Sea(6) inviting. This was a busy tourist season yet the beach did not feel overcrowded(7), unlike other more touristy European beaches while are often cramped while people vie for the best spot. I can remember we decided to take a dip straight away and strolling into the cool water was splendiferous - we both probably realised at that precise moment we were definitely going to enjoy this holiday of freedom and relaxation, where people are not judged by what they look like or by what they wear.

Like most people we encounter when telling the story of our naturist holiday you probably want to ask the question: how do you not look at other people's bits and pieces(8)? Obviously we do in the naturist environment as we observe people in life who are clothed generally, because neither of us is blind. The thing to remember is that we too are relaxed to be naked, and it's just a natural state of being. There is nothing to be embarrassed about, really, it's just a mindset. Perhaps naturism has created its own stigma because of those people who are exhibitionists as opposed to genuine naturists. I personally am not doing this to shock or offend, I am doing it either in privacy or in the appropriate environment because I choose to. Like many aspects of society naturism has been exploited for movies and televisions solely for titillation purposes, despite the sometimes genuine participation of the naturist to promote this way of life, but the media has to sell their programming. Often the life of a naturist is the same or similar as for most people, so without the nudity it might not be deemed interesting viewing. The problem arises when you have exhibitionists claiming to extol the virtues of naturism and use this as an excuse to expose themselves.

Rant over!

As you can well imagine there is a mixture all ages, shapes and sizes(9), on the beach, so we fit right in and nobody paid us any heed except for the fact we were not suntanned up to this point! But because of the sunshine and Mediterranean breeze it doesn't take much time to blend in on this score(10).

Our next task was to explore the rest of the complex, from the location of the restaurants, the supermarket, the health spa, and Johnny Watker's English bar - there were others available but we gravitated towards this one for reasons I shall explain later - before returning to our apartment veranda where we sat chatting about how this is going to be a brilliant holiday, which it will be, and our new neighbour Graham soon introduced himself. I cannot emphasise enough that Graham was brilliant. Hailing from southern England this was the beginning of his fortnight here on a holiday he has taken every year for fifty years. His friendliness and guidance were invaluable to making our holiday as enjoyable as it was, while he introduced us to his friends Jim and Irish Mike, plus all the patrons of Johnny Watker's where we would spend every evening in their company having a high(11) time, figuratively and literally.

We had dinner with Graham that first night in what he assured was the best pizza restaurant in the world and he wasn't wrong - these were proper, freshly-made pizza pies with every topping you could wish for, and I have never tasted anything similar or so good as those since.

Afterwards we met the friendly crowd at Johnny Watker's where the time seemed to simply fly by with banter, laughs and drinks, while Irish Mike and my wife would invariably mark men a score out of ten as they walked by, onward to whatever nightlife they were participating in(12), often dressed in gear to partake in their own fun and games which definitely weren't for the children(13) of the resort.

During the remainder of our holiday there we only left the complex twice - and yes, before you ask, we were clothed on those occasions. The first day-trip was a mini-bus excursion into Spain, which was very nice, while the second was a visit into the very picturesque harbour town of Cap d'Agde itself. But we couldn't wait to return to our base camp and bare our skin to the elements.

And that's all the detail I am giving, save to say that the entire stay was a fantastic experience all around.

You were perhaps expecting a sordid account of swinging, debauchery and S&M fetishes like you might have seen on television programmes? Sorry to disappoint you but during all the naturist experiences we have had there has been nothing salacious to report...except for this one time...!

Why the Roger Corman homage?

A naturist holiday might be considered in some eyes as quirky and different from the perceived lifestyle in which the "normal" person might partake, while the characters involved in naturism are often portrayed as eccentric individuals, and in some cases this is true because when a person has reached a state of oneness with body the mind often follows suit, and it can create an almost spiritual experience which can be perceived by others as eccentric. I am of course being more polite than what you read and view in the the media on this subject, but you know how narrow-minded and salacious tabloid press can be, so I see no need to go more in-depth with descriptions.

So whats the link between naturism and Corman's oeuvre?

Producer-director-writer Roger Corman is considered one of the foremost proponents of Independent Exploitation film production -

and of all the hundreds of films he has been involved with, only one has ever failed to recoup its budget. No other filmmaker can lay claim to this, not even someone as renowned as Steven Spielberg who sustained an early flop with 1941(14), which isn't really a bad film but failed to ignite the box-office upon its release, because of director expectations at that time: his reliance upon fantasy and sci-fi genres has produced his biggest monetary hits.

Corman began his movie life in the lower-echelons of the business but his passion for making films saw his rapid rise into directing and production, where he had his finger very much on the pulse of what audiences wanted, and brought in his films on time and on budget, exploiting the limited studio means which were at his disposal.

The exploitation industry itself involves a wide array of genres which became popular in their day from horror, sci-fi, creature feature, sex romp; and these productions were far from the normal or accepted studio fair, that is until the massive success of a certain 1975 Steven Spielberg creature-feature, and the science fantasy films which burgeoned at the box-office from 1977 onwards! From there on the exploitation film has merged into, and become, the mainstream. It is accepted on a par with other studio-backed productions and eventually gained the budgets to better serve the visual effects, while swiftly overtaking the profitability of those films which were once mainstays of the old system - now, the riskier films are those which are usually independently produced, lower financed, and possess the artistry of old school talent.

In other words: what used to be considered subjects of B-movies have become the new A-movie, or, the norm.

It was Roger Corman and others who were the first to touch on these more quirky subjects which the big studios wouldn't handle or finance, in a way that focused on profit over art, with Corman being the longest standing and most successful of these independents. Yet Corman himself, through his passion for the medium, often succeeded on both levels, producing films with artistic merits like The Pit and the Pendulam(15), based on an Edgar Allen Poe story, and The Intruder(16), a cutting-edge story about racial prejudice; just two good examples of these types. Corman was also a keen promoter of European arthouse films by the likes of Ingmar Bergman(17) and Federico Fellini(18) which the bigger studios wouldn't distribute.

There was no pretension behind these choices, Corman was a genuine lover of these little-seen at the time artists and wanted to give a mass audience the opportunity to view their work.

And if his foray into the comic book movie world had been successful in the 1990's with his version of the Fantastic Four(19), who knows what direction the industry would be taking right now. Once again, a cheaply made exploitation genre is now being milked for all its worth by the industry.

Roger Corman's multifaceted existence also nurtured the talent of others in the film industry who were fortunate enough to get their big breaks while working for him, a boon to us: Francis Ford Coppola, Ron Howard, James Cameron, Martin Scorsese, Pam Grier, Jack Nicholson, Sylvester Stallone, Jonathan Demme, Joe Dante, Penelope Spheeris, Gale Anne Hurd, Sandra Bullock etcetera.

So hopefully you can see why I chose this genre and this particular filmmaker to sit alongside the tale of my first quirky, not of the norm, naturist holiday, and will explore both styles for yourself with a new outlook...perhaps?

(1) Grand Theft Auto, 1977, directed by Ron Howard, starring Ron Howard, Nancy Morgan and Elizabeth Rogers. Poster tagline: "See the greatest cars in the world destroyed: Rolls Royce, Cadillac, Lincoln, Mercedes, Porsche and 43 screaming street machines."
(2) Suburbia, 1983, directed by Penelope Spheeris, starring Chris Pederson, Bill Coyne and Jennifer Cley. Poster tagline: "A new movie...about a new generation."
(3) The Arena, 1974, directed by Steve Carver, starring Pam Grier, Margaret Markov and Paul Muller. Steve Carver, from Crab Monsters, Teenage Cavemen and Candy Stripe Nurses: "Roger offered me my first features, The Arena, about slave girls who are forced to fight in a colosseum... It was sort f a female Spartacus... The script had several scenes in which the girls were undressed-one of Roger's prerequisites."
(4) Too Hot To Handle, 1977, directed by Don Schain, starring Cheri Caffaro, Aharon Ipale and Vic Diaz. Poster tagline: "Her mission -seduce and destroy! Her deadliest weapon is her body!"
(5) Attack of the Crab Monsters, 1957, directed by Roger Corman, starring Richard Garland, Pamela Duncan and Russell Johnson. Poster tagline: "From the depths of the sea...a tidal wave of terror."

(6) Monster From the Ocean Floor, 1954, directed by Wyott Ordung, starring Anne Kimbell, Stuart Wade and Dick Pinner. Poster tagline: "Terror strikes!...from the ocean floor."
(7) Viking Women and the Sea Serpent, 1957, directed by Roger Corman, starring Abby Dalton, Susan Cabot and Bradford Jackson. Poster tagline: "Fabulous! Spectacular! Terrifying! The raw courage of women without men lost in a fantastic Hell-on-Earth!"
(8) X, 1963, directed by Roger Corman, starring Ray Milland, Diana Van der Vlis and Harold J Stone. "The Man With X-Ray Eyes."
(9) Naked Angels, 1969, directed by Bruce Clark, starring Michael Greene, Jennifer Gan and Richard Rust. Poster tagline: "Mad dogs from hell! Hunting down their prey with a quarter-ton of hot steel between their legs."
(10) Angels Hard as they Come, 1971, directed by Joe Viola, starring Scott Glenn, Charles Dierkop and Gilda Texter. Scott Glenn, from Crab Monsters, Teenage Cavemen and Candy Stripe Nurses: "My first experience with Roger was Antels Hard as they Come. It was a subtle title. You had to show up on a motorcycle because otherwise they figured that any actor would say, 'Oh yeah, I ride a bike,' and they didn't want them showing up and not knowing how."
(11) The Trip, 1967, directed by Roger Corman, starring Peter Fonda, Susan Strasberg, Bruce Dern and Dennis Hopper. Poster tagline: "A Lovely Sort of Death." LSD...groovy.
(12) Screwballs, 1983, directed by Rafal Zielinski, starring Peter Keleghan, Kent Deuters and Linda Speciale. Poster tagline: "The nuts who always score."
(13) Rock'n'Roll High School, 1979, directed by Alan Arkush, starring P. J. Soles, Vincent Van Patten and Clint Howard. Poster tagline: "Will your school be next?"
(14) 1941, 1979, directed by Steven Spielberg, starring Dan Ackroyd, Treat Williams, John Belushi etc. Poster tagline: "A comedy spectacular." Not necessarily and exaggeration.
(15) Pit and the Pendulum, 1961, directed by Corman, starring Vincent Price, John Kerr and Barbara Steel. Roger Corman, from Crab Monsters, Teenage Cavemen and Candy Stripe Nurses: "I wasn't paying too much attention to the critics, but it feot good when the Poe films were appreciated."
(16) The Intruder, 1962, directed by Corman, starring William Shatner, Frank Maxwell and Jeanne Cooper. William Shatner, from

Crab Monsters, Teenage Cavemen and Candy Stripe Nurses: "He never told me why he wanted me for the part, but I'm sure it was because I was handsome, brilliant, and didn't need the money-because he didn't pay me!"

(17) Cries and Whispers, 1972, directed by Ingmar Bergman, starring Harriet Andersson and Liv Ullmann. Won the Oscar for cinematography from 5 nominations.

(18) Amarcord, directed by Federico Fellini, 1973, starring Magali Noel and Bruno Zanin. Oscar winner for best foreign language film plus two other nominations.

(19) The Fantastic Four, 1994, directed by Oley Sassone, starring Alex Hyde White, Jay Underwood, Rebecca Staab and Michael Bailey Smith.

CHAPTER EIGHTEEN

MY WEDDING DAY - BY SUSAN STARLING
(With an occasional interruption from me when I can get a word in!)

I remember saying to my work colleagues that after the weekend I would be a married woman, and we kept checking on the weather forecast all week until the Big Day - which was Saturday 3rd August, 2002. When the exciting day arrived the dark clouds formed above the venue, the Hilton Hotel in Norwich, and before we knew there was a rumble of thunder followed by rain. So typical of English weather that nobody can plan anything during the summer without taking a gamble, but never mind, Paul and best man were able to get have two photographs taken outdoors before the rains came, while I was able to turn the other cheek(1) and the enjoy what lay ahead for the rest of the day.

The mornings travel to the venue with my Mum, Dad and Sister, and the readying in our bridal suite at the Hilton, all went by so quickly the next thing I knew we were walking to the decorated Conference Suite where the registrar, guests, and - Paul were awaiting the brides arrival.

(Of course I was there already. If I recall David, my best man, and I arrived with my Mum, and his Mum and Dad, and friend Wayne who was to be the usher/doorman, just after lunchtime. I was, I think, filled with nervous anticipation but for no other reason that this ace high(2) wedding proceed without a hitch - see what I did there? - but because I was also determined to drink in every moment of the occasion, to remember everything, absorb all nuance and person present.

While waiting for Susan's arrival I selected a piece of music to play when she walked down the aisle, not a typical piece of wedding muzak, but a poignant and quirky classical composition which you can ask me about face to face because, on the page, it doesn't seem a romantic choice whatsoever.)

Paul's reaction was with tears of joy as I walked down the aisle on the arm of my Dad to the table/altar.

(My memory differs here. I think I remained composed. Maybe I daren't look at Susan as she walked toward me for fear of crying uncontrollably, which is the sort of thing I might do, until she was alongside me. I should also say there is a double-edged sword to my resistance for being emotionally in control, because my Dad had died not twelve months prior to my wedding.)

We went through the recital of vows without messing up our words, which was something I was worried about, but I thought go for it(3) and then it was done, before signing the certificate of marriage with two witnesses, those being Paul's best man and my lifelong friend Clarissa - who had cried happily when I asked to perform this task.

Plenty of photographs with family and friends were next taken, indoors of course, thanks to the weather, but the moods of all weren't dampened by what was falling outside and everyone chatted and laughed.

Next we went into the main area of the conference room which had been set out with tables reading for the meal, with the flower arrangements and colour schemes I had requested and, on a separate table with the kind wedding gifts, was the cake.

We had a lovely soup starter followed by roast chicken, then black forest gateaux for dessert. I didn't over-indulge on the food or drink, in fact Paul and I were the only ones who didn't have any drink from the bar-tab we had arranged, because my dress was snug around the waist.

After the short and sweet speeches from my Dad, Paul and David, Paul handed out the small gifts we had brought for Mum's, Dad, the bridesmaids and best man, plus one for Anne and Arthur, who are neighbours to Paul's Mum, and who supported her emotionally after losing his Dad.

(And who would continue to be supportive throughout the years.)

When the cake was cut and we mingled and chatted with all our guests, the room was turned around for the evening disco and other friends would arrive, usually beginning at the bar! It was great catching up with relatives, asking if they are having a good time, and seeing the faces if friends when they saw me in my dress. Everyone was getting along nicely, enjoying themselves and happy, there were certainly no trouble makers(4) at our wedding.

I found it amusing when I had to ask my sister for help to the bathroom because of the mounds of fabric I had to negotiate on my dress.

(Incidentally, Susan can still fit into her wedding dress now despite two children and fifteen years later.)

Lonestar's Amazed was our song of choice to dance to, and I think Paul was pleased when it was over because he doesn't like dancing.

(Especially not in front of over a hundred people with all of them watching!)

It was a great and special dance, and the night went from strength to strength, as with FAB days which you don't want to come to an end.

Films starring both Terence Hill and Bud Spencer:-

God forgives...I don't(1967) directed by Giuseppe Colizzi
(2)Ace High(1968) directed by Giuseppe Colizzi
Boot Hill(1969) directed by Giuseppe Colizzi
They Call Me Trinity(1970) directed by Enzo Barboni
Trinity is Still my Name(1971) directed by Enzo Barboni
The Black Pirate(1971) directed by Lorenzo Gicca Palli
All the Way, Boys(1972) directed by Giuseppe Colizzi
(1)Turn the Other Cheek(1974) directed by Franco Rossi
Watch Out, We're Mad(1974) directed by Marcello Fondato
Crime Busters(1977) directed by Enzo Barboni
Odds and Evens((1978) directed by Sergio Corbucci
I'm for the Hippopotamus(1979) directed by Italo Zingarelli
Who Finds a Friend finds a Treasure(1981) directed by Sergio Corbucci
(3)Go for It(1983) directed by Enzo Barboni
Double Trouble(1984) directed by Enzo Barboni
Miami Supercops(1985) directed by Bruno Corbucci
(4)Trouble Makers(1994) directed byTerence Hill

When Mario Girotti(Hill) and Carlo Pedersoli(Spencer) entered the movie business in the late nineteen fifties - the first film they were in together was 1959's Hannibal, directed by Carlo Bragaglua, but they were no more than extras - little did they know that during the seventies and early eighties their double act of action/comedy would make them International stars - who you perhaps haven't heard of.

Their team mixes up inoffensive humour, playful action with quirky stories and they have an undeniable chemistry which comes across clearly on-screen. You can see they are having fun and enjoying each other's company which is why they remained friends all their lives, and sharing time with their families - Hill celebrates fifty years of marriage to Lori Zwickbauer in 2017; Spencer was married to Maria Amato in 1960 until his death in 2016. Their dedication, tongue-in-cheek humour, talented yet bloodless fighting skills, enable viewers of all ages to watch their movies without worrying about being appalled by the content. They cover pretty much every genre except horror. Hill's vivid blue eyes are resplendent with joy, while Spencer's are heavy slits most of the time, conveying danger yet compassion. Hill is the tall Laurel, to Spencer's portly Hardy, if you will.

Watching this duo in action is like being amongst friends: a worthy hour-and-a-half of laughs and fun.

A marriage should be a friendship first and foremost, if it is to last, but I don't need to tell you that because you already know this fact...don't you?

CHAPTER NINETEEN

FIRST BORN

Best that I introduce myself to you first so we can dispense with any confusion: my name is Eli(1) Cobb(2), and I was what you might call an odd-job man, if you were being cagey, or strong-arm, if you were hiring me, or if we are being more particular then maybe 'henchman' might apply to my profession. Retired now, but when I was in that particular line of work I couldn't possibly conceive - no pun intended - of becoming a father, but here I now am while my wife is giving birth to our first. This seems a world away from the pain I've dished out on people over the years and I wouldn't miss it for all the coffee in Columbia - I don't drink tea, never liked it, the stuff gives me indigestion, especially when folk dilute the taste with milk or they barely touch the teabag into the water, blimey, some people are fastidious beyond belief, give me a Columbian black filter-coffee with half a tea-spoon of sugar any day!

Where was I-? Ah, yes, I remember now - not that Eli needs much help remembering because it was only the start of the previous paragraph when he began!

I realise now that the whole experience of childbirth is, for the father, very much like the best day and the worst day of your life rolled into the barrel of a gun and shot directly at you! And I should know the analogy! Not that I'm some sap like Dana(3) who can get suckered by wandering blindly into the simplest thing, no way, so I went eyes wide open to all the natal classes with my wife, and hence I had some idea what to expect. But nothing can prepare you for this!

When you go into the hospital with your partner, which you really must do, because believe it not she needs you like you needed her to get this result - yes, you did it, so take responsibility for your actions for the first time in your life! But it's okay to be nervous, scared, confused, and if you are squeamish I might point out you are in a hospital with people trained for this sort of thing! I might be a hulking man's man who used the rough-stuff before retiring but I too was frightened, which is okay because my active imagination invariably makes things worse in my mind than the eventual outcome, I just mask it well until afterwards.

Does it seem weird that a guy who has faced life and death situations on countless occasions can still be shaken and stirred by something which, in our case, fortunate folk that we are, lasted about an hour from arriving at the hospital to the birth itself? And can you believe I didn't Dwight(4)-out or do a Hopkins, neither. Nope, I was professionally calm...at least on the outside. Gotta pretend for the wife. Gotta be strong. Gotta be a man.

Don't get me wrong, folks, it is a terrific miracle of nature and completely life-altering, in a good way, but it's possible it can break a man too, at least for a man who has emotions and feelings towards his wife and child. I couldn't wait to become a parent, to be a Dad to a new life with all the sense if wonder and learning this brings with it. Okay, I know what you're thinking if you too are a parent, because I heard it a hundred times: wait until they can crawl; wait until they can talk; wait until the terrible-two's; wait until they to school; wait until the teenage years; wait until they say they hate you! That's right, ain't it? Children are so full of dread and horror, they become something of a sinister Peter Lorre(5) stereotype. And there's the illnesses, the projectile vomiting, the nappy changing, the inexplicable crying, the illogical tantrums, the food fussiness, the naive negotiating, copying their friends bad behaviour because they themselves are perfect, like you, right?

So if all this first-hand information from actual, real parents, were believed, then having kids must be a complete nightmare and why would any right-minded human being deliberately put themselves through such trauma? It would put anyone off. But like Elmer(6) chasing his quarry, we continue doing it despite everything.

Personally I think the only real challenge to overcome in parenting is one's own self.

You know, I'm kinda a tough guy in the mould of Oates(7) or Haig(8), unless I'm being too unkind on myself, maybe I'm more if a Widmark(9) man. I dunno. But I know that even tough guys can change when the situation demands the too, and this is one of those situations which implores every man to change for the better on some level. Sure, there are lots of really important things in life to distract a person from being a dedicated father: work, socialising, gaming, drinking, online selling, social media, must-see television... Yeah, lots of important time-consuming endeavours which your wife and kid appreciate are totally necessary in your life, so why should we sacrifice?

The things we fellas need to develop are patience and understanding.

Yeah, I admit, sleep deprivation makes me mighty crotchety, but sleep is overrated anyhow. My patience withers the more tired I become. But, hey, at least I can get some sleep, recognise when you are tired and get some, most of us have actually chosen wild nights without sleep so you know the consequences. My wife, she's getting way less than I am, so I gotta understand if she's got no time for me. One-hundred percent of her life at the moment is devoted to ensuring this child, our child, receives food, gets attention when required, is cleaned and kept comfortable. She is new to this as much as I am, but the onus is upon her to keep this life living, for heck sake! Which means our new understanding role is to be patient, supportive, helpful and committed, take over so she can get some rest and ain't driven completely outta her mind.

We chose this! Sorry, guys, but I really don't believe there's such a thing as accidental pregnancy between two consenting adults, so don't act too surprised when a baby arrives, it's not the kids fault you were stupid!

Becoming a parent...a Dad...is a miracle we should cherish.

Wow. We have sired a small human which is of our DNA. What a truly amazing miracle. From a baby, to a toddler, to a young adult, to adulthood itself.

Chances are that you have been through all these changes yourself at one time or other, unless you were fully formed at birth, so to a degree you already have the knowledge and experience to appreciate what your child is going through. I guess I was lucky, my parents were upstanding folk who worked hard to provide for me and by siblings. I realise not everyone had such support when they were growing up, but if that's the case, if your childhood were so bad, why would you wanna repeat the situation with a family of your own. We all need to adapt otherwise we become Joneses(10) or Wells's(11) in society, and pigeonhole ourselves. Who wants that? Who wants to repeat themselves unless they're really good at it?

Obviously the entire process of childbirth itself is unique because we all different human beings and react according to our own emotional responses and previous life experiences up-to this moment in time, so what I, with my career as a professional thug, cope differently to you when under-fire from emotional upheaval. Coupled with awe and wonderment, are helplessness and terror. Here is your wife, screaming in pain, and there really is nothing you can do or say to alleviate this distress. The doctor's and nurses's are professional, they know what they are doing, and you are not qualified to offer assessments or observations of your own, because Internet Search Engines are no substitute for years of actually doing this job. Unfortunately we now live in a society where everyone is an instant expert on all matters so we feel the need to throw in our ten-pennies worth, but I try to resist doing that, because I'm not as knowledgeable as the real experts. Let them do their job, like people let you do yours. How does it make you feel, how does it make you look, when others tell you what you already know? In reality you are not an expert on a subject just because you got the information on the Internet, and also, no one can truly inform you fully on what the experience is gonna be like. There's certain stuff, most definitely, common-sense stuff too like getting prepared for the journey home, ensuring you get everything baby needs.

But it is scary, this sense of utter helplessness, so an emotional outburst from Dad ain't nothing unusual. I don't mean get angry like Wincott(12) or Trejo(13), that's a bit extreme and irrational, and I would avoid doing a Hopkins(14), too. Just don't interfere or get in the way, that's not good for your wife or child. Although there were definitely many negative thoughts passing through my brain, I can tell you this much, I just the professionals get on with their job and it all worked out fine in the end.

Ultimately is my own life experiences which inform how I react to bringing up my kid in this crazy, face-paced and high-pressure we all live in, but I am willing to make the sacrifices in my own life because I feel deep down it is worth it. I want this family unit to work, I want my wife to feel supported, I want to nourish my child as they grow up with sustenance and knowledge, so they might mature into a better human being than I. Whether I will succeed in achieving this is something only time can tell, but in the long run, the rewards are unimaginable.

(1) Eli Wallach (The Magnifent Seven, 1960, as Calvera; The Good, The Bad, and The Ugly, 1966, as Tuco; Cinderella Liberty,

1973, as Lynn Forshay; Tough Guys, 1986, as Leon B. Little; The Godfather, Part 3, 1990, as Don Altobello, Wall Street Money Never Sleeps, 2010, as Julie Steinhardt.) Talented, ubiquitous character actor, the sly wiles of whom would often land him in trouble, began his career in Television which intertwined with his movie work for over sixty years.

(2) Randall "Tex" Cobb (Uncommon Valor, 1983, as a sailor; The Golden Child, 1986, as Til; Raising Arizona, 1987, as Leonard Smalls; Liar Liar, 1997, as Skull) This distinctive looking ex-Heavyweight boxer has created several memorable tough-guy supporting roles, once seen, never forgotten.

(3) Dana Andrews (The Ox-Bow Incident, 1943, as Donald Martin; Laura, 1944, as Det. Lt. Mark McPherson; The Best Years of Our Lives, 1946, as Fred Derry) Dependable leading man whose performances seem secondary to what is transpiring around him, often playing a character out of his depth.

(4) Dwight Frye (Dracula, 1931, as Renfield; The Maltese Falcon, 1931, as Wilmer Cook; Bride of Frankenstein, 1935, as Karl) Superb, underrated character actor primarily in the manipulated henchman mode, if you want to see what 'mad' is like just watch his scene-stealing performance as Renfield.

(5) Peter Lorre (M, 1931, as Hans Beckert; The Man Who Knew Too Much, 1934, as Abbott; The Maltese Falcon, 1941, as Joel Cairo; Casablanca, 1942, as Ugarte) Memorable and much imitated character actor whose performances are often the best part of the films he is in.

(6) Elmer Fudd (Many Warner Bros. cartoons, usually with Bugs or Daffy or both) The ultimate foil, a would-be henchman, inadequate tough-guy, best described in the book Warner Bros. Animation Art by Jerry Beck and Will Friedwald: "The most lasting image of Elmer Fudd is of a poor sap, so pathetic he fairly begs to be heckled. Or worse."

(7) Warren Oates (The Rise and Fall of Legs Diamond, 1960, as Eddie Diamond; Major Dundee, 1965, as O. W. Hadley; The Wild Bunch, 1969, as Lyle Gorch; 1941, 1979, as Co. Maddox) Intense and charismatic character actor who rose from the ranks of television and never achieved leading man status.

(8) Sid Haig (Point Blank, 1967, as a guard; Coffy, 1973, as Omar; Jackie Brown, 1997, as Judge; Bone Tomahawk, 2015, as Buddy) Tall

and menacing, bald and dangerous, a very memorable tough-guy in many films and television series.

(9)   Richard Widmark (Kiss of Death, 1947, as Tommy Udo; Pick-Up on South Street, 1953, as Skip McCoy; The Alamo, 1960, as Col. Jim Bowie; Judgement at Nuremberg, 1961, as Co. Tad Lawson) Masculine, conflicted, and unconventional leading-man turned dependable character actor in latter part of career.

(10) L. Q. Jones (Torpedo Run, 1958, as 'Hash' Benson; Hang 'Em High, 1968, as Loomis; Pat Garret and Billy The Kid, 1973, as Black Harris; Casino, 1995, as Pat Webb) Weathered and craggy faced character actor with a fifty year career across numerous genres.

(11) Vernon Wells (Mad Max 2, 1981, as Wez; Commando, 1985, as Bennett; Fortress, 1992, as Maddox; Dr. Jekyll and Mr Hyde, 2017, as Mr Enfield) Dark and menacing villain in bigger pictures, and a B-movie stalwart, star and character actor.

(12) Michael Wincott (The Sicilian, 1987, as Col. Silvestro Canio; Robin Hood Prince of Thieves, 1991, as Guy of Gisborne; Dead Man, 1995, as Conway Twill; Hitchcock, 2012, as Ed Gein) Always impressive, always memorable, craggy faced, gravel-voiced actor often pigeon-holed as a villain.

(13) Danny Trejo (Runaway Train, 1985, as Boxer; Desperados, 1995, as Navajas; Con-Air, 1997, as Johnny-23; Machete, 2010, as Machete) You wouldn't want to mess with this ex-convict turned actor, whose etched features are as unpredictable as his style.

(14) Bo Hopkins (The Wild Bunch, 1969, as Crazy Lee; White Lightning, 1973, as Roy Boone; Tentacles, as Will Gleason; Midnight Express, 1978, Tex) If you want to learn how to do 'crazy/funny' then just watch his earlier films/television performances, utterly brilliant scene-stealing character actor.

CHAPTER TWENTY

AN ADVENTURE IN THE KINGDOM

His Royal Majesty the King pensively stalks the corridor outside his Queen's bedchamber, eyes staring fixedly at the line on the floor which he subconsciously traces back and forth like an expectant father, probably because this is exactly what he is. His usual royal calmness, the one which he utilises to hide his deeper feelings, is being tested to the very limit today. The Queen has been in labour since the darkest hours of this summer's morning and there seems little respite from the pained moans which emanate from her bedchamber. The King has indeed run the full gamut of emotions while his tiredness threatens to spill forth with a spurt of frustration at the slightest provocation. This is the best and the worst day of his life, projected toward him like a hundred fiery arrows across the Castle Keep. He feels utterly useless in his own domain, completely inadequate to the task behind the door, forlorn for being alone in the corridor with everything now beyond his control.

Clopping feet resonate along the stone staircase behind the King and a messenger appears somewhat nervously from around the corridor, striding tentatively toward the King, who faces this man, his expression bordering upon intolerance.

"I thought I made it clear there are to be no disturbances." The King bellows when the messenger isn't forthcoming with his message.

"I am sorry, your Majesty." The messenger quivers with a fright which is palpable. "Vega(1) the tax-collector is in the courtyard, sire, and is insistent upon gaining an audience with your highness, claiming unpaid mortgage settlements."

Before the King can explode with rage, his face already in the process of turning red, a new scream, a much younger scream, replaces that of his wife's which momentarily changes the King's expression to one of tearful elation.

Lavasseur(2), the Queen's favourite hand-maiden and wet-nurse, opens the door to the bedchamber and curtseys, her face rosy red from tiredness and slick with sweat. The King hears not a word she says to him for he enters the room in a trancelike state, eyes transfixed on his wife and the fresh bundle which she is cradling gently in her arms: it is a truly powerful moment and his feeling of pride swells joyously within his chest.

"Charlotte." The Queen says simply to him when he bends over the bed in childlike wonderment. His wife's eyes are bright, watery and blood-shot, face pasty with sweat, mouth white, while the newborn baby girl's face is ruddy against the white swaddling. The King nods at them both with great pride and not a small amount of relief: Charlotte is an ancestral name shared with his Great-Grandmother.

From the doorway the King senses the messenger's presence beckoning him and it is with some effort that he leaves his wife's side, marches irritably out of the room without a sideways glance to this bringer of news with the messenger following in his wake.

As the King begins descending the stone spiral staircase his Mother-in-Law, Scarlett(3), is ascending. There is little love lost between these two even on happy occasions such as this.

"And where are you going?" Scarlett demands in her usual brusk, accusatory pitch. "Not leaving my daughter alone? How is she? Has the baby been born? I suppose I have to organise tonight's feast? I need a new gown! What am I going to wear?"

The King leans forward and plants a firm kiss on this woman's forehead, which takes her utterly by surprise, and says: "Frankly my dear, I do not give a dash!"

Without waiting to be rebuked for his rudeness and tossing the name 'Charlotte' over his shoulder, the King exits the tower into the stinging sunshine blazing upon the courtyard where the tax-collector, Vega, awaits him, messenger scurrying to keep up.

"The Lord of England demands your mortgage payment!" Says Vega haughtily, without any preamble.

Before the King of this rural county can respond it is the messenger who gains his attention by standing closely alongside him, apologetically handing over a scroll which the King irritably opens: Wogan(4) the Builder is requesting payment for the stable extension he carried out yesterday. This only causes the King's blood-pressure to soar.

"My King!" It is the chirpy voice of Squire Lenore(5) who bounds with dainty gaiety, unaware of what has passed between these men. "All fun and games, sir!" She says brightly, obviously having heard the news of the birth. "I have been instructed to remind you about Anne, sir."

"Jolly." Says the King dourly. "What now?"

"The dragon, sire?" Squire Lenore prompts. "Anne and the dragon."

"Splendiferous," the King sighs with exasperation. "Fetch my horse!"

Squire Lenore points to a pair of tethered horses saddled for the journey, the second being for herself.

"Well done, Lenore." The King says, permitting a smile at her preparedness, wishing he could laugh but the tax-collector might be offended.

"What about the mortgage?" Vega demands.

"And Wogan the Builder?" Prompts the messenger meekly.

The King mounts his horse.

"My banker will tend to both requirements." The King says confidently. "He deals with all my financial affairs and if payments are overdue it is no fault of my own."

Squire Lenore expertly mounts the second house and without saying a further word to either of the expectant men for fear of using language unbecoming a King, the pair ride hastily out of the courtyard through the main gate, following the Castle road until they reach the first field on his estate which they gallop across.

"Never a dull moment, sir." The squire says breathlessly when her mount has eventually caught up with that of the King's. "And congratulations."

That final word causes the King to smile at last because despite all those willing to bring down his mood, he is a father to his second daughter. He sighs deeply, happily. The rushing air against his face temporarily washes away the stresses, and the tears rolling down his face can be acquitted to the wind in his eyes should anyone ask. He believed that it would be easier to go through his wife's second pregnancy but, if anything, greater challenges present themselves with knowledge of that first, and it is daunting to contemplate how this new dynamic will affect the family. There is now more responsibility. Not just one young life to worry constantly about, even if that worry only plays out in the back of one's mind, but now there are two girls. And this is without taking the Queen into consideration. What is she going through? How will she cope? How will the King cope if she doesn't?

"Lord Richard(6) will be pleased." Lenore says sincerely, referring to the Lord of England.

"Thank you, Lenore." Says the King sarcastically. "Lord Richard will be placated by the news that I have another daughter who I will be taxed upon."

A cynical admission to be sure, but there we have it!

A familiar figure moves across the pathway which lay ahead of them and the two riders slow, gradually coming to a complete standstill when they reach the woman.

This is Bess(7). She resides alone in a cabin on the edge of the Landowners Township, and she is an ancient lady who some believe is a witch but the King only knows her for her past, and the wisdom she bestows upon those willing to listen.

"Your Majesty." The wizened woman says. "Please accept this gift for the Queen's newborn," she hands a wrapped parcel to the Squire. "I hope they are both healthy."

"Thank you." The King smiles his gratitude while a little perplexed that such news should travel so fast, which is what often happens these days, either through face, book or telegram. "Your knowledgeable wisdom in the old ways goes without saying."

"Careful on your journey, my King." Bess says, eyes glazing over as if seeing afar. "There are many unseen challenges and temptations in this life, do not easily be led."

"My King." Squire Lenore prompts. "Anne and the dragon."

Snapping out if his reverie, nodding acknowledgement and sensing the irony of Bess's words, the King digs his heals into the horses flanks and the two riders continue upon their journey across the next field where they reach the river, and are soon upon the Enchanted Bridge where the troll Porthos(8)lurks.

The fearful creature has heard their approach and blocks their path.

"I'm in a hurry." The King calls impatiently.

"Then pay the toll and you can continue on your way." Porthos splutters and hisses with equal irritability for this intolerable disturbance.

The King nods to Lenore who hands over ten silver coins, a generous donation to be sure, while trying her best not to touch the cursed troll for fear of catching whatever germs it is riddled with. When Porthos steps aside the two riders cautiously pass him by until they are safely across the bridge, before picking up the pace once more.

It isn't long before Squire Lenore is overcome by a fearful malady, her horse slowing before she slumps from it and hits the ground.

The King stops immediately and canters to her aid, silently cursing the fates and Porthos at this sequence of setbacks befalling what should be a simple journey, wondering why things cannot go his way for once.

They are upon the brink of Woodsher Forest which is at least some blessing, beyond which is their destination, the dragon's lair where his eldest daughter Anne is, but the King dares not move the Squire Lenore too much for risk of worsening what ails her. He is also unable to leave his most faithful servant to who knows what lurks nearby.

Tears of anguish finally burst forth unbidden as they have been threatening all day, despair racking his sides and the releasing of his emotions pour out.

While the King is knelt beside Lenore there is a soft disturbance in the underbrush of the Forest, leaves crunch and he swiftly leaps to his feet, sword drawn in a beat.

"Do not fear us." A woman says softly. "My name is Florinda(9)."

The King is captivated by the beautiful woman who appears like a vision from the trees, her golden hair radiating around her in the sunshine and her clear blue eyes penetrating with something new yet familiar, like a half-remembered dream. It is as if time stands still and nothing exists but her, unless this is wishful thinking on the King's part but during these brief seconds they share a spiritual connection to one another which is indescribable.

"My brother, Tournay(10)." She says to the King as a man of similar posture and grace appears. "We dwell here, within the trees."

"I- I did not realise people lived here." The usually composed King stammers, his heart beating faster, inspired by the very presence of Florinda, he wonders what can possibly be wrong with him to feel this way.

Florinda nods, moving toward him, placing a gentle hand on his shoulder as if to urge him to be strong and a spark of electricity passes into him, while her brother scoops Squire Lenore into his arms.

"We-" the King says, dazed, "don't have much time."

"Yes." The woman tells him. "Yes you do."

Somehow the ethereal conviction in Florinda's words captivate the King and he willingly follows them both to their forest village where other dwellers reside. But the King pays them no attention such is his complete focus on the enchanting Florinda, feeling besotted by this woman who takes him by the hand into her hut, while her brother tends to the squire in another existing in her presence in a way never felt before by him, this new familiarity causes his heart to sore with joyfulness.

"You are hungry." Florinda states and the King nods, sudden realisation hits him that he is in need of sustenance. "You must never neglect your body or mind." She says with certain wisdom which is beyond her years.

"How did you come to live here?" He asks, utterly in her spell.

While eating the nourishing hot broth which she serves him, they talk and talk and talk...

"Rest now." Florinda says after what seems like hours to the King, and she guides him to her bed, caressing his face like one might a child, suddenly kissing him on the mouth which sends an irrational explosion of familiarity through his brain, a dream recalled, a taste of palpable recollection. The King's body responds to her, the temptation threatening to completely overwhelm him. Euphoric, the King is sorely tempted to do just as this woman, this amazing muse who he has only just met wants, and his mind yearns for, but he thinks of his Queen and her newborn and also his eldest daughter Anne. These thoughts are enough to snap him back to the reality of his situation and the responsibilities of life, however testing a trial it has been.

"Thank you," the King says and he rises sluggishly from her bed, disorientated, unaware of the passage of time, "but I really must leave now." Feeling an illogical rush of devastation coarse through his every fibre.

Florinda turns her back on the King so he cannot see her tears, and it is with an abnormally heavy heart like the loss of a loved one that he departs, locating her brother's hut and Squire Lenore. His friend is prone, eyes shut, and the King is fearful until he remembers the gift which the old woman, Bess, gave him. He fetches the package which contains within it a tiny silk shawl which he lays upon Lenore's brow and by some wondrously divine magic the Squire is revived.

Wasting no more time they leave the enchanted village and its mysterious people behind them, continuing wordlessly through the great Forest, their path twisting and turning amidst the towering trees, the King mourning the departure Florinda from his life, until they reach the way out which is subsequently blocked by three highway robbers, swords drawn menacingly.

The King recognises the trio as the infamous Montoya(11) Bandits, fearless fighters who will give no ground in combat, not even to a respected King.

Swinging down from his horse the King bravely draws out his sword, having had his fill for today, his patience and anger tested to the limit, he makes the uncharacteristically reckless decision that enough is enough and he explodes.

First to strike is the younger of the Bandits, Dawg(12), and his skill is exemplary but no match for the highly trained, in the zone, King who dispatches him with the minimum of effort, conserving his strength for the others and there is no respite because Jacopo(13) is upon him straight away. The more experienced swordsman delivers some powerful blows but they are not good enough, and soon all that remains is Humphrey(14) leering at the King.

This opponent is more of a challenge for the King but after much clashing, hacking, slashing and parrying, sheer determination wins through in the end for the King.

"Here, my King." Says Squire Lenore, handing him a gourd-full of wine, which he gulps down victoriously.

"Now for the dragon." Says the King with a twinkle in his eyes, the knowledge that he has come this far spurring him onward, nothing can determine his fate for him now, life has presented many challenges and he has arisen victoriously.

"Hi, Daddy."

Anne runs into her father's welcoming arms.

"They grow up so fast." A man says.

"It doesn't seem possible." The father replies, lifting Anne up and propping her on his waist, she clinging to him joyfully, school-bag bumping to-and-fro. "I know this is going to sound like a bit of a cliche but time flies so fast its hard to believe Anne has started school already."

His wife, May, agrees with her husband - it has been an emotional day - looking briefly down at their youngest daughter Charlotte, the two year old asleep in her buggy.

"How was your first day, sweetie?" Mum asks Anne.

"Fine." Anne shrugs noncommittally, as if nothing fazes her.

"I think its worse for the parents!" The other man says, picking his own son up after his first day at school too.

"Being a parent is the best thing in the world." Anne and Charlotte's father says to his wife proudly, and he means it, too. "But the journey here is fraught with danger!" He grins mischievously while thinking that every day is worth more, every experience enhanced, all bad things temporarily forgotten, with each smile and all the laughter his daughters bring to him - splendiferous.

(1) The Mark of Zorro, 1920, directed by Fred Niblo, starring Douglas Fairbanks, Margueritte de la Motte, Robert McKim and Noah Beery. In comic-book annals this was the film which Bruce's parents, Martha and Thomas Wayne, took him to see prior to being murdered before his very eyes.

(2) Captain Blood, 1935, directed by Michael Curtiz, starring Errol Flynn, Olivia DeHavilland, Lionel Atwill and Basil Rathbone. Poster tagline: "Prince turned pirate to fight the King's armada and win a woman's kiss."

(3) The Adventures of Robin Hood, 1938, directed by Michael Curtiz, starring Errol Flynn, Olivia DeHavilland, Basil Rathbone, Claude Rains and Patric Knowles. Poster tagline: "The best-loved bandit of all time!"

(4) The Black Swan, 1942, directed by Henry King, starring Tyrone Power, Maureen O'Hara, Laird Cregar, Thomas Mitchell, George Sanders and Anthony Quinn. Dialogue quote: "Now put your shirt on, you look much too naked for a decent English gentleman."

(5) Scaramouche, 1952, directed by George Sidney, starring Stewart Granger, Janet Leigh, Eleanor Parker, Mel Ferrer and Henry Wilcoxon. From Film Review, 1952, by F. Maurice Speed: "Large-scale, lovely-to-look-at, rip-roaring Technicolored adaptation of the Rafael Sabatini story... Highlight of the film is a terrific sword duel between hero Granger and villain Ferrer."

(6) Men of Sherwood Forest, 1954, Val Guest, starring Don Taylor, Reginald Beckwith and Eileen Moore. Poster tagline: "All the glory and splendour of stirring adventure."

(7) The Pirates of Blood River, 1961, directed by John Gilling, starring Kerwin Matthews, Christopher Lee and Oliver Reed. Poster tagline: "Ransacking a lost tropic island...for a fabulous idol of gold."

(8) The Three Musketeers, 1973, directed by Richard Lester and starring Richard Chamberlain, Michael York, Oliver Reed, Frank Finlay, Raquel Welch and Christopher Lee. "One for all...and all for one!"

(9) Zorro The Gay Blade, 1981, directed by Peter Medak, starring George Hamilton, Lauren Hutton, Brenda Vaccaro and Ron Leibman. Poster tagline: "Zexy! Zany! Zensational!"

(10) The Scarlet Pimpernel, 1982, directed by Clive Donner, starring Anthony Andrews, Jane Seymour and Ian McKellen. This version is an Emmy Award winning television movie.

(11) The Princess Bride, 1987, directed by Rob Reiner, starring Cary Elwes, Robin Wright, Peter Falk and Mandy Patinkin. Poster tagline: "Scaling the Cliffs of Insanity. Battling Rodents of Unusual Size. Facing torture in the Pit of Despair. True love has never been a snap."

(12) Cutthroat Island, 1995, directed by Renny Harlin and starring Geena Davis, Matthew Modine, Frank Langella and Maury Chaykin. Tagline: "Discover the adventure if a lifetime." ...which is not the description I would use!

(13) The Count of Monte Cristo, 2002, directed by Kevin Reynolds, and starring Jim Caviezel, Guy Pearce, Richard Harris, Michael Wincott and Dagmara Dominczyck. Poster tagline: "Prepare for Adventure, count on Revenge."

(14) Stardust, 2007, directed by Matthew Vaughn, starring Charlie Cox, Claire Danes, Sienna Miller, Ian McKellen and Michelle Pfeiffer. Poster tagline: "A star falls. The chase begins."

CHAPTER TWENTY-ONE

CHECKOUT 13: UNLUCKY FOR SOME

"Why am I getting all the grumpy weird customers at my till." I ask Shakira, who is sat on the checkout behind me, semi-rhetorically. She is on 14 and having a jolly time. "I'm positive it's this till number which attracts them!"

Checkout 13(1).

Some people say that it possesses a curse because of the old market which used to be here many years ago, the spirit of disgruntled departed traders haunting their old stomping ground in Stalton-on-the-Broads, now the site of TAMS Supermarket. Locals who protested the placement of this supermarket fifteen years ago, and who can now not live without the convenience it provides them, claim to have seen ghosts of the livestock roaming its carpark at night. Some even state they have witnessed blood running across the ground as if the earth protests its own raping by the concrete consumerism upon it. While most people might say don't talk a load'a old squit!

Yet the facts remain and the records in the supermarket's Health & Safety bible, which management interpret according to their whim-of-the-day, records a variety of problems - or challenges to overcome, depending upon if your glass is half full or half empty - have indeed beset Checkout 13. They include numerous electrical breakdowns, inexplicable mechanic faults, computer glitches, consumables combusting, and operator bladder malfunctions! Even its recent upgrade has failed to correct the problems.

Staff complain about its position being too near the overhead air-conditioning unit making it too cold, or its facing the wrong direction, or the seat is too low, the seat is too high, the packing area is too small, the belt keeps stopping, there us a strange smell coming from the floor beneath it. Yes, all these and more are the gripes surrounding the mysterious Checkout 13.

Which us why I have been asked to man this checkout during a particularly busy time period, relinquishing my position overseeing the running if our entire departure point for the completely appreciative customers - sarcasm alert! Customers usually see me standing around, assume I am doing nothing and make some jibe regarding this, naively unaware of what it is I do, but never mind, I don't take this disrespectfulness to heart because if I did I might cry in my pillow every night or drink myself into an early grave, I am made of sterner stuff, my shoulders are metaphorically broad, so don't worry about your rudeness hurting me!

Anyway, I am on the checkouts now because they have forecast some weather - oh no! - and there is calmness to the air before the impending storm. Yes, I realise it's hard to believe people can act so utterly illogically, thinking they might get stuck indoors for weeks because of the weather based on forecasting which is speculative at best, instead of using one's own common sense, but this panic buying actually happens. Welcome to England, if you are new to weather! Oh yes, and don't get me started on the people who complain about how bad the weather is without realising the irony behind their words: if the weather were truly bad you might not be able to get to the supermarket in the first place, stoopid!

But that's enough about the weather, this is an altogether different tale of horror.

An unbidden shiver runs the length or breadth of my spine when the next customer appears at my checkout with wraith-like silence, jolting me from my reverie while redirecting my thoughts to the present. This man is in his early twenties, doe-eyed with vacant pupils staring into a void of his own creation, with a pale sheen to his skin and loose clothing bedecking his undernourished frame.

"Good afternoon." I greet him with my very best faked cheerfulness, because even though I try to keep my glass half full on the outside, on the inside I might be feeling something altogether different - I realise this story is full of surprises, you didn't expect people in retail might actually have feelings, did you, which is why you treat us like dirt most of the time!

My greeting elicits not a single flicker of response from this man who, I now notice, sports a blue-tooth device in his right ear which might explain his vacant expression. Undoubtedly he is busy taking a very important telephone call thus is too distracted to register my presence, so I proceed to serve him with funereal silence, trying my best not to be annoyed at his rudeness - don't forget, he was the one who came shopping, not me!

"Yeah, use my Wi-fi." The man says to the ether around us. "'I'm on level nine(2)."

And without even the slightest engagement with his server, that's me, the man slopes off at a pace which might be called snail-like if it were not disrespectful of snails.

Shakira turns about in her seat, smiling at me.

"It is Friday the thirteenth(3) today." Shakira says to me with her infectious chirpiness. "If that makes you feel better?"

"Might explain things, I guess." I reply.

When the next customer arrives at Shakira's checkout they greet each other wth polite and amiable friendliness, which isn't fair!

Maybe it is me! Perhaps I am in possession of a negative aura today, attracting those customers who are less than joyful, those with a pessimistic attitude to the whole shopping experience. I realise grocery shopping can be a chore, especially when one considers the stresses involved, whatever those stresses in life might be, yet all the same it's not as if you are tackling a fire or wiping a patients backside!

Thankfully, my next customers are a happily married middle-aged couple.

"Did you get my cereal?" The wife asks her husband with illogical panic, scouring the full trolley as if the world itself depends upon the revealing of this much needed product, while she simultaneously begins unloading the shopping onto Checkout 13's conveyor belt.

"No!" The husband replies with an irritably dejected sigh. "I thought you picked it up. We did spend ten minutes looking at the cereal, after all!"

"Well, I didn't." She informs him superfluously. "Get it for me while I unload."

"Yes, your Majesty!"

"Stop being contrary."

"Actually, I was being facetial!" The husband says, striding off to attend the errand.

I take this moment to say a polite hello and ask if she requires any help but I may as well be talking to myself, which I proceed to do, at least in my head, wondering about the important things in life such as the meaning of our existence on planet Earth! Maybe customers think we have a sixth sense(4) and automatically exactly what it is they expect from us!

"Is this it?" The husband returns with cereal and a bored expression.

"No." The wife replies. "But it will do! Can you get some 7-Up(5). You forgot to pick one up when you got your Pepsi. And stop staring at that woman on the checkout next to ours unless you are having an affair with her, which wouldn't surprise me, knowing you, you're embarrassing me."

At this point the husband's anger has reached a literal boiling point and he spontaneously combusts, leaving just a pile of burnt ash upon the floor.

"Selfish git!" The wife says without remorse, untroubled by the spectacularly luminous death which has befallen her husband, finally realising I am serving her and addressing me like I am there. "You might need to call a cleaner."

The wife mutters and complains about her lot in life which she packs, pays and leaves without fully focusing on what has actually transpired before her. I might have run up a bill of one thousand(6) pounds and she probably wouldn't have noticed.

Life just isn't fair sometimes. How is Shakira permitted friendly banter with her customers while I am allowed zero rapport with mine? I don't think I'm a bad person, really. I'm not evil incarnate - well, maybe some of the time I am! It's not a deliberate act on my part to make unavailable the items customers require to satisfy their consumerism. I aren't the one who made their trolley awkward to manoeuvre. I don't force you to get out of your bed the wrong side. My influence just isn't that omniscient.

No, there can only be one explanation and that's the curse of Checkout 13(7) working its black-magic.

"Are you all right, sweetie?" Shakira asks.

"I'll give you sweetie right up the..." Is not what I say because she really us a nice young woman. "Fine." Is how I really reply even if it is through gritted teeth. "Who's next please?" I ask no-one in particular in a loud voice which results in a meerkat response of head-turning from those people in ear-shot.

Bizarrely, my question has acted like some devilish supermarket pied-piper and a throng of customers lope up-to my till and firm a mumbling, orderly queue. I have gone from persona non grateful into a Zombie magnet!

"No beans." The first mature lady in the queue drones in an unnerving monotone, seemingly in a bizarre state of confusion or other malady affecting her speech. "No beans." She repeats.

"What sort of beans are you after, Ma'am?" I politely ask.

"No beans." Is her somewhat predictable response.

"No beans." Says the man behind her, eerily caught up in this almost religious mantra.

I glance from one to the other filled with a mixture of apprehension and concern, before I ask the lady once more in a patient voce what sort of beans she requires, hopefully that I can assist her.

"No beans!" Is her reaction.

This time it the dozen other people in the queue behind her who pipe up almost as one:

"No beans! No beans! No beans!"

After twenty seconds the unnerving choral chant abruptly ceases.

I swiftly tally up the ladies shopping.

"Two-thousand(8) pounds, please." I say, figuring that its worth trying anything to break this spell.

"Are you trying to be funny, Sonny?" She replies, much to my surprise.

"No, Ma'am." I offer, thinking quickly. "I don't have to try, its a natural gift."

She pays and walks away from my checkout with her followers trailing behind her, obediently repeating: "No beans! No beans! No beans!"

Sitting there on my high-chair, perplexed, I consider what might possibly cause such bean-worship. Maybe all those people were brainwashed by the same cookery programme on television the night before, and they all assumed they were chefs so sought out a particularly exotic ingredient so they might attempt a similar culinary experience. No, that's silly, something like that wouldn't occur in real life. They probably wish to rekindle their youth when baked beans on toast was considered a meal, perhaps the impending weather-bomb has them agitated to stock-up on essentials, like beans. What a delightfully colourful metaphor to describe rain clouds: weather-bomb. I wonder what the MET office will conjure up next to make forecasting rain seem interesting, obviously it wouldn't be good for the PC brigade if I were to be a weather presenter because I would tell people to stop watching this stupid nonsense and look out their window!

Speaking of which - or should that be writing of which? - is that a rumble of thunder I hear before me? After a thirty-second(9) delay there is a flash of lightening.

From behind me Shakira emits a tiny squeal if surprise, and when I promptly turn about to see what the disaster is, I discover that all the power has gone from her checkout except for 1970(10) eerily remaining etched on her screen.

"Spooky." She says, spookily.

"It's not me." I inform her. "I was born the year after."

"And I was born in 1972(11)." Shakira informs me tenuously.

"You aren't frightened by storms, are you?" I ask the poor girl with genuine concern, because some people can be really terrified by natures wrath, even to the extent that they still unplug their aerial lead from the wall - I think that dish on your house might act as a better conductor, don't you? "After all, the odds must be something like 200-1(12) that you will get struck."

"Thank you for your concern." Shakira says.

"Service." Says the grumpy man at my checkout.

"Yes, sir, certainly, sir," I reply facetiously, "polish you shoes, sir?"

The grumpy man looks down his nose snootily at me, not at all liking the taste of his own medicine and probably not realising I am mirroring his rudeness.

"Chop, chop," he says, adding fuel to the fire. "I'm in a hurry, I'm literally on a wild goose chase."

I look for the aforementioned fowl but see none, hurrying him through my checkout, concerned that his quarry might elude him, and the grumpy man has gone.

Another rumble of lightening and flash of thunder rattles the rafters, Shakira squealing delightfully, at least it sounds delightful to my ears, behind me.

"Are you all right?" I ask.

"It's okay," Shakira says, then adds fatally; "I'll be fine."

As if on cue by some devious scripting devil lightning flashes brightly once more, this time immediately followed by a thunderous boom - see what I did there! - and Shakira is struck by a blinding bolt of energy sending her 37,000(13) feet into the air, mainly because I am rapidly draining myself of plot ideas but still want to add a few movie titles to the list!

After what seems like thirteen(14) seconds but is nearer to five(15) the floor beneath Checkout 14 opens into a fiery cavernous pit, then like a group of nondescript lemmings customers walk over the edge without a single thought for their lives, following one another simply because it is the fashionable thing to do - not that I trying to imply anything about the Capitalist system!

This curious case of ritual immolation is carried out with the requisite amount of complaining, whinging and arguing, and will forever haunt my mind although twenty-eight(16) hours later everything is back to normal, life going on as if nothing had happened, while I realise that instead of all the doom-mongering, Checkout 13 had in fact been very lucky for me!

(1)   Dementia 13, 1963, directed by Francis Ford Coppola, starring William Campbell, Luana Anders and Patrick Magee. Poster tagline: "Are you afraid of death by drowning?...Have you ever attempted suicide?...Have you ever thought of committing murder?"
(2)   Session 9, 2001, directed by Brad Anderson, starring David Caruso, Stephen Gevedon and Josh Lucas. Poster tagline: "Fear is a place."
(3)   Friday the 13th, 1980, directed by Sean S. Cunningham, starring Betsy Palmer, Adrienne King and Jeannine Taylor. From Monsters in the Movies by John Landis: "In the first of this endless franchise, the monster turns out not to be the dead Jason Voorhees, but his mother, Betsy Palmer! Since then the indestructible hockey-mask-wearing ghost has slashed his was through 11 movies."
(4)   The Sixth Sense, 1999, directed by M. Night Shyamalan, starring Bruce Willis, Haley Joel Osment and Toni Colette. From Monsters in the Movies by John Landis: "Moving performances from Haley Joel Osment, Bruce Willis and Toni Colette help make this clever tale of a little by who can communicate with the dead so powerful."
(5)   House of Seven Corpses, 1973, directed by Paul Harris, starring John Ireland, Faith Domergue and John Carradine. From Nightmare USA, by Stephen Thrower: "John Ireland plays (a) mean-spirited doctor...in this tale of a film crew struggling to shoot a Gothic horror picture in a house where actual murders took place."

(6) House of 1000 Corpses, 2003, directed by Rob Zombie, starring Sid Haig, Karen Black and Bill Moseley. Poster tagline: "The most shocking tale of carnage ever seen."
(7) 13 Ghosts, 1960, directed by William Castle, starring Charles Herbert, Jo Morrow and Martin Milner. Poster tagline: "13 times the thrills! 13 times the screams! 13 times the fun!"
(8) Two Thousand Maniacs, 1964, directed by Herschel Gordon Lewis, starring Connie Mason, William Kerwin and Jeffrey Allen. Poster tagline: "An entire town bathed in pulsing human blood! Madmen crazed for carnage!"
(9) 30 Days of Night, 2007, directed by David Slade, starring Josh Hartnett, Melissa George and Danny Huston. From Monsters in the Movies by John Landis: "Danny Huston as Marlow, the leader of the vampires who besiege a small Alaskan town in the dead of winter, is terrific as a vicious vampire out for blood."
(10) Frankenstein 1970, 1958, directed by Howard W. Koch, starring Boris Karloff, Tom Duggan and Jana Lund. Poster tagline: "Warning! Frankenstein 1970 is the most blood-freezing horror ever created! This picture may he too dangerous for people with weak hearts! Beware!"
(11) Dracula A.D. 1972, 1972, directed by Alan Gibson, starring Christopher Lee, Peter Cushing and Stephanie Beacham. Poster tagline: "The Count is back, with an eye for London's hotpants...and a taste for everything."
(12) Dracula 2001, 2000, directed by Patrick Lussier, starring Gerard Butler, Christopher Plummer and Justine Waddell. Poster tagline: "The most seductive evil of all time has now been unleashed in ours."
(13) The Horror at 37,000 Feet, 1973, directed by David Lowell Rich, starring Chuck Connors, Buddy Ebsen and William Shatner.
(14) Thirteen Erotic Ghosts, 2002, directed by Fred Olen Ray, starring Julie Strain, Richard Gabai and John Henry Richardson. Poster tagline: "You'll wish you were dead.".
(15) Devil Times Five, 1973, directed by Sean MacGregor, starring Sorrell Brooke, Gene Evans and Taylor Lacher. From Nightmare USA, by Stephen Thrower: "Rick and his girlfriend...join (friends) at a winter hideaway... Meanwhile, five children...survive a road accident...and head for the house. It seems they were being transported from a mental institution, and the injured driver of the crashed vehicle is extremely anxious to stop them."

(16) 28 Days Later, 2002, directed by Danny Boyle, starring Cillian Murphy, Naomie Harris and Christopher Ecclestone. Poster tagline: "The days are numbered."

It's a funny thing how the inspiration for a story can come about. It can be as innocuous as a newspaper headline, a tale told by someone, a story passed down through generations, or just a phrase intoned with enough eeriness to produce a eureka moment. This last item was the case with Checkout 13: Unlucky for Some. My Tesco colleague, and friend, Matthew Fiddy said those very words about the self same Checkout with a gravelly horror movie trailer voiceover man tone, you know the type, you can probably hear his voice in your head. I was trying and failing to come up with a suitable story for tue horror genre, my ideas vying for a singular notion amongst the variety of ideas swirling in the murkiness of my imagination, and when Matt said the words "Checkout thirteen, unlucky for some," it was my eureka moment. Cheers, Matt.

CHAPTER TWENTY-TWO

USING YOUR LOAF OVER SPILT MILK!

Stalton-on-the-Broads is a small village with a population of just two-thousand but its central location between two better known villages, Stalham and Sutton, means it boasts a busy supermarket, TAMS, and a bustling community with a by-the-numbers estate of affordable homes with the better properties, and those possessing their fair share of land, on The Broads side of the village or the Rolling Fields side. These are the "better" neighbourhoods where the "normal" people live, although "better" and "normal" are equally subjective and debatable, because who decides what is "better" and who wants to be "normal?" Neither are definable yet both exist in our society.

At the end of a cul-de-sac overlooking Rolling Fields, itself pretentiously named Rolling Fields View, is a splendidly appointed four-bedroom detached house with Jacobean pretensions, in which reside the Wilder family – that's William, Marilyn, Anthony and Jackie(1). William works in the City and is home weekends, while his wife keeps house, tends the needs of their two school-age children and writes articles for a variety of Norfolk magazines. They are affluent, comfortable, but not to extremes, and have lived in their house for just under a year. Their home is based on Edwardian architecture, sheltered by lush trees and nature, being one with the environment as they claim, living off their own land and able to use solar- and wind-power so they are not reliant upon the greedy Utilities.

Their neighbours are the McCarey's of Irish descent – that's Cleo, Mark and Margaret(2). Margaret is the chief bread-winner, running her own Leisure Complex in the City. Their home is Jacobean is styling with the same resourcefulness as the Wilder's, hence the rapport which both families share.

The previous week, Wednesday to be precise, Marilyn and Mark met up for light lunch at the Edwardian self-sustaining house - before your narrow-minded prejudices get the better of you, it is possible for a man and a woman of similar age to just be friends!

This week, it is the turn of Mark to lunch in the Jacobean home of Marilyn, the beginning of which is where we join them.

"Would you like coffee?" Marilyn asks when the pair - not couple - enter the lovely, large kitchen.

"That will be lovely, thank you." Mark replies cordially. "What have you got?"

"Er-well, its coffee." She replies.

"Sorry, I don't want to seem like a fussy fusspot, but do you have ground or filter coffee?"

"Neither, just instant."

Mark mixes a disappointed/ apologetic gurning in his expression.

"I have some tea." Marilyn suggests helpfully.

"Splendiferous! Which varieties do you have?"

"Just PG Tips."

"Blast, I am sorry, I only ever drink Twinings. You must think I'm really fussy."

"I have some bottled water." Marilyn smiles politely.

"Lovely, thank you."

Marilyn is visibly relieved, not wishing to be a bad host by being unable to cater for her guest.

Mark smiles in a wistful way: "Did you see Mel with Little Gene(3) this morning? Didn't Gene look sweet? It's her first day at pre-school today."

"Yes, I did." Marilyn replies. "First day at school is always a bit exciting and heartbreaking at the same time, it's hard to believe they grow up so fast. The Zaz triplets, Jim, Dave and Jerry(4), had their first day today also."

"The people at the end?" Mark asks, referencing a family located at the end of the cul-de-sac who he is unacquainted with. "Strewth, they grew up fast!"

Marilyn nods, wistfully thinking about her own family.

"Go through to the conservatory, Mark." Marilyn says. "I've put out a plate of sandwiches, help yourself while I get the drinks."

"Thank you."

Mark walks out the kitchen backdoor and enters the sunlit conservatory with its delightful view across the Rolling Fields, feeling the gorgeous warmth inside compared to the chill of late Autumn outside, thinking what a splendiferous month they have been experiencing. Marilyn soon returns to him with his bottle of water and a glass to pour it into, while she has a large mug of steaming coffee for herself. When she takes a seat opposite him she cannot help but notice he hasn't touched the sandwiches.

"I hope you don't mind me asking, Marilyn, " Mark says apologetically, "but what type of bread are your sandwiches made with?"

"Hovis." She tells him graciously.

"Oh. Oh dear. You see, I only ever eat Warburtons Toastie and nothing else, sorry."

"That's no problem at all." Marilyn tells him. "That's what my husband prefers too so I've got some in the kitchen." She stands. "Would you like cheese or ham or both?"

"Sorry, I hope you don't mind." Mark tells her sincerely. "Is the ham off the bone?"

"Er- no, sorry, its wafer thin out of the packet."

"Oh, okay, no worries. Cheese, please, with real butter if you have some, I prefer it to the manufactured spread one can get these days."

Marilyn nods like the gracious host she is: "Cheddar cheese okay?"

"Yes, lovely, thank you," Mark replies with a little laugh, "as long as isn't the processed stuff which all the supermarkets churn out cheaply these days, and what is it with spreadable cheese too, are people so lazy they must spread Philadelphia(5) rather than cutting the real thing!?"

Marilyn laughs.

"I have the real thing" Marilyn replies with relief that at least she has got something acceptable for her guest, " from Kath & Cary Hawks's(6) Farmshop down the road."

"Splendiferous, thank you." Mark says. "I prefer their Farmshop to the other one, Lemmon and Matthau's(7), they don't seem to have the same quality. I don't suppose you have any chutney?"

"I've got some Keaton(8) and Chaplin(9) Sandwich Pickle."

"Oh well, no worries, just the cheese, please. And can you cut them diagonally for me too, please?"

Unfazed, Marilyn returns to the kitchen and makes the sandwich as instructed, handing it to a very appreciative Mark in the conservatory, who has been admiring an original painting of Ludham windmill and fen hung up on the wall.

"Is that an Oxer?"

"No, it's an Adams(10)."

Mark nods knowledgeably.

"Would you like some crisps?" Marilyn asks.

"Yes, please," Mark replies enthusiastically.

"What flavour do you prefer?" Marilyn asks, expecting the same rigmarole as was dished out with the other food and beverage before it.

"I really don't mind, thank you." Replies Mark somewhat unexpectedly.

Once more Marilyn tends to the matter, returning forthwith, while Mark stares wistfully at the Adams painting.

"One can almost imagine Being There(11)." He sighs ruefully. "Reminds me of my youth by the river, playing with my brother. We would sometimes go fishing there." Mark laughs. "A fish called Wanda(12), my brother would say when he landed a catch, trying to be funny."

Marilyn looks long and hard at the painting, a twinkle alighting her eye: "I lost my virginity to a boy called Harvey(13) next to that windmill."

They both laugh. Marilyn hands the crisps to Mark.

"Sorry, I don't want to seem like a fusspot," says Mark, "but do you have any Kettle Chips, they are all I ever eat?"

"No, I don't." Marilyn apologises sincerely. "I am getting a sense of Groundhog Day(14)! I do have some Walkers Sensations."

"Oh no, I never eat anything from a multi-national corporation," Mark tells her, "but the sandwich is fine, thank you."

(1) Some Like it Hot, 1959, directed by Billy Wilder, starring Jack Lemmon, Tony Curtis, Marilyn Monroe, George Raft and Pat O'Brien. Dialogue quote: "I'm Osgood Fielding the Third."..."I'm Cinderella the second."

(2) Duck Soup, 1933, directed by Leo McCarey, starring the Marx Brothers and Margaret Dumont. Dialogue quote: "I got a good mind to join a club and beat you over the head with it."

(3) Blazing Saddles, 1974, directed by Mel Brooks, starring Cleavon Little, Gene Wilder, Slim Pickens and Madeline Khan. Dialogue quote: "My mind is a raging torrent flooded with rivulets of thoughts cascading into a waterfall of creative alternatives."

(4) Airplane, 1980, directed by Jim Abrahams, Jerry and David Zucker, starring Robert Hayes, Leslie Neilsen, Julie Hagerty, Lloyd

Bridges and Peter Graves. Dialogue quote: "Looks like I picked the wrong week to quit sniffing glue."
(5) The Philadelphia Story, 1940, directed by George Cukor, starring James Stewart, Katherine Hepburn, Cary Grant and Ruth Hussey. Dialogue quote: (Hungover) "Aww...this is one of those days that the pages of history teach us are best spent lying in bed."
(6) Bringing Up Baby, 1938, directed by Howard Hawks, starring Katherine Hepburn, Cary Grant and Charles Ruggles. Dialogue quote: "When a man is wrestling a leopard in the middle of a pond he's in no position to run."
(7) The Odd Couple, 1968, directed by Gene Saks, starring Jack Lemmon and Walter Matthau. Dialogue quote: "I know him, he'll kill himself just to spite me. Then his ghost will come back, following me around the apartment, haunting and cleaning, haunting and cleaning, haunting and cleaning."
(8) The General, 1927, directed by Clyde Bruckman and Buster Keaton, starring Keaton, Marion Mack and Glen Cavender.
(9) The Gold Rush, 1925, directed by and starring Charlie Chaplin, co-starring Mack Swain and Georgia Hale.
(10) Adam's Rib, 1949, directed by George Cukor, starring Spencer Tracy, Katharine Hepburn, Judy Holliday and Tom Ewell. Dialogue quote: "No matter what you think you think, you think the same as I think."
(11) Being There, 1979, directed by Hal Ashby, starring Peter Sellers, Shirley MacLaine, Melvyn Douglas and Jack Warden. Dialogue quote: "This is just like television only you can see much further."
(12) A Fish Called Wanda, 1988, directed by Charles Crichton, starring John Cleese, Jamie Lee Curtis and Kevin Kline. Dialogue quote: "Let's make love."..."Well, if you absolutely insist."
(13) Harvey, 1950, directed by Henry Koster, starring James Stewart, Cecil Kellaway and Victoria Horne. Dialogue quote: "Well, I've wrestled with reality for thirty-five years, Doctor, and I'm happy to state I finally won out over it."
(14) Groundhog Day, 1993, directed by Harold Ramis, starring Bill Murray, Andie McDowell, Stephen Tobolowsky and Chris Elliott. Dialogue quote: "This is one time where television really fails to capture the true excitement of a large squirrel predicting the weather."

Retail is a funny thing and this is not a rant, just something for you to contemplate, because it would be reckless of me to bite the hand that feeds me.

Customers can be fickle.

One person's comedy can be another person's drama.

With all the items stocked, the hundreds of varieties of coffee and bread, for example, when people cannot find the exact one which they are after there is often very little thought toward trying an alternative just for once, because why should they?

Why change the habit of a part-lifetime just because the shop stocks two-dozen alternatives!? It isn't the point that we frequently take for granted that we often have more than one choice of any given item when there are people in this country, and the world, who cannot only not afford such consumerist opportunities but do not have such a grand choice.

"Who are you, Paul R Starling, to preach to me!?" Your sub-conscience quite rightly says.

It's a person's given right to complain to the nearest member of staff as if it is their fault entirely because, heaven forbid, other customers have been in prior to them and bought exactly what they wanted to purchase - and I won't mention queueing in a supermarket as opposed to queueing at roadworks, because how many times have you gotten out of your car and had a go at the nearest foreperson?

"But I have always drunk that coffee," or "eaten that bread," or "stunk after that Vindaloo."

Which isn't really true because you haven't "always" consumed these things - think about this for a moment and you will realise it is true, unless you haven't existed for more than five, ten, years - you know what I am saying.

Would you be this particular or obsessive about products if invited to a wedding breakfast, a restaurant, or even to a friend's for lunch as in the above sketch?

No, I didn't think so. Or, at least I hope not, but if you do, I imagine you won't be invited for a return visit!

CHAPTER TWENTY-THREE

LOCALLY FILMED PRODUCE!

I believe the title of this chapter is fairly self-explanatory, don't you?

Alan Partridge: Alpha Papa
2013- Declan Lowney, starring Steve Coogan, Colm Meaney, Tim Key, Karl Theobold, Nigel Lindsay, Felicity Montagu
    The fictional radio and television presenter Alan Partridge's station, North Norfolk Digital Radio, is held siege by a disgruntled ex-employee and it is up to our hero Alan to defuse the situation in his inimitable fashion with dashes of humour.
    Our Fine City is dominant in this film with many recognisable Norwich locations used such as the Train Station, Cathedral, some of its streets and Norfolk road network, and its appealing just for these to location-spot. But also worth looking out for is the River Bure at Wroxham and the extended chase and finale which takes on the road from Sheringham to Cromer, while the stand-off finale itself takes place on Cromer Pier.
    I am not a particular fan of Steve Coogan's brand of comedy but I have to say this is an enjoyable film. Colm(Star Trek The Next Generation/DS9)Meaney is always a watchable character actor and definitely adds gravitas to the proceedings, although the story is unexciting and in need of a sorely lacking sparkle of charisma, but the local production values and catchy music make this worth watching.

A Conflict of Wings
1954- John Eldridge, starring Muriel Pavlov, John Gregson, Kieron Moore, Harry Fowler, Guy Middleton
    This is a light comedy in the Ealing tradition set on the Norfolk Broads, telling the story of a Parish community who protest when their beloved bird sanctuary becomes a proposed target range for the RAF, and the point of view of a young local woman and her RAF engineer boyfriend who comes around to her way of thinking during this struggle with the authorities.
    Filming takes place in the high street of Ludham, at The Pleasureboat Inn in Hickling - the recreation ground in the village was

used as base-camp for the film crew - and on the Broads, while the train station seen in the film was at Catfield and is no longer in existence. Cinematographer's Arthur and Moray Grant utilise the Eastman Colour system to proudly capture the beauty and tranquility if the Broads and Cley, quaint community life and Norfolk generally, and although the countryside has altered remarkably since the 1950's many of the locations still remain recognisable.

Dad Savage
1998- Betsan Morris Evans, starring Patrick Stewart, Kevin McKidd, Helen McCrory, Joe McFadden, Mark Warren

A crime thriller trying in vain to fit the mould of others during the nineties by capitalising on the success of Tarantino and Pearce, it is basically about a local godfather who doesn't trust banks attempting to discover the person who killed his son and stole his cash, but there is much more going on besides this.

The muddled script hides a good film beneath it, and Patrick Stewart is fresh-faced after years of captaining the Enterprise on Star Trek The Next Generation, giving a stunning performance - one he will repeat years later in Green Room. The film itself is located in and around Hunstanton and at Wells lifeboat station, familiar and vivid and given a stark new lease of life by cinematographer Gavin Finney. Catch it if you can because this hidden gem is well worth your time.

45 Years
2015- Andrew Haigh, starring Charlotte Rampling, Tom Courtney, Geraldine James, Dolly Wells, Richard Cunningham

A gentle drama about a mature childless couple on the eve of celebrating their forty-fifth wedding anniversary when they receive unexpected news of the death of someone from their past, and the reevaluation of their relationship.

The subject isn't as bleak as it sounds and the film is driven by two very fine lead actors at the peak of their abilities - Rampling was Oscar nominated for her role - so don't be put off if you think this isn't your cup of tea, because this reaps many rewards upon viewing, plus much of the action takes place in Norfolk including The Broads at Hickling, Norwich's London Street, the Royal Arcade, St. Benedicts and Assembly Rooms; plus Great Yarmouth and Martham.

So a simple bitter-sweet love story directed unhurriedly and with exceptional internalisation of emotions from the leads, not a ground-breaking film but one which will linger long afterwards.

The Go-Between
1970 Joseph Losey, starring Julie Christie, Alan Bates, Margaret Leighton, Michael Redgrave, Michael Gough, Edward Fox
 Based on the novel by L.P. Hartley with a script by Harold Pinter, this is a romantic period drama about neighbours who become forbidden lovers and enter into a torrid affair, and the affect this has on their lives and those they surround themselves with.
 Norwich train station is seen briefly and the two lovers dine at The Maids Head in Wensum Street, as well as taking a walk around the Cathedral and its grounds. The privately owned village of Heydon is also featured along with Melton Constable Hall, while the cricket match takes place at Thornage and the swimming scene at Hickling, so much to see here.
 This film was nominated for twelve BAFTAS, winning four, and Gerry Fisher's gorgeously opulent cinematography captures our county at its best.

The Grotesque
1995- John-Paul Davidson, starring Alan Bates, Theresa Russell, Sting, Lena Heady, Jim Carter, Anna Massey, John Mills
 The films strap line: "Beneath the surface of respectability lies the shadow of our darker side," aptly sums up this muddled horror comedy with its pseudo-psychological pretensions and bleak story.
 The beautiful private village if Heydon, near Reepham, is used in this movie as is Heydon Hall itself, and these locations are filmed with a refinement that contrasts the film and makes it worth watching, unless you really do want to see Sting's er- stinger! Other points of note amongst the mediocrity are Anne Dudley's eerie score, an early appearance from Game Of Thrones actress Lena Headey, and a brilliant performance from Theresa Russell.

In Love With Alma Cogan
2012- Tony Britten, starring Roger Lloyd Pack, Niahm Cusack, Gwyneth Strong, Neil McCaul, Christian Brassington, Keith Barron

This is a contemporary light-hearted, bittersweet romantic comedy which we British are best at producing. Norman struggles to maintain his position as manager of the end of the pier theatre when a lookalike of his childhood sweetheart, Alma Cogan, is enlisted to play there, while his assistant, Sandra, tries to gently persuade him that retirement might be his best option against all the opposition.

Beautifully capturing the seafront at Cromer, and Cromer Pier itself, plus various streets in the town, this harks back to older story-telling times when comedy was gentle and times were slower of pace, more in keeping with British television tropes of the seventies and eighties than the easy vulgarities of today's comedies.

The Reeds
2010 Nick Cohen, starring Anna Brewster, Jeff Bell, Daniel Caltagirone, Emma Catherwood, OT Fanbegle

A supernatural stalk'n'slash movie with a very basic premise: a group of innocent young adult's holiday in an unfamiliar and isolated region subsequently becoming psycho-killer fodder in the process.

Apart from the first few minutes all the action in this movie is filmed on Hickling Broad and surrounding roads and boatyards, so there is certainly a lot of appeal to over 18 year-old Norfolk-watchers in this regard. If you like this no-brainer style movie evoking late 90's studio B-movie's without the self-referential in-jokes also indicative of that era, then this is definitely for you, and the photography by Dennis Madden does possess a quasi-stranded-in-nature Deliverance look, but this isn't the most original independently produced horror movie on the market.

A Warning to the Curious
1972- Lawrence Gordon Clark, starring Peter Vaughn, Clive Swift, Julian Herington, John Kearney, David Cargill

Not a movie, this is a fifty-minute television production made by the BBC for its series A Ghost Story for Christmas, based on the short story by MR James, but it's better than some horror films and a definite must for Norfolk local's because it covers several villages.

The story centres on Mr Paxton's quest to unearth one if three legendary Anglican Crowns said to protect our coastline, with the aid of Dr. Black, but his search produces a ghostly stalker who wants the crown returned.

Beginning with a prologue filmed on the edge of woodland at Holkham where the main story returns on several occasions, this plot unfolds along the quayside at Wells-next-the-Sea, the marshes of Cley to the dunes of Waxham beach, taking in Happisburgh church and the North Norfolk Railway on its travels. Mr Paxton conducts much of his journey by bicycle which makes his quest all the more impressive - time-constraints and editing produce his Olympian-level cycling! Most of the locations are instantly recognisable while the story repels toward its conclusion satisfyingly.

Wilt
1990- Michael Tuchler, starring Mel Smith, Griff Rhys Jones, Alison Steadman, Diana Quick, Roger Lloyd Pack, Jeremy Clyde, Roger Alam

A broad comedy based on Tom Sharpe's satirical novel about inept school tutor Henry Wilt who inadvertently gets accused of murdering his wife, a crime which is investigated by equally inept Inspector Flint and the humorous bumbling scenarios upon which they embark.

Norwich City is used quite frequently, the streets during a car chase especially, City Hall and St. Augustine's, along with much-filmed but unrecognisable in this case Hickling Broad for the boat scene, and the climax of the film takes place extensively at the remote church in Horning.

Funny but straining to be more humorous, which is a pity.

For video overviews of these films and locations look on YouTube: Paul R Starling Norfolk at the Movies

CHAPTER TWENTY-FOUR

ORIGINAL SIN-
A FRANCHISE BIOPIC BASED ON THE SEQUEL TO A NOVEL

"Familiarity breeds contempt." At least that is how one saying goes, whereas: "absence makes the heart grow fonder."

So what are the multi-national profit oriented studios supposed to do when tempering these conflicts of interest, particularly when failure creates contempt for the product? Admittedly some people in society also sneer at success, frowning upon the mainstream because its made for the lowest form of cinema-goer and not for us high-minded cineastes. Cinema began life as a money-spinning venture for businessmen looking to earn a healthy income by churning out film for the masses without much thought given to the art.

Nobody is wrong, really, but I believe I have mentioned this fact earlier, maybe more than once. There is equal value in Fellini as Bay, it just depends on which side of the entertainment as art fence you sit.

Story in key and is the nature of story by which we gain insight into a person, factual or fictional, and if that person is interesting enough we might want to learn more about them, oftentimes discussing them with someone else who might themselves tell the story using their own voice, sometimes with embellishments of their own creation.

Not that I am advocating lack of originality, I am just paying homage to my own experiences and observations!

Film producing companies need to make a profit: fact.

Studios need a revenue stream so other, more artistic fare, can be created, either alongside or independent to them: fact.

Ultimately, movies are products which need an audience, irrespective of whether that audience is a single person or millions of people.

Movies were a technical innovation which immediately caught the eyes of multiple entrepreneurs who developed, nurtured and effectively created the industry which exits today, albeit with numerous changes on route.

The modern phenomenon of multi-platform merchandise-heavy expanded franchises began to fully form throughout the 1980's, after the success of Star Wars(1) in 1977 alerted movie producers to the potentials. And so the '80's saw the beginning of "event" film blockbusters, "tent-pole" studio productions with high concepts, higher expectations, and often an inbuilt audience. By 1989 the success of three particular films with these inbuilt audiences, huge cross-promotions and lucrative soundtracks, effectively launched the "blockbuster" season of today.

    Many digital innovations have aided the visual creativity of filmmakers in the last thirty years, with some critics claiming that reliance on CGI and other gimmicks has brought the artistry of the industry to a new low. Others might say it has freed up the imagination which is why we are now seeing effects-heavy franchises dominating the box office.

    At this point I should like to reiterate the point I made about paying homage to the past through my own observations. All eras extol the virtues of the past.

    While these bigger productions are drawing in an audience failure is also inevitable, and these failures are not through lack of razzle-dazzle, but through a lack of audience engagement. Mainstream movies have been forced to become more savvy and sophisticated with their storytelling as the audience becomes more aware of details, plot and character, which might very well have existed in the past but often bypassed the mainstream. This is another reason why fewer independent studios exist; the smarter the audience means the mainstream has to up its game.

    But thankfully, if you search, there are still challenging, artistic, freeing-the-mind movies out there which offer the experience of unique vision.

    So the traditional Hollywood studios, corporations now, more often than not need to generate their revenue using the familiar the (comparatively) safe option - I say comparatively because spending $200million plus on something which audiences may or may not pay to watch is still an expensive gamble. This reliance upon the familiar is increasingly more lucrative to each successive production generation, which is why 2017's box office if filled with "safe bets," although not all will make money despite the numbers you might read which they bring in.

    Let's begin with the franchise movie, and there are many: Son of Frankenstein(2) is the third entry in Universal's Frankenstein series, themselves a part of a horror cycle which saw interchanging characters and actors appearing in each other's film; while The Hound of the Baskervilles(3) saw the stars reprising their roles as Holmes and Watson a further thirteen times together.

Then there are the remakes: Gunga Din(4) was first filmed in 1911 as a silent short, and is based on an 1892 Rudyard Kipling poem; The Cat and the Canary(5), based on a John Willard play, had been filmed before in 1927 and 1930; Destry Rides Again(6), based on a novel by Max Brand, was first filmed in 1932 starring Tom Mix; while the Hunchback of Notre Dame(7), based on the novel by Victor Hugo, was famously filmed in 1923 with Lon Chaney memorably playing the title role.

Goodbye, Mr Chips(8) is a semi-autobiographical account of James Hilton, and is based on his 1934 novel; while Young Mister Lincoln(9) is a biopic.

The stage is always a good source of material: Dark Victory(10) from the 1934 play by George Emerson Brewer Jnr and Bertram Bloch; The Women(11) from a play by Clare Booth; and Babes in Arms(12) was based on a 1937 stage musical by Richard Rodgers and Lorenz Hart.

Short-stories have also occasionally leant themselves out, such as Stagecoach(13) from the 1937 story "Stage to Lordsburg" by Ernest Haycox.

Novels of course are a ripe source to take advantage of: Emily Bronte's Wuthering Heights(14); The Wizard of Oz(15) was based on a novel by L. Frank Baum; while Lewis R Foster's "The Gentleman From Montana" was the basis for Mr Smith Goes to Washington(16); but most famously of all is the adaptation of the 1936 best-seller by Margaret Mitchell, Gone With The Wind(17).

All the films mentioned above except Star Wars, obviously, were released in what is now considered by many film historians to be Hollywood's Golden year: 1939. And all these films have reached some part of Classic status among cineastes.

Now, I'm not trying to suggest that in 80 years-time The Hunger Games(18) franchise will be revered as much as Frankenstein(19), but I am sure that if producer David O. Selznick were alive today he would consider Gone With The Wind has multi-platform expanded universe potential - not that its returns were shabby, because when adjusted for inflation Gone With The Wind still rules at the box office.

Also, there were far more films being made in 1939 than 2017 and the industry was still comparatively new so audiences and critics were less likely to complain about yet another remake or sequel or reimagining. Yes, films based on something which came before them is not a new phenomenon, it simply appears this way because of the publicity which is now behind them, each one having to outdo the next in its inventiveness in order to draw punters in.

Modern cinemas comic-book phase is not dissimilar to early cinemas reliance upon the stage adaptation; both are creative arts and appropriate for their generation.

And who can blame the companies who have to finance these things if they want a built-in audience to buy tickets, because if you or I were to write a novel which became a huge success and your readership demanded more of the same we might be tempted to revisit our creation - purely for artist reasons, of course!

(1) Star Wars, 1977, directed by George Lucas, starring Harrison Ford, Mark Hamill, Carrie Fisher and Alec Guinness.
(2) Son of Frankenstein, 1939, directed by Rowland V Lee, starring Boris Karloff, Bela Lugosi and Basil Rathbone. IMDb rating: 7.2.
(3) The Hound of the Baskervilles, 1939, directed by Sidney Lanfield, starring Basil Rathbone and Nigel Bruce. IMDb rating: 7.6.
(4) Gunga Din, 1939, directed by George Stevens, starring Cary Grant, Douglas Fairbanks Jnr and Joan Fontaine. IMDb rating: 7.5.
(5) The Cat and Canary, 1939, directed by Elliott Nugent, starring Bob Hope, Paulette Goddard and Gale Sondergaard. IMDb rating: 7.3.
(6) Destry Rides Again, 1939, directed by George Marshall, starring Marlene Dietrich, James Stewart and Charles Winninger. IMDb rating: 7.7.
(7) The Hunchback of Notre Dame, 1939, directed by William Dieterle, starring Charles Laughton, Maureen O'Hara and Thomas Mitchell. IMDb rating: 7.9.
(8) Goodbye, Mister Chips, 1939, directed by Sam Wood, starring Robert Donat, Greer Garson and John Mills. IMDb rating: 7.8. 72nd on the BFI Top 100 British movies list.
(9) Young Mister Lincoln, 1939, directed by John Ford, starring Henry Fonda, Alice Brady and Marjorie Weaver. IMDb rating: 7.6.
(10) Dark Victory, 1939, directed by Edmund Goulding, starring Better Davis, George Brent and Humphrey Bogart. IMDb rating: 7.6.

(11) The Women, 1939, directed by George Cukor, starring Norma Shearer, Joan Crawford and Rosalind Russell. IMDb rating: 8.0.
(12) Babes in Arms, 1939, directed by Busby Berkeley, starring Mickey Rooney and Judy Garland. IMDb rating: 6.6.
(13) Stagecoach, 1939, directed by John Ford, starring Claire Trevor, John Wayne and Thomas Mitchell. IMDb rating: 7.9.
(14) Wuthering Heights, 1939, directed by William Wyler, starring Laurence Olivier, Merle Oberon and David Niven. IMDb rating: 7.7.
(15) The Wizard of Oz, 1939, directed by Victor Fleming, starring Judy Garland, Frank Morgan and Ray Bolger. IMDb rating: 8.1. 10th on the AFI Best 109 American movies list.
(16) Mr Smith Goes to Washington, 1939, directed by Frank Capra, starring James Stewart, Jean Arthur and Claude. IMDb rating: 8.2. 26th on the AFI Best100 American movies list.
(17) Gone With The Wind, 1939, directed by Victor Fleming, starring Vivian Leigh, Clark Gable and Olivia de Havilland. IMDb rating: 8.2. 6th on the AFI Best 100 American movies list.
(18) The Hunger Games, 2012, directed by Gary Ross, starring Jennifer Lawrence, Josh Hutcherson and Liam Hemsworth.
(20) Frankenstein, 1931, directed by James Whale, starring Clive Colin, Boris Karloff and Mae Clarke.

CHAPTER TWENTY-FIVE

CONTACTLESS, PART 2

"Gene's friend Cathy is girlfriend a me best mate, Drake(9)." Burt continues his explanation from the beginning of the book, much to Doug's and my relief, even if his sentence structuring leaves something to be desired. "He's a dodgy something-and-so and he found out about Gene's money-fluffing brother-in-law on account of the business Drake does with him."

At least this partly explains how Gene and Cathy came into possession of a gun, but Doug doesn't share this information with Burt just yet, in the same way I don't remind you what happened earlier because you can reread it for yourself.

"Drake did dodgy scams until he hooked with Jean(10)." Burt explains poorly. "That's Jean with a jay not a gee." - after all, we can see the text but Doug cannot, which doesn't really explain the grammatical errors unless it's just me! - "You follow?"

Doug shrugs as if to say not exactly!

"Jean is Ty's sister." Burt explains as if this is the most obvious thing in the world. "Jean got Drake involved in this contactless card scam. You see, some Russian mafia dude equips her with a dozen zapper things which look like mobile phones but are really designed to scan for contactless cards. They only have a range of about five feet but that's enough in a crowd of people to extract thirty quid a pop. A fiver goes to the geez who carries the phone, five to Jean, the rest to this mafia guy in Russia. It's untraceable and very lucrative."

Wishing that his mind was devious enough to concoct such an ingenious and quite foolproof scam, Doug smiles at the relative simplicity of the thing - in this technology laden culture a criminal doesn't have to forge a signature or remember a four-digit code, he just swipes your card! How's this for banks thinking about our security! A person would only have to work for this organisation for a couple of weeks and he might net thousands of pounds! Bankers, hey!?

"And, um-" Doug says, returning to the moment, "Ty is complicit?"

"No," Burt says, confused, "but he knows all about it. You better go kill him," he says matter-of-factly after consulting his watch. "He's gonna be finished soon."

Staggering away, Burt leaves Doug watching the big man, perplexed, alone at the rear of the speakeasy, the kitchen lights illuminating his pale face, wondering about the influx of information and which to discard as totally superfluous. Should he return to Gene, confront her with these revelations? Can Doug actually remember everything he has been told? He realises possessing the gun puts him in fairly deeply without ever having committed a murder. Undoubtedly both Cathy and Gene would testify against him should he fail his task. Will they anyway, if he succeeds? If he goes to the police with all this knowledge will it do him any good? Alternatively, what about confronting Ty with all this, see what he has to say? Could Doug broker some kind of a deal there, blackmail him, perhaps? Or, alternatively, should I just let him get on with it instead of babbling on about the what-if's because it might ruin the twist ending, if there is one, and render all this rumination stupid?

Doug consults his watch. He hasn't much time. It's now or never. No time like the present. Do today what one can put off tomorrow.

Doug pulls a coin from his pocket: Heads he confronts Ty; tails he returns to Gene.

Heads it is, then.

Pocketing the gun because it would be inadvisable to enter a busy supermarket with it drawn unless one wishes to deliberately attract attention – there's a tip for you - Doug eyes the interior from the foyer, lids narrowed to slits, surveying the scene with hawk-like studiousness which doesn't cast any suspicions upon him whatsoever.

"Can I help you?" Asks the stores alert security guard, Otto(11).

"No thank you." Doug replies politely yet with a lop-sided expression. "Is Ty here?"

Otto checks his necktie before realising what Doug is really asking, and telling him that yes, Ty is here, but he is now leaving by the back exit so Doug needs to hurry if he wishes to catch the guy.

Doug thanks Otto and quickly leaves the store, the excitement palpable, gun knocking heavily against his thigh like an object of equal male potency which can be deadly in the wrong hands, and he strides around the rear of TAMS Supermarket where he can see the dimly-lit back passage - stop sniggering!

Ty is indeed here, recently out the door, phone illuminating his handsome features. Doug can understand why this man is irresistible to women, wishing he swung both ways himself in this crazy world. Doug strides on from Where The Sidewalk Ends(12) and into the passageway, drawing out the loaded gun, remaining concealed in the shadowy underworld for as long as he is able.

"Jumping beans!" Ty swears when he first notices the whites of Doug's eyes then the glinting gun barrel. "Is This Gun For Hire(13)?" He laughs, not taking Doug seriously. "So who are you supposed to be?"

"My name is Doug." Replies...Doug - obviously!

"I've seen you skulking around here before," Ty claims. "I wondered who the prowler(14) was! I'll call the coppers, you drunken imbecile!"

Doug realises this man thinks this is some kind of joke.

"This is real." Doug states, waving the gun threateningly in front of Ty's face for emphasis. "I've been asked by your sister-in-law to kill you because you beat up your wife and have muscled in on someone else's contactless card scam. They want you put on ice, big boy, and I'm here to do the job."

Ty looks from the gun to Doug's serious expression and realises this Gun Crazy(15) loon is seriously serious about this seriousness.

"Okay, okay, okay," Ty says, holding his hands up defeatedly, "lets calm down a bit, shall we? And, thank you for calling me big boy, I didn't realise it was that obvious."

Doug takes a step back defensively, suspecting this man hasn't cowed so easily in the face of danger, the lights from TAMS reception casting enough of a glow for Doug to be able to read the full extent of Ty's expression and something is definitely amiss - which is really a rather good observation from Doug, considering his earlier naiveté, unless he was actually putting it all on as a ruse to fool us too.

Something moves across the frosted glass of the window, catching Doug's attention; the silhouette if a woman is inside and she is holding what can only be described as a gun, with Ty in the Crossfire(16) should they both shoot.

"Who is that?" Doug asks.

Ty looks to the window behind him to the right, but by now the silhouette has disappeared from view. Ty asks Doug what he is talking about.

"The woman in the Window(17)?" Doug prompts. "Who is she?"

Ty shrugs his shoulders, unconvincingly feigning ignorance.

"Something fishy is going on." Doug states. "And I aim to find out what the set-up(18) is." He ponders the situation for a moment. "This gun has blanks in it, doesn't it? Yes, that's it. I am supposed to shoot you but when I leave you scram, leave the country, and your wife and sister-in-law claim a hefty life insurance sum before joining you on some far-flung island somewhere, but there's just one pitfall(19) to your plan, see, because you all thought I would be a stupid sap and not work it out for myself."

Ty looks befuddled by this curious turn to his evening.

"Sounds to me," Ty said, "that you have gotten a raw deal(20)."

Just then the door to TAMS reception opens and out steps Gene looking seductive, lovely, and all the superlatives you can conjure. She holds a gun in her gloved hand and aims it at Ty, bloodlessly shooting him in the chest because this is a PG story, before taking aim at Doug next.

"You could've had me," Gene tells Doug, "body and soul(21) but you are too much of a wimp that I figured I had to do this myself. Your finger prints are on this gun, Dougie, so I suggest you run while the going is good, and don't think about telling anyone the truth because who is going to believe you," she says, smiling sweetly, "over me?"

Doug weighs up his options along with the gun in his hand, realising the weapon must be loaded after all- unless... He kneels down to the body on the floor and gives it a prod, followed by a second, firmer nudge with a bit of brute force(22) which Ty cannot ignore, the previously dead man springing to life, and to his feet.

"Okay, you passed the test." Ty says.

"You wanna join our operation?" Gene asks. "All this subterfuge was your recruitment test, and like Ty says, you passed, and you wanna know something else, Dougie, you are gonna get the girl too."

Doug smiles, his eyes lighting up victoriously, two cars abruptly pulling up along the street side of the passage at the rear of TAMS, and out jump four uniformed and two plain-clothed police officers, much to the surprise of the two perpetrators of this crime in progress who are cornered(23) in the act - and the reader who was also fooled! He produces the enforcer(24) of the law badge from his inside pocket.

"Fooled you." Doug gloats. "Arrest them." He tells his fellow officers, and thus ends this tale of deception, double-cross and denouement.

(1) Out of the Past, 1947, directed by Jacques Tourneur, starring Robert Mitchum, Jane Greer, Rhonda Fleming, Richard Webb and Kirk Douglas. A private eyes past catches up with him while he tries settling into a quieter life.
(2) In a Lonely Place, 1950, directed by Nicholas Ray, starring Humphrey Bogart, Gloria Grahame, Frank Lovejoy and Martha Stewart. A screenwriter becomes the prime suspect in a murder, while his neighbour slowly has doubts about his innocence.
(3) Night and the City, 1950, directed by Jules Dassin, starring Richard Widmark, Gene Tierney, Googie Withers, Herbert Lom and Hugh Marlowe. A chancer entering the big-time bites off more than he can chew as a promoter.
(4) Nightmare Alley, 1947, directed by Edmund Goulding, starring Tyrone Power, Joan Blondell, Coleen Gray and Taylor Holmes. A successful carny's lies and deceit become his downfall.
(5) Cross-Cross, 1949, directed by Robert Siodmak, starring Burt Lancaster, Yvonne DeCarlo, Dan Duryea, Stephen McNally and Alan Napier. A lorry driver conspires with his ex-wife to have his own armoured truck hijacked.
(6) The Killers, 1946, directed by Robert Siodmak, starring Burt Lancaster, Ava Gardner, Edmond O'Brien, Charles McGraw and Albert Dekker. An investigator uncovers intrigue and treachery after a man is murdered.
(7) They Live by Night, 1949, directed by Nicholas Ray, starring Farley Granger, Cathy O'Donnell and Howard Da Silva. An injured escaped convict falls for the woman nursing him back to health.
(8) Scarlet Street, 1945, directed by Fritz Lang, starring Edward G Robinson, Joan Bennett, Dan Duryea and Margaret Lindsay. Lovers plot to steal a man's assumed fortune when he falls for the woman.
(9) Detour, 1945, directed by Edgar G Ulmer, starring Tom Neal, Ann Savage and Claudia Drake. When a hitch-hiker assumes the identity of a man who dies on him, his life spirals out of control.
(10) Pick-Up On South Street, 1953, directed by Samuel Fuller, starring Richard Widmark, Jean Peters, Thelma Ritter and Milburn Stone. A pick-pocket becomes the target of Communists when he inadvertently lifts a message destined for them.
(11) Laura, 1944, directed by Otto Preminger, starring Dana Andrews, Gene Tierney, Clifton Webb, Vincent Price and Judith Anderson. A

detective falls in love with the woman whose murder he is investigating.

(12) Where the Sidewalk Ends, 1950, directed by Otto Preminger, starring Dana Andrews, Gene Tierney, Gary Merrill, Tom Tully and Karl Malden. A troubled detective accidentally kills a murder suspect.

(13) This Gun for Hire, 1942, directed by Frank Tuttle, starring Alan Ladd, Veronica Lake, Robert Preston, Laird Cregar and Marc Lawrence. An assassin is paid off in marked bills by the foreign spies employing him.

(14) The Prowler, 1951, directed by Joseph Losey, starring Van Heflin, Evelyn Keyes, John Maxwell and Madge Blake. From Film Review, 1952, by F. Maurice Speed: "Renegade American cop Van Heflin murders Evelyn Keyes' radio producer husband so he can get his hands on his wife and cash, but the lady's unborn child-of which the cop is the guilty father-brings about the failure of the plan."

(15) Gun Crazy, 1950, directed by Joseph H. Lewis, starring John Dall, Peggy Cummins, Berry Kroeger and Morris Carnovsky. A deadly marksman wife persuades her husband to go on a robbery spree.

(16) Crossfire, 1947, directed by Edward Dmytryk, starring Robert Mitchum, Robert Ryan, Robert Montgomery and Gloria Grahame. Soldier friends become murder suspects in a twisted plot.

(17) The Woman in the Window, 1944, directed by Fritz Lang, starring Edward G. Robinson, Joan Bennett, Raymond Massey and Dan Duryea. Blackmail and murder ensue when a professor falls for an unscrupulous woman.

(18) The Set-Up, 1949, directed by Robert Wise, starring Robert Ryan, Audrey Totter, George Tobias and Alan Baxter. A boxer must throw a fight to save his corrupt manager.

(19) Pitfall, 1948, directed by Andre deToth, starring Dick Powell, Lizabeth Scott, Jane Wyatt and Raymond Burr. Two men fall for the wife of a convict with dire consequences..

(20) Raw Deal, 1948, directed by Anthony Mann, starring Dennis O'Keefe, Claire Trevor, Matsha Hunt, John Ireland and Raymond Burr. A convict in double-crossed while formulating and escape plan.

(21) Body and Soul, 1947, directed by Robert Rossen, starring John Garfield, Lili Palmer, Anne Revere, William Conrad and Hazel Brooks. A boxer falls in with the wrong crowd.

(22) Brute Force, 1947, directed by Jules Dassin, starring Burt Lancaster, Hume Cronyn, Charles Bickford, Yvonne De Carlo. A convict plans a revolt.

(23) Cornered, 1945, directed by Edward Dmytryk, starring Dick Powell, Walter Slezak, Nina Vale and Morris Carnovsky. A flyer discovers his wife has been murdered and sets out to investigate.

(24) The Enforcer, 1951, directed by Bretaigne Windust, starring Humphrey Bogart, Zero Mostel, Ted de Corsia and Everett Sloane. A DA gets the chance to prosecute a big league organisation.

Bibliography: (and other miscellaneous stuff) because even though lots of information is available on the Internet, creating instant experts on every subject, personally I prefer a good book.

CONTACTLESS
The Art of Noir - The Posters and Graphics from the Classic Era of Film Noir
By Eddie Muller
Overlook Duckworth, Peter Mayer Publishers, Inc. ISBN 978-1-4683-0735-1

The 101 Best Film Noir Posters from the 1940's - 1950's
By Mark Fertig
Fantagraphics Books. ISBN 978-1-60699-759-8

A STAR(ling) IS BORN

The Act of Seeing
By Nicolas Winding Refn and Alan Jones
FAB Press. ISBN 978-1-903245-79-0

Blaxploitation Cinema: The Essential Reference Guide
By Josiah Howard
FAB Press. ISBN 978-1-903254-44-8

The Picture House in East Anglia
By Stephen Peart
Terence Dalton Limited. ISBN 0-900963-56-5

1981 - MY SPORTING LIFE

The Oliver Stone Experience
By Matt Zoller Seitz
ABRAMS. ISBN 978-1-4197-1790-1

BONDING

The James Bond Archives
Edited by Paul Duncan
Taschen GmbH. ISBN 978-3-8365-2105-5

ADVENTURE OF THE ROLE-PLAYING FANTASY GAME

The Third Reich's Celluloid War - Propaganda in Nazi Films, Documentaries and Television
By Ian Garden
The History Press. ISBN 978-0-7524-6442-8

Ray Harryhausen An Animated Life
Written by Ray Harryhausen and Tony Dalton
Aurum Press Ltd. ISBN 1-85410-940-5

POSTER!

The Art of John Alvin
By Andrea Alvin
Titan Books. ISBN 9780857689290

The Art of the B-Movie Poster!
Edited by Adam Newell
Gingko Press. ISBN 978-1584236221

Clint Eastwood - Icon!
By David Frangioni with Essays by Thomas Schatz
Titan Books. ISBN 9781848565883

MGM Posters - The Golden Years
Text by Frank Miller
JG Press, Inc. ISBN 1-57215-269-9

Oeuvre - Drew Struzan
Written by Drew & Dylan Struzan
Titan Books. ISBN 9780857685575

Russian Movie Posters
With an introduction by Maria-Christina Boerner
Vivays Publishing. ISBN 978-1-908126-15-3

1990: GONE IN TWENTY MINUTES -
PASSING MY DRIVING TEST

The Most Famous Car in the World
By Dave Worrall
Solo Publishing. ISBN 0-9517509-1-7

Motor Movies - The Posters!
By Paul Veysey
Veloce Publishing. ISBN 978-1-845841-27-0

KASSIOPI
FIRST FLIGHT HOLIDAY

Eurocrime! The Italian Cop and Gangster Films that Ruled the 70's
Documentary feature directed by Mike Malloy

MILLENNIUM COUNTDOWN

Casablanca - As Time Goes By... 50th Anniversary Commemorative
By Frank Miller
Virgin Publishing Ltd. ISBN 1-85227-411-5

The Complete Making of Indiana Jones
By J.W.Rinzler and Laurent Bouzereau
Ebury Publishing. ISBN 978-0-09-192661-8

What I Love About Movies, Volume No.1
Presented by Little White Lies
Faber & Faber Ltd. ISBN 978-0-571-31208-5

NAKED BABES IN BEACH TOWN

Crab Monsters, Teenage Cavemen, and Candy Stripe Nurses - Roger Corman: King of the B Movie

By Chris Nashawaty
ABRAMS. ISBN 978-1-4197-0669-1

Doomed! The Untold Story of Roger Corman's the Fantastic Four(2015) documentary feature directed by Marty Langford

CHECKOUT 13: UNLUCKY FOR SOME

Monsters in the Movies - 100 Years of Cinematic Nightmares
By John Landis
Dorling Kindersley Limited. ISBN 978-1-40536-697-7

Nightmare USA - The Untold Story of the Exploitation Independents
By Stephen Thrower
FAB Press. ISBN 978-1-903254-46-2

Universal Studios Monsters - A Legacy of Horror
By Michael Mallory
Universe Publishing. ISBN 978-0-7893-1896-1

ORIGINAL SIN-
A FRANCHISE BIOPIC BASED ON THE SEQUEL TO A NOVEL

Hollywood's Golden Year, 1939 - A Fiftieth Anniversary Celebration
By Ted Sennett

Other novels by
Paul R. Starling

SCOTT DALTON ADVENTURES

Living on the Edge
Danger on the Edge
Over the Edge of the Abyss
....

Life in the Shadows
....

All available from Amazon in hardcopy format or Digital.
....

COMING SUMMER 2018

British Bulldog
"The fourth Scott Dalton story."

....

"I work to serve you. I work *for* my family."